THE STORY
OF THE WESTERN RAILROADS

THE STORY
OF THE
WESTERN RAILROADS

From 1852 Through the Reign of the Giants

BY

ROBERT EDGAR RIEGEL

University of Nebraska Press
Lincoln and London

Copyright © 1926 by the Macmillan Company
Library of Congress catalog card number: 26–9772
International Standard Book Number: 0–8032–0903–7
International Standard Book Number: 0–8032–5159–9 (pbk.)
Manufactured in the United States of America

First Bison Book printing May, 1964

Most recent printing indicated by first digit below:
6   7   8   9   10

University of Nebraska Press edition reprinted from the
Macmillan Company 1926 edition by arrangement with
Robert E. Riegel

TO

FREDERIC L. PAXSON

PREFACE

Good transportation was a vital necessity for the American West throughout its history. While there were a few men who went West because of a desire for solitude or to avoid the clutches of the law, and hence wanted to cut connections with the East, or were unconcerned about them, the great majority felt otherwise. The average westerner—and his wife—wanted to keep in contact with his friends and relatives back East. Even more he wanted to be able to market his crops as cheaply and as rapidly as possible, and in return to obtain the manufactured goods that were not produced in the West—silks and fashion magazines for his wife, broadcloth and Havana cigars for himself, and in fact all the trappings of civilization as he had known it in the East. He had gone West to make his fortune, not to become a hermit.

The demand for better connections between East and West existed as long as there was a frontier, and was supported enthusiastically by all Americans from whatever part of the country. A whole series of transportational advances—improved roads, steamboats, canals, railroads, and automobiles—appealed in succession to the American people. Of these the most important until well into the twentieth century was the railroad, and particularly so for the region west of the Mississippi, which in general lacked the proper building materials for roads and the necessary water for steamboats and canals. The railroad offered the best opportunity for spanning the large distances of the West and of bringing it prosperity.

The building of railroads west of the Mississippi was one of the great feats of history. New lines were constructed over thousands of vacant miles, with only hopes for the future. True the process was at times wasteful and often involved various types of chicanery, but the basic facts are that the feat was accomplished and that the West developed rapidly as a result. Not only were the major transcontinental lines constructed in about a generation, but, equally important, a network of feeder lines came into existence to lure the farmer to occupy western farms and then to bring him within reach of markets.

Even before the western railroads were completed, they were being criticized by their farmer-customers, who found wealth disturbingly elusive. Some of the farmers' criticisms were true, some were exaggerated, and some were false, but in any case the railroad was transformed in popular opinion from a life-giving fountain to a blood-sucking octopus. Today these extremes of sentiment no longer seem either valid or important, and we have come to the time when the contributions of the railroad to American civilization can be evaluated more firmly.

ROBERT E. RIEGEL
Dartmouth College
December, 1963

TABLE OF CONTENTS

CHAPTER V

Military use of railroads—development of army control—
effect on western roads—Minnesota beginnings—early construction further west—chartering of the Union Pacific—route
—federal aid—organization—further aid by Congress—lobbying—difficulties—Credit Mobilier operations.

CHAPTER VI

Union Pacific—early work—labor—Indian troubles—method
of construction—local influences—race with the Central
Pacific—Central Pacific—early efforts of Judah—formation of
company—Contract and Finance Company—difficulties—
joining of lines—situation of the companies—developments
to 1873—Union Pacific change in ownership—Central Pacific
monopoly of California.

CHAPTER VII

Chicago and Northwestern extensions—Chicago, Rock Island
and Pacific and the Mississippi River bridge—Chicago, Burlington and Quincy—development of the Joy lines—Chicago,
Milwaukee and St. Paul—Illinois Central—Pacific Railroad
of Missouri—North Missouri—shorter roads—Missouri,
Kansas and Texas—St. Louis and Iron Mountain—Cairo and
Fulton—International and Great Northern—Utah roads.

CHAPTER VIII

Kansas Pacific—Denver Pacific—completion—Santa Fe—
early history—first construction—struggle with Denver and
Rio Grande—Atlantic and Pacific—lease of Missouri Pacific
—Texas and Pacific—Southern Pacific—Northern Pacific—
incorporation—Jay Cooke—early construction—financial arrangements—foreign security sales—changes in management
—failure of Jay Cooke and Company—panic of 1873—result
on Northern Pacific and its branches.

CHAPTER XIII

Union Pacific—government debt—Thurman Act—relations
with Iowa Trunk Lines Association—"Tripartite Agreement"
—Colorado Railways' Association—Utah connections—Oregon
situation—Villard—Oregon Railway and Navigation
Company—Villard's "blind pool"—Oregon and Transcontinental—Completion
of Northern Pacific—Canadian Pacific
—Pacific Mail Steamship Company—Transcontinental Traffic
Association and its difficulties.

CHAPTER XIV

Minor roads—Hill and the Great Northern—completion—
"Soo"—Chicago Great Western—Chicago and Northwestern
—Chicago, Burlington and Quincy—Chicago, Rock Island
and Pacific—competitive areas—southwestern pool—Omaha
pool—subsidiary pools—transcontinental pool—Iowa and
northwestern pools—Texas pool—Chicago-St. Louis pool—
common management—rebates and other troubles—shippers'
organizations—attitude of public—effect of state laws.

CHAPTER XV

Migration from the East—early foreign immigration—Chinese
labor—early skilled labor—Civil War developments—
after the war—immigration—migrants from the East—attitude
of the railroads—technical education.

CHAPTER XVI

First importance—engineers—conductors—firemen—trainmen
—other groups—features of early organizations—Knights of
Labor—Gould strike of 1885—Gould strike of 1886—effect
on Knights of Labor—brotherhoods—Debs and the American
Railway Union—attitude of the railroads—attitude of
the public—injunctions—"Coxey's army"—labor legislation.

CHAPTER XVII

CHAPTER XVIII

CHAPTER XIX

CHAPTER XX

THE STORY
OF THE WESTERN RAILROADS

THE STORY
OF THE WESTERN RAILROADS

CHAPTER I

THE BEGINNING OF RAILROADS

The triumphant opening of the first railroad west of the Mississippi River occurred on December 23, 1852, when the first train on the Pacific Railroad of Missouri steamed proudly from St. Louis to Cheltenham—the immense distance of five miles. It was a moment of exaltation for the citizens of Missouri. Flags waved, bands played, and orators prophesied the flowering of the West under the beneficent influence of the steam locomotive.

For once the orators were right. An epoch was marked. Twenty-five years earlier the musical whistle of the locomotive was as yet unheard in the United States. Twenty-five years later steel tracks spanned the continent from New York to San Francisco. The railroad conquest of the United States was completed within the traditional life span of three score years and ten.

The railroad was one of the products of the industrial revolution. Large scale production with its attendant specialization destroyed the old economic self-sufficiency of small groups; the movement of persons and products was increased immensely. Existing means of transportation on land and water were improved and extended; canals were dug in large numbers; and finally steam was applied to both water and land transportation.

The first extensive use of steam as a land motive power occurred in England, where the industrial revolution was first apparent. Here and there stationary engines were installed to haul a string of cars over wooden planks. Side boards were soon placed on the planks to keep the cars from sliding off. The first important improvement came with the idea that it would be possible to put the engine on an additional car, attach the motive power to the wheels, and thus move the whole train. In spite of the skepticism of many good people this absurd theory was vindicated in the famous trials of 1829, when George Stephenson proved that his "Rocket" could pull a train of cars faster than a horse could pull a carriage. In consequence locomotive engines were introduced on the Liverpool and Manchester Railway, and subsequently over the whole of England.

American development of the locomotive was in large part independent and parallel to that of England. As early as 1800 the inventor Oliver Evans tried to interest people in steam locomotion. Four years later he had his idea sufficiently developed to produce a sort of boatlike steam Juggernaut which propelled itself over the road by its own power. Evans' idea was still very crude, so that Latrobe, one of America's first engineers, commented upon it unfavorably in his transportation report to Secretary of the Treasury Gallatin in 1808. During the next decade John Stevens made sufficient progress to secure some interest on the floor of Congress, but no definite action was taken. The first "railroads" opened in the United States were installed by certain quarries and coal mines during the latter twenties, and were operated by horse power. The first important railroad in the United States was the Baltimore and Ohio, begun in 1827. The locomotive engine had not as yet come into use, so various kinds of motive power were tried. Horse traction was used, and experiments were made of putting the horse inside the car on a treadmill. At one time sails were put on the cars, which were then operated like boats. None of these methods having proved successful, experiments were continued further with steam locomotion. Peter Cooper produced the first successful steam engine in the United States—an upright boiler on a flat car. Thereafter steam soon superseded all other forms of traction. The growth of the Baltimore and Ohio was not rapid; when the 133 miles of the railroad between Charleston and Hamburg were completed in 1833, it immediately became the longest stretch of track in the world.

The first American railroads were modeled after the earlier forms of transportation—turnpikes and canals. The cars were built (and sometimes propelled) like boats. The theory of private toll roads was taken over for their operation. Each user furnished his own carriage and horse, and paid a fee for the use of the road. This conception of the nature of the railroad disappeared very early, but can be traced as far west as Arkansas in the legislation of the thirties.

Improvements in motive power were paralleled by changes in track and equipment. Wooden ties soon replaced those of stone. Wooden rails were improved by putting an L shaped piece of iron on the top, which improved the wearing qualities immensely. The flanges were soon transferred to the wheels, thus decreasing the

expense and saving friction. The remaining iron strips
had a bad habit of curling up and running through the
floor of the wooden car; this danger was removed when
the rails were made entirely of iron. The early upright
boiler was soon replaced by a vertical one with steam
coils. The carriages soon began to look less like boats
and more like the present day railroad car.

These first railroads were not a self-evident improvement over other forms of transportation. Considering
cost, speed, convenience, and safety, the canals were
able to wage a vigorous struggle for supremacy. Turnpikes were also a factor of importance. Mail contracts
were sometimes awarded the turnpikes in preference
to railroads because of their greater speed. An average
of fifteen miles an hour was considered very fast, and
most trains ran a great deal more slowly. Not until
1838 were all railroads made post roads.

By the early forties the railroads were securely pre-
dominate as a means of transportation. Construction
was gradually gaining momentum and continually extending further west. A New York-Chicago line was completed in 1853, and a Philadelphia-Chicago line in 1858.
Railroads began to reach the Mississippi, and the eastern
railroad net began to assume permanent form.

The further west that railroads were built, the greater
were the difficulties encountered in their construction.
Eastern construction had at least the advantage of
being carried on in well established communities with
facilities for securing material and labor, and sufficient
traffic to support the road when it was built. The West
had no such advantages to offer new lines.

A good share of the West was still unorganized and

without settlement by 1850. The Indians had been moved west of Missouri during the twenties and the thirties, to the land that was to be "eternally" theirs. It was considered that all this territory was a desert. Even as late as 1850 the federal government experimented with Syrian camels as a possible means of transportation. The moving of the Indians was the precursor to the organization of the freed territory as territories and then as states. Missouri was admitted as a state in 1820, Arkansas in 1836, and Iowa in 1846, while Minnesota attained a territorial status in 1849. At the same time, new territory was being gained in the Northwest and the Southwest. The annexation of Texas, the settlement of the Oregon dispute with Great Britain, and the acquisitions of the Mexican War all served to round out the continental possessions of the United States. By 1850 Texas and California had been admitted as states, while Oregon, Utah, and New Mexico had become territories. The remainder of the West remained unorganized Indian country.

The territorial organization and statehood of the greater part of the West did not indicate a large population. The census of 1850 showed only about a million and a quarter inhabitants in a territory that today has thirty million. Missouri, the most populous state, had about half of the total population. Minnesota could boast of only 6,077 souls, in a larger territory than today supports nearly two and a half million. A population of a million and a quarter, spread over half a continent, was hardly a field for successful railroad operations. The redeeming features were that such population as existed was limited in the most part to fairly small areas, and that the total number of inhabitants were increasing so rapidly that a great deal of the country would soon be well settled.

The basic difficulty of western railroad construction, however, was that of securing capital. The westerner was such because he had not become wealthy in the East. Whatever property he possessed was in the form of land, machinery, buildings, and stock. Surplus capital was practically non-existent, which meant that all money-raising schemes depended for their ultimate success upon interesting eastern capital.

The western railroad promoter found only one problem easier to solve than had his eastern predecessor. By 1850 railroad materials and equipment had become fairly well standardized, so that only a few points remained open for individual solution. The principal of these was the matter of gauge. Prior to the Civil War there was practically no attempt made to create a standard track width, and those in common use varied from 3' 6" to 6'. The westerner's decision as to gauge depended on his estimate of the comparative economy in construction and operation. The importance of having the same track width as the connecting roads was not evident, since there were practically no connecting roads.

After capital had been secured and materials decided upon, came the difficulty of getting the materials where they were to be used. Not until 1854 did any railroad reach the east bank of the Mississippi, although seven roads were completed that far in the next eight years. Through lines were practically unknown. Short roads of varying gauge were the rule. Little attempt was made to correlate the various standards of time in use and to have the trains make connections. Each new line meant reshipment, and for a long haul the waits were interminable.

The "Erie war" of the middle fifties was a striking example of the disorganization then existing in the railroad field. The New York Central was trying to produce a through line, and one of the points at which two short lines were to be connected was Erie. All the people benefiting through the reshipment protested—draymen, freight handlers, hotel and restaurant proprietors. The friction resulted in open warfare and riots before the New York Central finally succeeded in its object.

A great part of the railroad supplies used in the West did not come overland at all, but rather by boat through the Gulf of Mexico and up the Mississippi. Practically all such supplies came either from New England or England. The water route was somewhat longer, but avoided the frequent handlings which were so excessively costly, especially with the heavier items.

Water transportation also avoided the necessity of ferrying across the Mississippi. The only bridge built south of St. Paul before the Civil War was the one at Davenport, completed during the middle fifties. The St. Louis bridge was not completed until after the war. If the road under construction began at the Mississippi it could haul its own supplies from that point. If not, they were further reshipped as far as possible by water and then carried overland by wagon. At best the process was exceedingly expensive.

A final difficulty lay in securing the man-power necessary for construction and operation. Labor was scarce. Every westerner hoped to become a landowner or merchant, and as long as land was cheap and opportunities many, a supply of unskilled labor was hard to secure and even harder to retain. At best the unskilled labor was performed by those who wanted to save a little money to buy land or open a store for themselves. Such labor was necessarily fluctuating and unsatisfactory.

Positions requiring skill and managerial ability were even more difficult to fill. Practically all the skilled mechanics, engineers, firemen, surveyors, construction engineers, superintendents, and general managers secured their training in the East. In ordinary times the demand for such men exceeded the supply, and many western railroad troubles can be traced to the absence of well trained and capable men in the better positions.

American optimism, and particularly western optimism, dismissed all these difficulties lightly. The latter forties and early fifties was everywhere a period of expansion, and the westerner was by nature a "booster." He had come from the East because he chafed under the restrictions of a well-organized society, and because he had faith in himself—that with an equal chance in a new country he would be able to amass the wealth which he had failed to secure in the East. Each individual westerner expected to become wealthy and famous; each city expected to become the metropolis of the West; and each state expected to become the industrial and artistic center of the nation. Before this spirit obstacles disappeared as if by magic. Some of them later reappeared with increased force and potency, but others were gone forever.

The threefold desire of the West was for land, capital, and transportation. With these three desires satisfied the millennium would ensue. In railroads it saw the necessary transportation, and the resulting enthusiasm was unlimited. No serious check came to the feeling until the original debts incurred so gladly began to come due

—usually in twenty years. Then the settler or his son began to reconsider the advantages of railroads from the bitter light of experience, and the results were frequently disheartening.

When the West became interested in any project it turned naturally to the government for assistance. Railroads were no exception, and towns, cities, townships, counties, and states contributed their quota toward improved transportation. Even the national government was persuaded to donate large tracts of land from the public domain, and even in one case to lend money. This hope of government action was largely non-political, for the West felt that it was but the duty of government to help it attain the desires closest to its heart.

Western enthusiasm was reinforced and made productive by a similar feeling in the East. The expansion of business and credit produced surplus capital seeking investment. Everyone had confidence in the future of the United States, and nothing was more natural than that a large portion of this surplus capital should be invested in western railroads. Some went into purely western projects, while others went to expand more easterly lines in order to draw tributary business from the ever-growing West.

The rapid growth of the West with its ever expanding business opportunities gave a tinge of color and romance to merchandizing, which was ordinarily more prosaic. Vast stretches of the West remained an open page for the pen of the adventurous and romantic. Even ordinarily hard-headed businessmen caught the vision of a future country of cities, farms, and mines, and did their part toward making the dream a reality. There was a gripping romantic feeling to the thought of the ever-extending steel fingers, which would one day reach the golden land of California and tap the mystic richness of the Far East.

The possibilities and advantages of trade with the Far East were a golden Mecca for the thoughts of the people of the thirties and forties. China and Japan were just becoming known, and no tale of their wealth was too exaggerated for credence. Railroad enthusiasts early became enamoured with the idea of trade with the Far East, and adduced this possible commerce as one of the important reasons why a road linking the Atlantic and Pacific coasts should be built.

Years later, after the transcontinental railroad was an established fact, it became a favorite after-dinner sport for elderly gentlemen to lay claim to the original idea. They were ably seconded by painstaking historians, until finally it was shown that the idea of a transcontinental railroad antedated the railroad itself. Regardless of the varied claims to priority, it may be said that the visionaries had the idea of a transcontinental railroad many years before the longest-haired and wildest-eyed could conceive of construction as being possible.

The transcontinental idea was purely chimerical until the middle forties. As yet it was a mechanical impossibility. The United States had only a small and uncertain hold on the Pacific coast, and the intervening land was for the most part unknown and desolate. Ultimate finality lay in the fact that any trade with the Far East was very precarious until treaty arrangements could be made with the countries concerned.

From the middle of the forties conditions began to change rapidly. The first commercial treaty with the Far East came in 1844, when Caleb Cushing secured such a treaty with China, which was comparable to the one made a few years before between China and Great Britain. A decade later occurred Commodore Perry's expedition to Japan, leading to the opening of that country to western trade. With these two contacts assured, trade with the East was something more than a chimera. The opening of the Far East to trade vastly increased the interest in China and Japan and their products. Caleb Cushing and other travelers drew large audiences to their Lyceum lectures on the Far East and business men began to look forward to the silks and spices of Cathay.

The one man who typified the combination of railroad enthusiasm and the lure of the East to the greatest extent was Asa Whitney, a merchant of New York. Practical, yet with a touch of mysticism and romance in his nature, he was indefatigable in urging the importance of the eastern trade and its possible acquisition if a transcontinental railroad were built. For the decade after the Cushing treaty was signed he spent most of his time and money in advancing this pet project. He visited practically every state in the union to secure support, went over a large share of the route himself, and nagged Congress incessantly for aid. More than any other man he was responsible for the development of the transcontinental project; the history of the idea is linked inextricably with his name.

Whitney's plans, as well as those of practically all transcontinental enthusiasts of the forties and fifties, were based fundamentally on government action. His first proposition was that he be given a sixty-mile strip of land from Lake Michigan to the coast, which he would sell as necessary to pay the cost of construction. Any remaining proceeds would constitute his profit. The land involved in this plan would have been somewhat more than is included in the present state of Illinois. At a later time Whitney modified his original plan by offering to pay 16 cents an acre for the land. The House Committee on Roads and Canals reported the project favorably in 1850, but decided that he had offered an excessive price for the land and proposed 10 cents an acre as the proper figure. Congress took no action on this report. Whitney found his chief opposition in Congress in Benton and his "national road" advocates, who wanted the government to build the road with the proceeds of the land sales. The majority of Congress was apathetic to the whole project, and no action was taken.

Necessarily Whitney was limited in his early plans to the northern route. The acquisition of the entire Southwest and the whole seaboard during the latter forties gave a choice of route which had not existed before. A transcontinental railroad was at least possible, and the interest became more general. The Gadsden purchase was consummated in order to give a southern route entirely within the limits of the United States.

The railroad movement played a large part in the rapid organization of the new acquisitions into states and territories. Douglas's support of the Kansas-Nebraska bill was undoubtedly influenced in large part by his plans for a Pacific railroad. The only territory remaining unorganized by the middle fifties was the present Oklahoma, and a strip lying between the western boundary of Minnesota and the Missouri River.

Settlement in the new territory at first proceeded very slowly. The Santa Fe trail, and the California and Oregon trails by way of South Pass brought a few hunters, traders, and later settlers, but a real impetus was lacking. The needed spur came with the discovery of gold in California in 1848. Miners, traders, and settlers began to go west by the thousands instead of by the tens, so that within a year it was estimated that there were nearly 300,000 people on the Pacific coast.

Increased population immediately necessitated better transportation. The Overland Mail and later the Pony Express made possible the delivery of mail and passengers, but the inconveniences of travel hardly encouraged that type of business, while the expense was too great for the hauling of heavy freight. The overland service was supplemented by the route across Panama. The railroad across the isthmus was completed in 1855, and connections at each terminal were made by the Pacific Mail Steamship Company, which had a monopoly of all such business. This route necessitated two reshipments, but was a good deal more convenient than traveling overland. All heavy non-perishable freight was shipped around the Horn. While slow and somewhat dangerous, this route was a good deal cheaper because it was entirely by water and no reshipments were necessary.

Increased population in the Far West meant the nearer approach of transcontinental railroad building, and in consequence the various possible routes began to assume definite form in the minds of railroad enthusiasts. By 1849 *DeBow's Review* could list eight well defined routes lying between Panama and Oregon. The number of such routes within the territory of the United States was distinctly limited by the barrier of the Rocky Mountains. In general only three variations were advanced. The first was to run from Lake Michigan by the northern route to Oregon; the second was to run by way of South Pass to San Francisco; the third was in the south, to pass the mountains either at Yuma or the Needles.

During the forties and fifties the advantages and disadvantages of the various routes were urged endlessly. Many people considered the Oregon route too far north, and felt that it would be blocked by snow most of the year. It had the advantage, however, of being an easier engineering operation than the central route. Further south there was considerable fear of the "Great American Desert," which was thought to occupy a great part of the Middle West.

At the time of the first proposals for a government aided railroad to the coast, constitutional objections were raised to the right of the federal government either to charter or aid such a project. This obstruction, however, was dead by 1850, so that it played no real part by the time the idea had reached a stage where it was no longer chimerical. The real difficulty lay in the choice of a route.

The northern route had the least serious consideration. Climatic conditions and lack of population were reinforced by the fact that its western terminus was not desirable. It was true that a northern point such as Portland was advantageous in trade with the Far East, but more important was the consideration that the majority of the Pacific coast population was in California.

As a rule northerners favored the South Pass route, which would give a direct line to San Francisco from either Chicago or St. Louis. Southerners were equally emphatic in favor of the southern route. This sectional division, reinforced by the division in Congress, made legislation impossible, and both Benton and Douglas

were balked in the schemes which were close to
their hearts.

Numerous compromises were suggested both inside
Congress and out. The usual plan was to suggest the
line desired and then to include branches to other sections. Benton favored the St. Louis route, with branches
to Chicago and Memphis; Rush (Texas) favored the
New Orleans route, with northern branches; Gwin (California) favored the Memphis route, with branches to
Dubuque, St. Louis, Matagordi, New Orleans, and Fort
Nisqually. Any such solution was bound to remain one-
sided, and by no stretch of the imagination could it be
considered acceptable to all parties.

The North was unwilling to agree to any line which
would produce a closer connection between the old South
and the new Southwest. Southern leaders were equally
unwilling that the new West be brought into close and
direct contact with the North. Many of them were looking forward to the eventual breakdown of the union, and
were unwilling to help build a railroad which would later
be entirely northern. For many years it seemed that
nothing short of a political or economic cataclysm would
make agreement possible.

Although the building of a transcontinental railroad
was made impossible by conflicting sectional interests, a
considerable groundwork of information was secured prior
to 1860. Beginning with the Lewis and Clark expedition many scouting and exploring parties covered the
West, and their numerous reports furnished a much-
needed basis of fact for railroad speculation.

Some of these surveys were for military purposes, some
for the building of turnpikes, and some for railroads. The
most important single survey was carried on under Sec-

retary of War Davis, and the results submitted to Congress in 1855 in ten bulky volumes. As was to be expected the recommendation favored the southern route. The significant part of the report, however, was the immense amount of information, which proved invaluable at a later time.

The transcontinental enthusiasm of the fifties had a twofold importance. Besides producing the information which later enabled the building of a railroad to the Pacific coast, it reacted in favor of the plans for local lines west of the Mississippi. Enthusiasts for a transcontinental road were bound to be in favor of local lines, and practically every small trans-Mississippi road that was begun during the fifties had visions of some day completing its line to the Pacific coast.

CHAPTER II

THE FIRST CONSTRUCTION

Universal prosperity combined inextricably with the growth of the West and the growing interest in a transcontinental railroad to produce the first trans-Mississippi railroads during the fifties. Especially important was a long series of internal improvement conventions which brought the railroad question to the point of action. Interested either in internal improvements as a whole, or later in the transcontinental idea, their reflex action was to encourage local railroad enthusiasm and construction.

The first important convention which concerned itself with railroads was the one held at Memphis in 1845. The venerable Calhoun was the presiding officer, and gave the keynote address. His emphasis was mostly on internal improvements in the old South, and he barely mentioned the situation further west. Following his lead the convention devoted very little time to the consideration of western matters, and was content with putting itself on record as favoring a transcontinental road by the southern route.

A parallel convention was held at Chicago in 1847 as a protest against Polk's veto of the River and Harbor Bill the preceding year. Little attention was devoted to railroad matters, but after the main convention had adjourned, Horace Greeley took the chair and resolutions were passed favoring a transcontinental railroad by the central route. The Chicago convention was particularly notable for its widespread publicity.   Greeley published extensive accounts of it in the widely read New York *Semi-Weekly Tribune,* and naturally did not omit giving very favorable mention to the extra meeting of which he was chairman. Thurlow Weed reported the convention for the *Albany Evening Journal.*

The first convention interested entirely in railroads met at St. Louis in October, 1849, to discuss ways and means for a transcontinental road. It was widely attended, but the largest delegations came from the two closest states—Illinois and Missouri. There was very little doubt as to which route the convention would favor. The real excitement came in the struggle of Douglas and Benton for control of the proceedings. Douglas won the contest and became chairman. The final resolutions favored the San Francisco-St. Louis route, with branches to Chicago and Memphis.

The corresponding southern convention was held a week later at Memphis. The Tennessee and Mississippi delegations disputed the control of the meeting, with the former finally victorious. Lieutenant Maury, who claimed to have originated the idea of the southern route, was elected chairman. Both Asa Whitney and Jefferson Davis were present as visitors.

As was expected, the Memphis convention recorded itself in favor of the southern route, with a terminus at Memphis. It also favored the organization of the entire West into states in order to avoid any possible constitutional objections. No attempt was made to provide for a compromise route, except that one of the members, Albert Pike of Arkansas, subsequently gave publicity to a plan to build both the St. Louis and Memphis lines.

These conventions marked the beginning of a long
series of similar meetings, of which notable ones were
held at Philadelphia in 1850, Iowa City in 1851, New
Orleans in 1852, and Little Rock in 1853. They were
all mass conventions attended by public spirited citizens
who were willing to devote their time and energy to public undertakings. Railroads were not considered as purely
business ventures but rather as public works benefiting
the state and nation.

Conventions of the magnitude of the Pacific railroad
gatherings were evidences of a widespread interest and
enthusiasm. Prevented by sectional differences from attaining its legitimate object, it turned into other chan-
nels. Particularly was it important in intensifying the
desire for local railroad construction, which it fanned to
a white heat during the prosperity of the early fifties.
The resulting wave of enthusiasm swept over the entire West, and produced innumerable attempts at railroad
construction.

The beginning of the railroad movement is impossible
to localize, but the first actual construction is more easily
documented. Quite naturally it occurred in the oldest
and most populous of the trans-Mississippi states—Missouri. Railroad agitation in Missouri went back at least
as far as the thirties, for as early as 1836 an internal improvement convention meeting in St. Louis had favored
railroad construction. In accordance with its recommendations the state legislature chartered a number of
small lines the following year, to afford an adjunct to
water transportation. Few thought that the railroad
would ever be able to compete seriously with the rivers.
At best it could only be a collecting agency.

At the same time a Board of Internal Improvements

was created, which was to have the oversight of the railroads as one of its duties. It was abolished before any railroads came into existence. This early and abortive movement came to an end with the panic of 1837; up to this time no railroad had even been begun.

When railroad agitation revived in the forties its principal object lay in securing a transcontinental road which would run directly west from St. Louis. Senator Benton was the outstanding protagonist of the scheme. Early in 1849 he introduced a resolution into Congress favoring his project, and from that date events began to move rapidly. In March of the same year the Pacific Railroad of Missouri was chartered by the state; in October the St. Louis convention assembled; and in the following January the company was organized and books opened. A chief engineer was hired from the East, surveys were started across the state, and contracts were let for the first part of the road.

The first ground for the new enterprise was broken by Mayor Kennett of St. Louis, on Independence Day, 1851. This epoch-making event was duly celebrated by the citizens of St. Louis with parades, fireworks, and speeches. Orators proclaimed the past, present, and future glories of the great state of Missouri, and of its capital and principal city, St. Louis.

The Pacific Railroad of Missouri was chartered to run from St. Louis to Kansas City, with the hope that it would eventually make transcontinental connections. Its patrons, headed by Thomas Allen, were the wealthy and public spirited citizens of St. Louis. Civic and state pride were the dominating motives in its early construction.

The greatest difficulty of the Pacific Railroad of Missouri, as of every other western road, was the securing of adequate capital. Stock and bond subscriptions were not limited because of lack of confidence or enthusiasm, but rather by the even more potent lack of capital. Even when capital was subscribed in considerable quantities, it frequently occurred that a large part of the subscriptions remained unpaid for many years, and sometimes never became available.

The one great prospect for all railroad security salesmen was the government. Local or state subscriptions, or a federal land grant, were possibilities which no railroad promoter overlooked. No matter what form of government aid was secured, its value still depended on the availability of eastern capital. Local and state subscriptions were made in bonds, which had to be sold in the East. Their value to the railroads lay in the difference in value between their selling price and that of the original railroad securities. In any event they were but slightly more salable in the West than railroad stocks and bonds. Even the land from a federal grant was sold for the most part to eastern settlers and land companies.

The difficulty of securing capital meant that such money as was raised had to be made to cover as much ground as possible. Grading, track, and equipment were of the poorest, which meant that wrecks were of common occurrence, and the cost of maintenance and operation high. A very common way of husbanding the company's cash resources was to pay the construction company partly in stocks and bonds. Such securities were always issued at a discount while at the same time the construction company padded its cost accounts to take care of any further depreciation.

This sort of financial practice normally produced an

over-capitalized and poorly constructed road, with very little profit in operation. Many promoters foresaw this eventuality and secured their profit in the construction. By organizing their own construction companies they were able to make satisfactory contracts with themselves on their own terms. If the promoter was then not too moral or too stupid, it was easily possible to corner all the available capital as well as the control of the company by the time the track was constructed. While this procedure was eminently satisfactory in some respects, it had the disadvantage of destroying any possibility that the road would be able to pay dividends for years to come.

These general propositions apply in most part to the Pacific Railroad of Missouri. Paid up individual subscriptions were meagre, but were supplemented by town, county, state, and federal aid. Construction was paid for in part with the securities of the company, issued below par. The track was poorly constructed and the road badly equipped.

Even with all the aid that could be secured for a popular cause, the Pacific Railroad progressed slowly. Five miles were completed by the end of 1852, but by 1857 the track extended only as far as Jefferson City, a distance of 125 miles. At the same time the resources of the company were practically exhausted, so that future construction was exceedingly problematic.

The Pacific Railroad was soon followed by others. The determining factor as to which roads were built was the attitude of the state of Missouri, which pursued an extensive policy of state aid during the fifties, attempting to produce an adequate railroad system by the use of the credit of the state. Considerable loans were made, secured by a first mortgage on the road concerned. These loans were in the form of state bonds which found their sale in the East at a somewhat higher rate than the railroad first mortgage bonds would have brought. For example, the Pacific Railroad received a total of $7,000,000 in state bonds, from which it realized $6,026,427, or approximately three-fifths of the total cost of the main line to 1860.

Five principal lines were contemplated by the state legislation—(1) the Pacific Railroad of Missouri, running due west from St. Louis to Kansas City; (2) the North Missouri, running northwest from St. Louis in the direction of Omaha; (3) the Southwest Branch of the Pacific Railroad, running southwest from St. Louis and having transcontinental aspirations; (4) the St. Louis and Iron Mountain, running due south from St. Louis; (5) the Hannibal and St. Joseph, connecting the Mississippi and Missouri rivers between the points named in the title.

All of these lines benefited by the state encouragement and started construction. Their progress was uniformly slow, the best record being made by the Hannibal and St. Jo. Both this line and the Pacific Railroad participated in a federal land grant, but even this additional aid did not appreciably hasten construction. Land was plentiful and cheap, so that the immediate return from land sales was not large.

The panic of 1857 put an end to the Missouri policy of state aid. The results up to that time were disappointingly meagre in comparison to the effort. Missouri was the oldest and most prosperous of the western states, had the earliest start, and had contributed generously to railroad construction. In spite of these advantages only three hundred miles of line had been constructed by the end of 1857.

Offsetting the three hundred miles of railroad were a depleted state treasury, bankrupt roads, and a business depression. All available funds seemed to have been spent and work was in abeyance. Missouri's splendid plans had so far only materialized into a few fragments of poorly constructed and badly managed roads. The future of Missouri railroad construction indeed looked dark.

The first trans-Mississippi railroad line to be put into use after the memorable opening of the Pacific Railroad, was situated in Texas. As in the case of Missouri, the interest of Texas in railroads went back to the thirties, at which time Texas was independent. Railroads were combined with canal projects and banking operations. Plans were even advanced to the point where work was begun, but the disorganized condition of the country put an end to operations at that time.

When prosperity again returned after the panic of 1837 the banking and canal schemes had disappeared, and the railroad projects became all-important. Most of the projected roads contemplated the tapping of the rich country back from the Gulf, and the carrying of its products to some available Gulf port. A speculative eye was turned toward possible connections east to Memphis and New Orleans, north to St. Louis and Chicago, and west to the Pacific coast.

The most populous portion of Texas was the district tributary to Galveston Bay, and it was here that railroad projects first began to assume definite form. The Harrisburg and Brazos Railroad began work as early as 1840, but many interruptions occurred before the work produced any important results. After several transfers the property finally became the Buffalo Bayou, Brazos

and Colorado, under which name it was the first Texas
railroad to be put into operation.

The first rails were laid on the B. B. B. and C. in 1852,
antedating the Pacific Railroad by several months, but
the formal opening of the first stretch of twenty miles to
traffic did not occur until August, 1853. From this time
progress was slow, but steady. Thirty years later this
road, then known as the Galveston, Houston and San
Antonio, had the poetic justice of being the first southern
road to make transcontinental connections.

Most of the other Texas lines built before the panic
of 1857 also centered in the Galveston-Houston district.
The total construction by that time was not even as
great as that of Missouri. The population of the state
was small, and state aid was given conservatively. The
miracle was that any railroads were built at all. Probably the answer lies in the concentration of population
and in the character of the hardy pioneers who settled
Texas and wrested it from the control of Mexico.

Lying between Missouri and Texas was the unfortunate state of Arkansas. Either too far north or too far
south to become an important commercial center, its
land did not prove very attractive to settlers. In consequence it increased in population and wealth but
slowly. It was further unfortunate in entering the Union
just in time to be involved in the banking craze of the
thirties, and as a result it hopelessly impaired its credit
in the first few years of statehood. During the fifties
it had neither the private or state credit, nor the wealth
or population to start railroad construction.

In spite of all drawbacks railroad enthusiasm was as
strong in Arkansas as elsewhere. The number of railroad projects per square mile compared very favorably

with that of other states. The spirit was willing but
the flesh was weak. Money was scarce, credit was non-
existent, and the economic urge was not pressing. The
only railroad to start construction prior to 1857 was the
Little Rock and Memphis, which was aided by a federal
land grant. Even with this assistance it was unable to
put any track into operation.

Arkansas's chief hope was the building of a transcontinental road which would have its terminus at Memphis. If such a line materialized it would cross the
entire state from east to west. Citizens of Arkansas attended all railroad conventions and did all in their power
to further the project. The one road that was enabled
to start building was projected in the hope that it would
one day constitute part of such a through line to
the coast.

The conditions in Iowa were somewhat unique. A potentially rich state, it was yet very slow in developing.
Population had a tendency either to go down the Mississippi from the mouth of the Ohio, or to follow the
Great Lakes route. In either case Iowa received only
a small and indirect stream of settlers. The result was
that the early development of Iowa was very slow;
but once the country was made accessible its progress
was rapid.

Iowa railroad progress followed the same tendencies
as did the general settlement of the state, a slow start
but a fast finish. Railroad agitation existed to some extent during the thirties, but only came to a high point
about the time of the Iowa City railroad convention of
October, 1851, presided over by ex-Governor Lucas of
Ohio. Proposed railroad routes were mainly east and
west, from the Mississippi toward the Missouri. A few

north and south lines were favored, particularly to include the state capital at Des Moines. Railroad construction in Iowa had an unusual deterrent in the lack of governmental encouragement. The constitution of 1846 forbade any state debt of over $100,000 except for some specific object and secured by a provision for payment, while county aid was limited by the law of 1855. Even federal aid was slow in coming, and Iowa was the last of the first tier of trans-Mississippi states to receive a land grant.

The principal advantage of Iowa beside its fertile land, was its geographic position. As long as river transportation was dominant Iowa was not in the direct line of travel, but when railroads became important the situation was reversed. The early preëminence of Chicago as a railroad center made it inevitable that a large share of through lines to the West would pass through Iowa. As soon as the Chicago railroads reached the Mississippi the future of Iowa was assured.

The first Iowa railroad was completed in 1855, and from that time construction was steady. For a number of years Iowa's railroad mileage was roughly equal to that of Missouri, but once she drew ahead she never lost the lead. Less government aid meant decreased speculation, which combined with geographic advantages served to produce a railroad system in Iowa that was better constructed and more efficiently operated than those elsewhere.

Minnesota, with its population of 6,000 in 1850, can be compared most easily with Arkansas in its mileage of "projected" railroads in contrast to its lack of funds for their construction. Handicapped by a negligible population, territorial status, a total absence of credit, and a geographical position too far north to attract many through lines, it overcame its difficulties by ignoring them. To its inhabitants Minnesota was the center of the United States, a potentially rich country with a beautifully mild climate, and unavoidable for the building of through lines to the Pacific. The one minor detail which could not be imagined into existence was the capital necessary to build and equip the much-to-be-desired railroads.

The principal routes for the "projected" railroads of Minnesota centered in St. Paul and Minneapolis, north to Duluth (then a small village), south toward St. Louis, and west toward Nebraska Territory (then including all of the Dakota territory). Direct east and west roads were suggested from such Mississippi river points as Red Wing, Winona, and La Crosse, and from some northern point such as Duluth. None of these routes were any more than contemplated; no road was built prior to 1857.

Minnesota during the fifties is the most excellent example of simon-pure railroad enthusiasm, unalloyed by the least possibility of any immediate construction. Prior to the panic of 1857 it was a territory and had no population, no capital, no credit, and no government aid. In spite of these drawbacks railroad enthusiasm reached such a high point that as soon as federal aid came and statehood was achieved, the state embarked upon an extensive policy of subsidized construction, entirely oblivious to the existence of such a minor detail as a national financial panic.

The general railroad enthusiasm of the early fifties was bound to find echoes in the remoter portions of the West. Settlers in Kansas and Nebraska began to think seriously of railroad construction to be undertaken in the near future, while even in the Far West the railroad feeling had its reflection. A small wooden horse road was installed at the falls of the Columbia River in 1850, but can hardly be considered significant. Iron rails and locomotives were not added until 1861.

One railroad in California was able to find the funds for construction prior to 1857. The rapid increase of the state's population since the discovery of gold had concentrated itself particularly in the rich Sacramento-Placer mining district. Transportation from the mines to the Sacramento River was essential, and for the purpose of satisfying this need the Sacramento Valley Railroad was organized in 1852. Its opening excursion, from Sacramento north to Placer, occurred on November 13, 1855. A year later it was extended as far as Folsom. The Sacramento Valley Railroad was the product of unusual conditions, and remained the only railroad in California until after the Civil War. For many years it was one of the best paying roads in the United States, but its success did not lead others to emulate its example.

Western railroad enthusiasm was always a facsimile of a similar situation in the East. Railroad interest reached its high points simultaneously all over the country with periods of economic prosperity. The amount of construction varied directly with the population and wealth. The prosperous period of the thirties brought the first eastern construction, and the first interest in the Middle West. The boom period of the latter forties and the early fifties saw the area of construction expand further west and the creation of a non-productive interest in the Far West. Later periods of prosperity saw the process repeated further and further west, until finally the railroad net had reached the Pacific coast.

The interest of the trans-Mississippi West in railroads during the thirties was only an auxiliary to water transportation. Lines were chartered to connect the large inland towns and to transport freight to the rivers. Many of these charters were made on the assumption that the roads would be a sort of glorified toll road, with each farmer furnishing his own horse and wagon. In many cases maximum charges were specified, and in later years they proved an important type of precedent for government regulation of rates.

By the time that the panic of 1837 had receded the West was much better prepared for railroad construction. Population and wealth had increased enormously, while additional eastern construction had developed the mechanics of railroading so that it was no longer an experimental science. It still remained true that capital was not available in the West, but the prosperity of the East produced a sufficient surplus to permit of many western investments. Economic prosperity explains the building of the first trans-Mississippi railroads, but it was reinforced and assisted by the movement for transcontinental communication, which in turn was advanced by the territorial expansion of the United States, the rush of population to the Far West, and the opening of trade relations with the Far East.

This early construction was entirely on a state basis, each state endeavoring to foster a complete transportational system for the use of its citizens. The only important exception to the policy of state encouragement was in the case of Iowa, and here the excellent geographical position more than offset any lack of state assistance.

Railroads were uppermost in everyone's mind as the true economic panacea. Projected lines were innumerable, and construction was carried on considerably faster than economic conditions warranted. Together with this overbuilding and overexpansion of credit went its usual concomitants of speculation, mismanagement, and corruption. Only a pin's prick was necessary to break the bubble.

The pin prick came in 1857. The end of the Crimean War brought the renewed competition of Russian wheat, while the continued expansion of British shipping curtailed American business. Banking houses were overloaded with unredeemable paper, and credit was strained to the breaking point. The crash came with the failure of several important banking houses, and soon the country was in the midst of a financial depression and economic hard times.

The financial panic meant the cessation of western railroad building. Loans were called, and the further sale of stocks and bonds was impossible. Even state and local bonds in the hands of the railroads declined to such a figure that their sale was impossible. Many of the roads went into the hands of the receiver, while the remainder curtailed their elaborate building programs.

In many ways the railroad enthusiasm of the fifties paralleled the banking craze of the thirties. Business was good, credit was expanding, everyone was optimistic. In the thirties the people and their various governmental agencies had placed their confidence in banks, and when they collapsed the whole financial fabric of the country went with them. In the fifties it was the railroads that were looked upon as the apostles of a new order. When the saturation point had been reached and the market overflooded with poor securities the whole financial structure again collapsed and the country was plunged into another business depression.

CHAPTER III

The most observed trait of westerners has always been their sturdy individualism and self-reliance. It has been commonly remarked that the crude and unsettled conditions of the West led to a self-completeness that was lacking elsewhere. In spite of this consensus of opinion, which is probably well founded, the West has always been the first section to ask for government action. In times of prosperity it has looked for encouragement, and in times of depression for relief.

The early settler who went through the period of territorial organization, and then the formation of a state government and its acceptance by Congress, was in a frame of mind to appreciate fully the powers and uses of government. He was in close contact with an institution which he himself had helped to form for his own advantage. When he wanted cheaper land, more money, roads, canals, or bridges, it was to the government that he looked first for assistance.

The westerner's attitude toward government grew first out of his contact with local and state institutions, but was carried on to the federal institutions. He had the feeling that the central government was directly responsible for good times, and equally culpable in times of distress. Since western life was one continuous struggle it usually occurred that the Washington government was blamed rather than praised. Relief was sought from all kind of difficulties, real and imagined, preventable and inevitable.

When railroad construction became the popular economic panacea, the western states at once looked to Congress for assistance. They looked at the large area of the public lands lying within their boundaries, and felt that at least this portion of their territory should be used for their own benefit. It seemed manifestly unfair that they could not use their own land for their own advantage. Why should not land be given at least to aid important projects for internal improvement within the state?

Having persuaded themselves that they had a moral right to at least a considerable portion of the public domain lying within their own borders, the western states argued further that if their pet projects were assisted the main advantages would accrue to the nation as a whole. Railroads, for example, would be of tremendous commercial and military advantage to the entire United States.

It was even argued further that such gifts of land to aid the railroads, instead of being a drain on the resources of the government would actually be an asset. The remainder of the land near the railroads would be doubled in price, while settlement would be encouraged. In fact, such land aid was not only a duty to the West, but also a duty to the rest of the country in the benefits which would accrue to everyone.

Citizens of the Northeast and Southeast were not so easily persuaded of the desirability of giving western land to aid internal improvements. They held to the idea that the public domain was the original possession of the first thirteen states, and that they had given it to the central government for the advantage of the nation as a whole. They could not feel that the giving of transportation facilities to the West was of sufficient common benefit to justify the gift of a large portion of the public domain. The theory that the proceeds from the sale of the public domain should be used to pay off the national debt died a lingering death, and was partially replaced by the idea of distributing the proceeds of the land sales among the various states of the Union.

The Southeast was even more solidly opposed to land grants for western internal improvements than was the Northeast. Constitutional arguments had their root in economic conditions. Slavery was on the defensive and feared the creation of transportational systems which would make the North dominant in its trade relations with the West. Even the immediate control of the western railroads was bound to be vested in the North eventually, because it was there that the surplus capital of the country existed.

The East went just as far in its opposition to land grants as the West did in its support. It was argued that such gifts would only produce speculation. The majority of the valuable land would be cornered in the hope of future advances in price. Instead of the West being benefited it would actually be injured by the operations of the large monied interests.

The advocates of government aid had a powerful argument in precedent. Examples of government aid to internal improvements went as far back as 1796. Land was the one valuable surplus possession of the government. At first it was given to aid turnpike projects, and later during the canal enthusiasm of the twenties it had been given in considerable amounts for that purpose. It was fairly well established in principle, with certain limitations, that the government had the power to aid internal improvement projects by gifts of land.

The principal limitations of early federal practice lay in constitutional theory and state rights doctrine. It was generally assumed that while the government had the right to aid or construct internal improvements it did not have the power to maintain and operate them. Furthermore, Jackson's veto of the Maysville road bill crystalized the feeling that the government should not give aid to a project which was entirely local in nature.

Numerous proposals for railroad land grants were introduced into Congress during the twenties and thirties, but with one exception they failed to get further than to be reported from committee. In 1833 a grant which had formerly been made to the Illinois and Michigan canal was transferred to a railroad. It was never utilized.

During the early forties the sectional division of Congress was so obviously adverse to the passage of land grant legislation that but comparatively few bills were introduced. Representatives of the Southeast were definitely opposed. The Northeast was equally well committed to a policy of opposition except for a scattering of back-country Democratic members. Even the West was not entirely unanimous. There were a few Whigs who were in favor of Clay's plan to distribute the proceeds of land sales among the various states, and this group was joined by those who had an interest in river transportation and feared the competition of the railroads.

The advancing forties brought economic prosperity and a revived interest in railroads as well as a lessening of constitutional objections. Additional western members in Congress toward the close of the decade produced a continually increasing pressure because of the added importance of the West in the sectional struggle between the North and the South. More northern members began to be won over to a support of railroad aid on the basis of the additional commerce that it would bring to their section. The principal remaining difficulty, as in the case of the project of a transcontinental railroad, was to find the route or routes that would make a sufficiently wide appeal to secure a majority support in Congress.

By the time that Douglas entered the Senate in 1847 the movement for railroad aid was growing rapidly. As a westerner he was deeply interested in railroad projects, and had spent considerable thought in trying to conceive a plan that would appeal to all sections. The result of his cogitations appeared in the bill that he proposed for the aid of the Illinois Central. The line to be aided extended directly south from Chicago across the state of Illinois, with several branches. The West was already committed in favor of such projects. The North could be persuaded that it would receive some benefits, and the South could be appealed to because the road was to make southern connections.

Douglas's political sagacity was confirmed when enough eastern votes were accumulated to insure the passage of the bill in 1850. The state of Illinois was given a land grant for the use of the Illinois Central. A precedent was made, both in the giving of the land grant and in its terms. The way was opened to future similar legislation.

As soon as the passage of the Illinois Central act broke the Congressional deadlock, each of the public domain states began to clamor for its share of the booty. It seemed manifestly unfair to them that one state should receive what was denied the rest, and so by dint of persistent log-rolling other states began to share in the distribution of the public domain for railroad use. Western members were willing to trade their votes with other western members, and also with eastern Congressmen in order to procure for their state the advantages of a federal land grant.

All of the first tier of trans-Mississippi states, with the exception of Texas, received land grants for railroad use during the fifties. Texas had retained the control of her own land when she entered the Union, and in consequence was not included. During the same period, however, she evolved a land system of her own.

These grants of the fifties were all similar in their terms. Alternate sections of land, six sections in width, were granted along the line of the proposed road. In the event that settlers had already taken up any of this land there was a provision for an indemnity selection within fifteen miles of the road. Each line was to be completed within ten years or the land was to revert automatically to the public domain.

The administration of the land grants was mostly in the hands of the General Land Office, a part of the Department of the Interior. As soon as the railroad decided on its approximate route it sent a map of the project to the General Land Office, which thereupon withdrew from settlement all of the land within the indemnity limits of the grant. As fast as the line of the road was made definite the railroad selections were made and the remainder of the land reopened for settlement. Final deeds to the land were issued as fast as the road was completed and accepted by the President.

The theory back of the general application of the acts was sound, but complications arose in practice. The most serious difficulty lay in the tendency for settlers to take up land in spite of its withdrawal by the land office. The average emigrant could not see the justice of being prohibited from settling on the public domain wherever and whenever he wished. His attitude seemed especially justified when the railroad was slow in building. Most of the land was not taken up for quite a number of years, and in some cases the road was never built. Much Congressional legislation was necessary to take care of illegal settlers, and of conflicting claims between the settlers and the railroad companies.

An unexpected difficulty was encountered in the attitude of the courts toward the recapture clause of the land grants. It had been assumed that in case the railroad did not build within the specified time the land reverted to the public domain without further ado. The Supreme Court, however, in the case of Schulenburg v. Harriman, decided that the grants were made *in praesenti* and unless forfeited by a special act of Congress could be taken up whenever the railroad finished building its line, regardless of the time limit in the original grant. This decision was a prolific cause of misunderstanding and dissatisfaction in the West.

The railroads which were aided during the fifties were expected to form complete state transportational systems with the aid of a few short lines, which were expected to be built entirely by local effort. In general the main lines followed the routes suggested in Chapter II. Only incidental attention was paid to the connection of the lines of one state with those of its neighbors. Possible transcontinental routes were given a little more attention, but were never foremost in consideration.

As was to be expected, the grants were acclaimed by the West in terms of unstinted praise. As each state received its grant it began to foresee a comprehensive railroad system and began work in that direction. Enthusiasm was unbounded, and all of the railroads started construction, most of them with additional state and local aid. Necessarily many of the projects were abortive and the work that was done was purely formal.

The general feeling of buoyancy and hope received a sad shock in the panic of 1857, which caught most of the roads in the midst of extensive plans for building. Some of the roads continued their construction in spite of economic depression, while others discontinued building entirely. Instead of the hoped-for period of rapidly increasing railroad building came a period in which construction was barely sustained at its former rate.

Sober second thought disillusioned many people concerning the value of land grants. Land was not valuable until settlers appeared, and settlers would not come into the remoter portions of the West until railroads were constructed. The whole process was a vicious circle. The railroads were necessary before the land grants became valuable, while the roads could not be built until the proceeds of the land were available. In consequence the roads had to look elsewhere for the majority of their capital, and to sell their land as fast or as slowly as conditions warranted.

The panic of 1857 had hardly begun to recede before the Civil War opened. With the withdrawal of the South and the opening of hostilities conditions changed rapidly. The sectional division in respect to the organization of new territories and the building of a transcontinental road disappeared. The North was left free to follow its own devices.

The North proceeded at once to the territorial organization of the free Northwest. Dakota Territory was cut away from Nebraska (1861) and organized to include the formerly unorganized strip just west of Minnesota. Colorado and Nevada were organized as territories and Kansas was admitted to the Union. Later during the sixties Nevada and Nebraska were admitted as states, while Arizona, Idaho, and Montana were organized as territories. In consequence, all of the West except Indian Territory was made available for railroad expansion.

With the withdrawal of the South it became more desirable than ever that western railroads should be built. Political, economic, social, and military reasons all dictated the closer connection of the West and the North. Both local lines and a transcontinental line became more desirable, and if for no other reason, then to show the good will of the East toward the hopes and aspirations of the West.

As soon as Congress was able to spare time from pressing war exigencies it turned its consideration to the railroads of the West. Its most important action was the chartering of the first transcontinental project, and this action acted as an opening wedge to other similar roads, so that before the war was ended Congress had embarked quite definitely on a course of aid to all possible routes to the Pacific coast.

The grants of the sixties presented notable differences from those of the preceding decade. The policy of making lavish gifts to each state in order to foster a complete transportational system for each one was abandoned. The Kansas grant of 1863 was the only exception. In part this change of policy was dictated by the smaller population of the states further west and by the failure of earlier gifts to accomplish their purpose. More than this, however, the Civil War marked a change from local to national construction. The war itself was a factor in breaking down the separatism which had existed at an earlier time, and in building up a national spirit.

The later land grants were made for the most part to transcontinental lines, to their connections, and to particular strategic roads. State boundaries were frequently overlooked. Whereas the older grants were made to the states, which in turn gave them to the roads, the new grants were frequently given directly to the roads to be aided. A number of the roads to whom aid was given were chartered in the act providing for the grant.

The terms of the acts also changed somewhat. The Kansas act increased the amount of the land to the odd sections within ten miles of the road and broadened the indemnity selection to within twenty miles of the road. Later grants followed this precedent, and were nearly all of increased scope, some providing for a fifty mile indemnity limit in the territories. Increasing population did something toward increasing the scope of both the grant and the indemnity limits. In the states further east it was necessary to make a larger grant in order to produce the same return to the road. More important was the lack of inhabitants and the poorer quality of the land further west. The less the population, the less the probability that the road would pay dividends in the near future. Then too, the land in the mountain states was not good, and for the most part had very little, if any, value.

Starting with the grant to the Union Pacific in 1862,

practically all the future transcontinental roads were aided during the next decade—the Union Pacific and its branches, the Central Pacific, the Atchison, Topeka and Santa Fe, the Northern Pacific, the California and Oregon, the Atlantic and Pacific, and the Texas and Pacific, as well as numerous less important lines. In addition to these, some of the earlier grants were changed, sometimes being expanded.

The Texas and Pacific act of March 3, 1871, brought the list of trans-Mississippi grants to an end. Only one later grant was ever made, that to the Chicago and Northwestern in 1872. A total of some 180,000,000 acres had been given to various lines of road. Of this total amount more than 100,000,000 acres were finally patented by the railroad companies. The remainder was either unavailable because of previous settlement or was returned to the public domain by act of Congress upon the failure of the road concerned to build its line.

The value of the land given to the railroads is extremely uncertain. The price at which it sold varied greatly. Probably the average price received by the railroads was around $5 an acre, making $500,000,000 in all. Viewed from present day standards, this sum does not seem excessively large, but at the time that it was given it amounted to about the cost of three lines like that of the Union Pacific-Central Pacific from Omaha to San Francisco. It must be remembered, however, that much of the land was unsalable at the time that the grant was made, and depended upon the building of the railroad for its value. If all the land grant roads could have waited fifty years to sell their land they would have been extremely wealthy, but due to the exigencies of the case they sold as fast as possible.

The influence of the land grants in hastening construction is even more difficult to ascertain than the value of the land given. In all probability the building of the Union Pacific was hastened from ten to fifteen years. It is improbable that other roads were benefited that much. Such a road as the Santa Fe would probably have been built within a very few years of its historical date, regardless of the land. Such was the case of the Southern Pacific, and later of the Great Northern. It is entirely possible, however, that these few years were vital, for otherwise construction might have been indefinitely delayed because of the depression of the latter eighties and the nineties.

Whatever good results were produced by railroad land grants can not quite obliterate the evil effects. Lobbying had a rapid growth, while bribery and corruption were omnipresent. Many of the most prominent of the country's politicians were involved in questionable practices, and the moral tone of the government was distinctly lowered. Railroad land grants were certainly not entirely to blame for the situation, but their influence was bad enough to make it very questionable whether or not they were worth more than they cost.

The railroad land grants were the outstanding, but by no means the only evidence of government interest. At the same time as each grant was made, provisions as to the management and building of the road were added. In every case the bond issue was limited, the price of stock settled, the use of American iron and steel made mandatory, and the fixing of fair and reasonable rates compulsory. Specific provision was made that rates were to be under the control of Congress. The Texas and Pacific was further prohibited from any kind of discrimination.

At the same time that the government was chartering, aiding, and regulating the land grant railroads it embarked on its one venture in monetary assistance. The idea that the government should assist financially in the building of the first transcontinental railroad had been firmly planted in the minds of most people by the early agitators for such a road. With this idea as a background, and the desirability of rapid construction as a foreground, Congress was led to include financial assistance in the Union Pacific act.

Both the Central Pacific and the Union Pacific were given assistance to the extent of from $16,000 to $48,000 a mile, depending upon the difficulties of construction. The loan was made in the form of government bonds, and was to constitute a first mortgage on the properties concerned. The government had plenty of time to regret its bargain in the thirty-five years of litigation and legislation which followed.

The transcontinental roads were also aided by the considerable body of information that the government had collected in its various explorations and surveys. The Gadsden purchase was consummated largely for the benefit of a southern transcontinental railway. The transportation of government mail and property furnished monetary assistance for many a needy road.

Other roads than those aided by Congress found it necessary to traverse the public domain, and for this purpose it was necessary to secure the consent of the federal government. This right was never refused, but had to be granted by special act of Congress. In 1852 a general law was passed which removed the need of special legislation and gave the right-of-way to any road which desired it. The only exception was in land set aside for the use of the Indians.

Starting with Louisiana in 1849 many of the western states were given the swamp land within their borders. In all, about 20,000,000 acres were donated in this way. In some cases, as in Iowa and Arkansas, the state re-granted this land to favored railroad companies. Frequently, with the construction of levees and the installation of proper drainage the land became as fertile and productive as any in the West.

In addition to the land given directly, Congress adopted the plan, with the admission of Ohio, of giving each state a percentage of the proceeds of the land sold within the state as recompense for the absence of state taxation of the public domain. This percentage varied, being either 2, 3, or 5%. Most of the trans-Mississippi states received 5% (California received none), and much of this money was spent either directly or indirectly in aiding railroad schemes.

Congress also presented each new state admitted after 1841 with 500,000 acres of land for the encouragement of internal improvements. This land was also frequently used for aiding railroads. While the direct gift in these latter cases was from the state, the land or money came originally from the central government.

The attention of Congress was also called to the situation in regard to railroad iron. Iron production in the United States was very small during the thirties and most of the iron used for railroad purposes came from England. Consequently the people interested in railroads desired the removal of the existing tariff, and in response to this demand Congress in 1832 removed the 25% ad valorem duty on iron, which had been assessed by the tariff of 1830. As the amount of iron produced in the United States continued to increase the pressure of the producers in favor of a tariff became stronger than the opposition. The act of 1843 provided for a 20% ad valorem duty, and when the new tariff bill of the same year went into effect no exception was made for railroad iron.

The end of direct government aid to the railroads was produced by a rapid shift in feeling on the part of the people of the United States. Early railroad projects were considered as semi-public in nature, and the citizens who aided them were considered as public benefactors. Government assistance not only seemed desirable and fitting to everyone, but was only objected to because it was not given soon enough or in adequate amounts.

Once the initial difficulty of sectional differences had been overcome there was little limit to the enthusiasm of Congress. During the fifties and sixties the public domain was given away with a lavish hand. Various types of aid were considered, but they always eventually gave way to the ubiquitous land. Land was the one possession which the central government held in profusion, and it was impossible to conceive of a time when the public domain would be exhausted.

The reaction came in the early seventies when people began to become resentful of the failure of the railroads to bring a utopia, and began to fear large aggregations of capital and absentee ownership. Political corruption and demoralization, which were frequently linked with the railroads, served to advance the feeling still further. In popular fancy the railroads were transformed from gifts of a beneficent providence to dreadful vampires, the product of Satan, sucking the life blood of the country.

The revolting Liberal Republicans of 1872 stated their objections to further land grants, and the other parties echoed their sentiments. At the same time other forms of railroad aid were being stopped. The year 1872 may well mark the division point between the old period of unbounded enthusiasm and the new period of suspicion and opposition.

CHAPTER IV

The individual states were even more interested in railroad projects than the national government. Railroads meant wealth and prosperity. It was felt that the first state to acquire an adequate railroad system was bound to be more prosperous than its neighbors. Terminal cities attracted additional roads, and progress was then by geometric progression. Railroad promoters by no means overlooked this attitude of mind, and played upon it to the best of their ability, with the result that most of the unattached land and money of the community accrued to the interest of the railroads. Railroad men sincerely believed that more railroads meant more wealth, more wealth meant more railroads, and so on indefinitely.

Westerners as a rule accepted and even expanded the optimistic statements of the railroad enthusiasts. Legislators, themselves frequently farmers, felt keenly the desirability of good transportation, and were willing to vote for any measure which they felt would secure that object. Neither the legislators nor the railroad promoters felt that any obligation was unsound if it was guaranteed to produce a railroad, for would not a 90% reduction in the cost of transportation cover any debt?

The most unanimous movement in favor of railroads came before many were built, but when their construction looked possible—that is, in the fifties. A wave of emotional enthusiasm swept over the West between 1849 and 1857 that has its closest counterpart in the banking craze of twenty years before. To some extent this feeling continued to exist wherever new railroads seemed possible, but it never again was as unanimous as in the early fifties.

As in the case of railroad construction, Missouri was the first state to arrive at the point of giving monetary assistance to make railroad dreams become a reality. State credit was comparatively good, the people had no doubt as to the value of railroads, railroads could not be built without capital, and so Missouri embarked upon the project of furnishing the capital which was to start the train of events leading to prosperity.

At the time when railroad interest became paramount Thomas Allen, being a public spirited citizen, was both president of the Pacific Railroad of Missouri and chairman of the state Senate committee on internal improvements. Combining business with both pleasure and public interest, he introduced a bill calling for state bonds in the aid of the Pacific Railroad. Not to be selfish in the matter he included the Hannibal and St. Jo. in his bill, to receive similar assistance. The bonds were to be issued as a loan to the roads and to be secured by a first mortgage on the property. Little opposition developed and in due course of time the bill became a law.

The general principles governing the first act were sound. The bonds were to be issued at 6% for a term of twenty years, and were to be secured by a first mortgage. They were to be issued in $50,000 lots, but only after the company could show bona fide subscriptions to indicate that it was a going concern and had expended an amount equal to the state aid offered. The terms of this first loan were irreproachable. Under competent administration and supervision the interest of the state was assured, and any loss practically impossible. Unfortunately the supervision was slight, and by the time that the experiment ended every safeguard provided in the original act had been either modified or removed.

This first loan led to others, until soon Missouri was fairly embarked on a policy of aiding all the significant state railroads—the Pacific Railroad of Missouri, the Southwest Branch of the Pacific Railroad, the Hannibal and St. Jo., the North Missouri, the St. Louis and Iron Mountain, the Cairo and Fulton, and the Platte County. The first four were the through lines discussed in Chapter II. The fifth made eastern connections at Cairo, Illinois, and then continued the line of the St. Louis and Iron Mountain toward Texas. The sixth furnished western connections for the Hannibal and St. Jo.

The total loans authorized by the state of Missouri were in the neighborhood of $25,000,000. Only $19,-000,000 of the bonds were actually issued, from which the railroads realized something over $16,000,000, which meant that the average price of Missouri bonds was 85. The railroads lost the difference, because they accepted the state bonds at par, but they were so confident of their own futures that they were willing to saddle themselves with this excessive capitalization.

Construction progressed slowly even with the aid of the state. By the close of 1857 only three hundred miles had been put into operation, although of course additional work had been done. Most of this mileage was on the Pacific Railroad and on the Hannibal and St. Jo.

This figure means that the state had spent something over $60,000 for every mile of construction, to say nothing of the additional sums spent by the individual companies. Allowance should be made for work which does not show in the mileage figures, and also for some of the money which did not become available until later. This excessive cost was particularly discouraging when taken with the fact that every road was continually on the verge of bankruptcy, and only managed to struggle along because of the continuance of state aid.

The small amount of work done for the amount of state capital invested led to an ever increasing volume of charges of fraud and mismanagement. A legislative investigation resulted in whitewashing everyone concerned, but did not completely satisfy the citizens of Missouri. There was little doubt in most people's minds that at least a portion of the state aid had been put to improper uses.

More important than the charges of fraud were the existing economic conditions and the current ways of doing business. Missouri did not have the wealth or traffic to support its proposed railroads, which meant that construction costs were supplemented by a continual operating deficit. Much of the funds of the various companies went to keep the roads running after they had been built.

State bonds which had to be sold at a discount meant an excessive capitalization and an unwarranted increase in fixed charges. A weak financial condition meant high prices for materials and construction, which in turn were poor and needed frequent repairs. The stock of the companies was worth less than par and was given in part payment of construction contracts, which had the effect of further weakening the financial status of the companies.

The inverted pyramid of Missouri finance was pushed over by the panic of 1857. State bonds which had been selling in New York for 83 in March fell to 65 by the end of the year. The legislature took fright and refused any further assistance except to portions of line already partly constructed. The various companies, with their main support removed, showed signs of distress. With what remained of the state aid final bankruptcy was averted for several years. The North Missouri and the St. Louis and Iron Mountain succumbed in 1859, the Pacific Railroad and the Cairo and Fulton in 1860, and the Southwest Branch and the Platte County in 1861. The Hannibal and St. Jo. managed to retain solvency, partly because it was better managed, partly because it was able to dispose of some of its land, and partly because it was in the path of the overland traffic.

A final attempt was made to resuscitate the Missouri railroad system in 1860, when a bill for further assistance passed both houses of the legislature, but was vetoed by the governor. No future serious attempt was made to continue the policy of state aid. The outbreak of the Civil War caused a temporary suspension of the interest in railroads. The Hannibal and St. Jo. still managed to maintain solvency, but the other roads were in very bad shape. Military reasons led to the revival of interest toward the end of the war, and in 1864 the Pacific Railroad and the North Missouri were allowed to retire the state lien to the position of a second mortgage and to issue their own first mortgages in order to complete their main lines.

The constitution of 1865 made provision for the creation of a sinking fund by the railroads to retire their debt to the state. Failure to create any such fund led to the foreclosure of the roads concerned and their sale at public auction. These sales were later made the subject of a whitewashing investigation, which, as in a former case, hardly convinced anyone of the justice of the proceedings.

The entire debt of the railroads to the state of Missouri was finally released unconditionally because of the seeming improbability that it would ever be paid. The entire amount was charged to the account of experience, and the last of the bonds were finally paid in 1903. The constitutions of both 1865 and 1875 provided against any future experiment of the same kind by prohibiting the use of the credit of the state for the benefit of a private corporation.

The Missouri experiment was typical of that of the other states. All of the first tier of trans-Mississippi states except Iowa ventured into the realm of state railroad aid. Iowa was restrained by a state constitutional prohibition and by her favorable geographic position, which made state aid unnecessary.

In Minnesota the railroad excitement coincided with the statehood movement. The year before Minnesota was admitted to the Union (1858) she received the usual railroad land grant from Congress. It was impossible for a territory to vote railroad aid, and so the Minnesota railroad enthusiasm had to wait. Being a repressed desire it took especially virulent form when it was allowed to come to the surface.

As soon as statehood was achieved the railroad enthusiasts went into action. By a large popular vote a constitutional amendment was adopted which called for a state loan of $5,000,000 to go to the roads which had benefited by the Congressional land grant. This loan was to be made in state bonds, and was to be secured by a first mortgage on the property concerned. $100,000 was to be advanced for each ten miles graded and an additional $100,000 for each ten miles opened for business.

Minnesota's intense railroad enthusiasm entirely overlooked the little matter of the panic of 1857. Work was started and bonds issued just as energetically as though the period were one of prosperity. To be sure the most of the work was done in the form of grading, but the important thing to the inhabitants of Minnesota was that a state railroad system was actually in the course of construction.

The objections of critical outside observers to the Minnesota experiment were too obvious to need enumeration. All of the criticisms which applied to the Missouri policy were ten times as applicable, to say nothing of the existence of a financial depression throughout the country. The railroads were not at all oblivious to the defects of the situation, and in consequence devoted most of their energies to grading. In most cases grading meant driving a few stakes and running a scraper over the surface of the future road. Grading secured all the advantages of the loan a great deal more rapidly and cheaply than construction would have done.

Minnesota's experiment lasted for just about a year. By that time the price of state bonds had fallen to an impossible figure. Two hundred miles of road had been graded, but the only track in existence was a stretch of 1400 feet which the Minnesota and Pacific used to store its only engine. Completed railroads looked almost as far distant as ever.

The rapid failure of the loan produced an equally rapid revulsion of feeling on the part of the citizens. The amendment authorizing the loan was repealed in 1860 by a larger popular majority than had put it into effect two years before. As far as that generation of Minnesota voters was concerned the repeal of the $5,000,000 loan amendment was the end of the episode. No effort was made to provide for the payment of the outstanding bonds.

For over twenty years the holders of the repudiated bonds tried to secure a settlement. In 1870 the state offered to exchange them for land, but the bondholders refused. After several other unsuccessful negotiations a compromise was finally effected in 1881 by which the state assumed the payment of both principal and interest at the rate of fifty cents on the dollar.

Arkansas came very near to duplicating the experience of Minnesota. Its somewhat larger population was offset by the existence of a considerable debt incurred in the banking business of the thirties, and consequently credit was non-existent for any effort at railroad aid during the fifties. Not until after the Civil War did conditions seem propitious. Arkansas was then without a single complete line of railroad, and felt that if something were not done about the matter, she would be completely overshadowed by her more prosperous neighbors.

A bill for state railroad aid was passed by the legislature but vetoed by the governor. Railroad enthusiasm was sufficiently high to secure the necessary majority to pass the bill over the veto. Just at this time the convention for the formation of a new state constitution was in session, and so it was deemed advisable by all parties to wait for the provisions of the new constitution before further action was taken.

The constitution of 1868 made provision for either state or county aid upon the vote of the people, and within a year a law calling for state railroad aid had been ratified by the electorate. The roads to be aided constituted a total of 850 miles, to be designated by a Board of Railroad Commissioners, the majority of which were ex-officio members.

Land grant roads were to receive state bonds to the amount of $10,000 a mile and non-land grant roads were to receive $15,000. This money was to be made available only after the road concerned had sold enough stock to pay for preparing one-third of its entire line for the rails. As soon as the road had prepared ten miles for the rails it received state aid for that distance, and as the line progressed the process was repeated. These loans were to constitute a first mortgage on the property concerned.

The roads which were aided by this authorization of bonds were planned to produce a complete railroad system centering at Little Rock, and the road running from Memphis through Little Rock to Fort Smith was actually completed. It is to be noted, however, that the road which did the greatest amount of building during the period refused the proffered state assistance. The Cairo and Fulton had had a touch of the earlier Missouri venture and saw that it was an easier and more profitable matter to sell its own first mortgage bonds than to sell the depreciated state issue. Weaker roads found it impossible to secure adequate funds either with their own bonds or with those of the state.

The Arkansas railroad venture ended with the constitution of 1874, which prohibited future loans of state credit. Remarkable to relate, this constitution also provided that all existing debts should be repaid dollar for dollar, and the railroad bonds were refunded. An amendment was adopted in 1885 by a vote of 8-1 which provided for the repudiation of three internal improvement bond issues, among them being the railroad issue. The sovereign state of Arkansas had vindicated her right to forget troublesome obligations.

California was the only far western state to be in a position to be interested in the aiding of railroads. The state constitution prohibited any financial aid to private corporations, but in spite of this prohibition California presented rights-of-way, land for terminals and wharves, and guaranteed some of the bonds of the Central Pacific.

Texas deserves separate consideration because of its unique position and history. When Texas entered the Union it retained control of its own land, which meant that Texas railroads had to look to the state government for both land and money. The development of Texan policy, however, parallels fairly closely that of the central government and of the other western states.

The first large Texas land grant was made in 1853 to the Mississippi and Pacific—eventually to become the Texas and Pacific. The federal policy was followed in giving twenty alternate sections per mile, but instead of giving a larger area for indemnity selections, a tract of land in southwestern Texas was laid aside for that purpose.

As early as 1854 Texas took a step which was never taken by the federal government. A general land grant act was passed by which any road built received aid in land. Sixteen odd sections were given per mile, this land to become available as fast as the road was finished in twenty-five mile strips. The expense of the surveying had to be paid by the railroad benefited.

The financial assistance given by Texas, as provided in the law of August 13, 1856, was also general in its application. Any road desiring aid could receive $6000 per mile from the public school fund. This money was available only as the road was put into use, and was to constitute a first mortgage on the property. The idea was that the company should raise the money for the completion of the first strip of road, then the state would aid the second strip, and so on.

Texas was the one state to make a success of its policy of railroad encouragement, probably in large part because it did not force the development too fast. The terms of both the land and money aid were such as to do away with any possible favoritism and thus avoid the concomitants of eternal lobbying and corruption. The surveying clause of the land law saved the state a considerable amount of expense. The bond aid, administered with even ordinary intelligence, was nearly fool proof. Twenty-five miles of road open for business was always a safe investment for $150,000.

The success of the Texas plan was well attested by its continuation throughout the fifties, sixties, and seventies. Some strategic lines were even given additional assistance. The monetary aid was finally brought to an end by the constitution of 1876, and the granting of land was discontinued in 1882. The state railroad debt never exceeded $5,000,000 at any one time, and the total land grants were about 25,000,000 acres.

Texas was notable in proving that it was possible to hasten railroad construction without injuring the credit of the state. Railroad progress in Texas, although not excessively rapid, continued steadily. Naturally it was stopped by the Civil War, but the progress both before and after that event was satisfactory. In consequence the episode of Texas railroad aid stands out as the one bright star in the night of state assistance.

These various experiments in state monetary assistance were supplemented here and there by other forms of aid. The earliest form of favoritism was special charter privileges, but these disappeared in the early fifties when all of the states passed general incorporation laws. Federal swamp land and internal improvement grants were frequently given over to the railroads. The right of eminent domain was always allowed, and frequently building sites for stations and yards were donated. California guaranteed the interest on some of the bonds of the Central Pacific. Exemption from taxation was a common form of aid until it was declared unconstitutional by the Supreme Court.

By the early seventies the period of state aid was at an end. The virginal enthusiasm of the fifties had been dampened by the panic of 1857 and even more depressed by the Civil War. It had again taken heart after the war, only to receive its final death blow from the panic of 1873. A growing anti-railroad feeling made a future revival of state assistance improbable.

Government railroad aid was by no means limited to that of the federal and state agencies. Every legal subdivision—city, town, county, and township, was looked upon as a possible source of assistance. Complaisant legislatures of the fifties placed practically no restrictions on such subscriptions.

Local aid was a widespread phenomenon, being a compound of railroad enthusiasm, local pride, and the hope of personal gain. It was a hard-hearted county that would not subscribe to one or more railroad projects. Each citizen felt that the railroad was the apostle of economic salvation. No debt was too large to contract, because it was thought that the advent of the railroad would so increase economic prosperity that it would make the payment of any amount very easy.

The railroads played upon local pride and cupidity with great success. Communities were pitted against each other, and railroad agents would visit each one in turn to encourage competitive bidding for the privilege of having the road. Sometimes the roads went even so far as to survey two or three parallel lines in order to encourage larger competitive local subscriptions. Competitive bidding did not always mean that the highest bidder got the road. Frequently the route was decided upon in advance, and the competition was used only to work up enthusiasm.

The larger towns and cities sometimes sponsored their own roads, and frequently gave assistance to as many as eight or ten. In such cases the purpose was the creation of railroad and distributing centers rather than merely securing adequate transportation. Besides subscriptions in money there were often gifts of right-of-way, and of land for stations and yards.

Local aid was ordinarily in the form of the bonds of the locality, which were used for the purchase of the stock or bonds of the road to be aided. Usually it was bonds that were purchased. Frequently the aid was altogether out of proportion to the property values, and the only hope for future payment lay in a rapid growth of population and wealth. Sometimes there was no adequate provision that the road would ever be built or that it would pass through the community concerned, although usually some such guarantee was insisted upon.

Local subscriptions were fairly satisfactory until the bonds became due. Twenty-year bonds issued during the fifties became payable during the depression of the seventies. Excessive debts created under favorable conditions did not appear any smaller in a time of business depression, and the second generation felt that their collection was almost pure extortion.

Many counties and towns tried to meet the situation by following the example of Minnesota and Arkansas— either by repudiating the entire issue or by finding some legal technicality for its avoidance. Unfortunately for the counties, but luckily for the bond holders, minor political subdivisions were not sovereign and could not repudiate debts. Even when a technical flaw in the method of issuing the aid could be found the courts ordinarily protected the innocent purchaser and declared the issue valid.

The most notorious effort to avoid payment was that of Yankton, Dakota Territory. Yankton refused to pay its debt even after the United States Supreme Court held it valid and collectible. Whenever a process was served, the official on whom it was served was willing to swear that he had just resigned, thus producing the general effect of a game of hide and seek. A compromise was eventually effected and the debt paid, but the bad odor of the whole affair to the East served to delay the admission of the Dakotas into the Union several years. Most of the western local histories are permeated with a feeling of resentment against the railroads for forcing the payment of local bonds. Undoubtedly they were a heavy burden on people who had little or no part in contracting the debt. It was equally true that the debts were made in good faith and were valid, and that the purchasers of the bonds were not the persons to be made to suffer for the excessive optimism of those who had originally voted for their issue. Many of the debts dragged on for years. Clark County, Missouri, only completed its payments in 1918, and remnants of the debts of other localities still remain.

The dangers and bad effects of local railroad aid are fairly obvious, but the offsetting advantages should not be overlooked. Westerners were right in their feeling that the future depended on railroads. Hundreds of towns were killed by their failure to secure railroad connections, while a corresponding number grew from small villages to large commercial centers under the powerful impetus of the railroad. It was largely due to the initiative of the early settlers that particular towns secured adequate transportation and became important.

The necessity for state assistance is not so clear. Whereas in the case of the towns the building of one or more railroads might mean the difference between prosperity and obscurity, such was not the case with larger districts. Here economic desirability was the more important factor and dictated the building of railroads quite irrespective of financial assistance. The experience of Iowa is illuminating. Offering no special concessions, and later securing the undivided hate of the railroads because of its adverse legislation, it still had more mileage than any other trans-Mississippi state (up to 1887). On the other hand Arkansas, with its poorer geographical position and lesser wealth, was unable to obtain railroads even with the most lavish grants of aid.

State and local aid show very similar features. Excessive debts were created in a spirit of buoyant optimism, with little thought as to their amount, their probable effect, or their payment. Many of the schemes were ill-advised and predestined to failure. Lack of adequate supervision, insufficient knowledge, waste, incompetence, and corruption played their parts. Many of the loans were either completely lost or the holdings sold later at a low figure. Part of the debtors tried to avoid payment. The whole experience constituted one of the important causes of a revulsion in feeling and the creation of the later anti-railroad movement.

The panic of 1857 was the first object lesson which gave the West pause for thought, and with the exception of Kansas (1862), the constitutions from that time until the end of the war prohibited local railroad aid—Minnesota, Iowa, Oregon, and Nevada. The comparative prosperity after the war encouraged further assistance, and the constitutions of Missouri, Arkansas, Nebraska, California, Minnesota, and Texas reflect this feeling. Some restrictions on the earlier freedom were made, however. The most common restriction was that any bond issue had to be ratified by a two-thirds vote of the electorate.

The Granger movement and the panic of 1873 finally brought an end to local aid. With the exception of Nebraska (1875) the constitutions of the seventies prohibited such assistance—California, Arkansas, Kansas,

Missouri, Texas, and Colorado. Later constitutions followed this precedent. Exceptions can be made of the Dakotas (1889) and Utah (1895), which permitted a limited amount of aid. Even in these three cases the surrounding restrictions amounted practically to a prohibition. The period of local railroad aid had passed.

CHAPTER V

The panic of 1857 called a halt to the extensive plans for railroad construction. Most lines attempted to keep on building, in the hope that the depression would soon subside. Others discontinued work entirely. The most notable exception was the Hannibal and St. Jo., which prosecuted its work vigorously, with the result that it completed its line to the Missouri River within the next two years. For six years it remained alone in this accomplishment.

The effects of the panic were still visible when the Civil War broke out and further complicated affairs. The results of the war on railroad building were exceedingly complex. In some ways construction was hastened and in other ways it was retarded. The ravages of the war were a very real drawback in many sections of the country, while in many other sections the conflict brought a feverish interest in economic advantages and an increased importance to the railway.

Both the North and the South made use of their railway systems in the prosecution of the war. The South was under the initial difficulty of having several strategic portions of her railroad system missing, and of having little time or capital to remedy the defect. In spite of the recommendations of General Lee these gaps were not closed, and the southern railroad system never became effective. An army railroad administration was built up, but continually labored under the disadvantage of a lack of centralized independent control.

Southwestern railroads were even further handicapped by the prosecution of the war in that district. The campaigns for the control of the Mississippi were fatal to the railroads of that portion of the country. Lines in Texas, Arkansas, and southern Missouri were not only hampered by the obstruction of their traffic, but also suffered from raiding operations of the two armies. In some cases the track and equipment were taken away to be used elsewhere, while in other cases they were destroyed. Sometimes the northern armies took over a useful road, and usually by the time they left, it was unrecognizable.

The northern part of Missouri had its worst difficulties during the early part of the war, but was able to assume a more peaceful aspect by the time of the end of hostilities. The Pacific Railroad was even able to continue construction so that it reached the Missouri during the last year of the war. With this one exception southwestern railroad construction was non-existent during the war period.

The North utilized its railroads to better purpose than did the South. With the closing of the Gulf route it became necessary to ship all food products by rail, and the roads which tapped the old Northwest received a large increase of business. Roads further west reacted to the same influence and benefited by the cessation of water competition. Unfortunately the lines west of the Mississippi were still fragmentary and lacking in effectiveness, so that their importance was only a fraction of what it would have been ten years later.

The most significant advance made by the North in the field of railroad economics was in the phase of military administration and utilization. Most of the war was carried on in southern territory, and in consequence it became highly important to secure adequate transportation for a considerable distance from the base of supplies. All operations were harassed by continual raids, and in most cases the southern army destroyed all railroad facilities before it left any territory. Before the end of the war a highly centralized and effective northern military railroad control had been built up, and this organization was fully equipped to build, repair, and operate all lines captured.

The effect of northern military control on the West was very indirect. Few western lines were used by the organization. Economies in railroad construction and operation, however, as well as time-saving devices which were so necessary for the work, very soon came into widespread use, and their effect was rather marked on future western construction. Many of the officers and men who worked for the government during the war later became interested in western railroad projects.

The cessation of railroad activities in the Southwest during the war was not paralleled in the Northwest. The closing of the Gulf route made railroads an absolute necessity, while the prevalence of war prices made the farmers eager to secure better transportation for a larger crop. There was little fear of military operations to act as a deterrent. A rapid expansion of the currency had given everyone more money than in the past.

The incentives to construction during the war period were paralleled by certain difficulties. While it was true that the increased amount of currency in circulation and the higher prices paid for grain had resulted in the existence of more ready cash in the West than usual, it was equally true that the price of railroad materials had advanced correspondingly. Furthermore, labor was unusually scarce, both because of the drain of the army, and because it was attracted to the East to secure the high wages then being paid.

A large part of the war construction took place in the state of Iowa, where the strong Chicago lines which had reached the Mississippi during the fifties started their march across the state. None of them were completed before the end of the war, but the Chicago, Burlington and Quincy, the Chicago and Northwestern, the Chicago, Milwaukee and St. Paul, the Chicago and Rock Island, and the Illinois Central had secured their Iowa extensions and had begun work. The first road to enter the state capital was the Keokuk, St. Louis and Minnesota, which was completed in 1866 with the aid of the state swamp land grant.

Minnesota railroads had been left stranded by the repeal of the $5,000,000 loan amendment. The governor, authorized by the state legislature, foreclosed them all in 1860 and then bought them all in for the benefit of the state at the nominal price of $1000 apiece. Later they were rechartered by new companies, and by the end of the war all of them had started construction.

The first Minnesota road opened for traffic was the Minnesota and Pacific (1863)—later the Great Northern. The dominant figure in its later history was James J. Hill, who entered the employ of the road in 1865 as local agent at St. Paul. At a later time he secured control of the system and used it as the foundation for his railroad empire in the Northwest.

The war period also saw the real beginning of railroads in the second tier of trans-Mississippi states and in the Far West. Construction was begun in Kansas and Nebraska as soon as there was any hope of eastern connections. On the Pacific coast the chief work was done on a number of small lines in the San Francisco-Sacramento district in California.

While there was considerable railroad development in the Northwest and in the Far West the most important field of endeavor was that of transcontinental building. Sectional differences had blocked any action in the early fifties, but the latter part of the decade saw a revival of interest. Older men and measures were passing. One or more roads were conceivable, sentiment for their construction was increasing, and the West was growing in size and importance.

Both the Democrats and the Republicans favored the building of a Pacific railroad in their platforms of 1856, and in the following year President Buchanan recommended the project to the consideration of Congress. The Senate was willing to pass the necessary legislation in the succeeding year, because of the large proportion of western members. The House was slower to act because it was more completely dominated by eastern interests. Finally in 1861 the House came to the point of passing a two-route bill, but the session expired before the Senate amendments could be acted upon.

Just at the time when it looked possible to secure the necessary transcontinental legislation the South seceded from the Union. With it went the chief opposition to railroad aid and there was no longer any question as to the passage of the Pacific railroad bill. The only uncertainty was as to its terms. This phase of the situation, as well as other western problems such as territorial organization and the sale of the public domain, came to the attention of Congress as soon as it had considered the most pressing of the military needs.

The railroad problem was inseparable from other western wants. The final organization of all the West except Indian Territory and the division of the Dakotas occurred during the sixties, and was intimately bound up with the railroad situation. The passage of the Homestead Act gave the basis for the final partitioning of the public domain. With the encouragement to the transcontinental railroads the stage was set for the drama of the final conquest of the West.

The chartering of the Union Pacific on July 1, 1862 represented a compromise in routes. Necessarily the road was projected to run by way of South Pass to the Pacific, because that was the only practical route open at the time, which would have been generally acceptable. Instead of deciding between the rival claims of Chicago and St. Louis, Congress evaded the whole point at issue. A trunk line was planned from a point on the hundredth meridian, about midway across the state of Nebraska, to the Pacific coast. The Union Pacific was to build to the eastern boundary of Nevada and the Central Pacific of California was to complete the line.

As originally planned the road was to have five branches from the hundredth meridian to the Missouri River—to Kansas City, Leavenworth, St. Joseph, Sioux City, and to some place on the western boundary of Iowa to be designated by the President of the United States. This last connecting link was to be built by the Union Pacific itself, whereas the other branches were distributed to other companies.

The terminus of the fifth branch, which was really a continuation of the main line, was finally fixed at Omaha. Colonel Dodge, later in charge of the construction of the Union Pacific, claims the credit for this decision. In his early surveys for lines in Iowa he had been impressed with the future possibilities of Omaha, and praised the town whenever he had an opportunity. In 1863 he had an interview with President Lincoln, who was then undecided as to the terminus of the Union Pacific, and Dodge claims that it was because of his influence that Omaha was selected as the proper site.

The only branch of the Union Pacific to be built as originally planned was that to Omaha. The Sioux City branch was eventually built south instead of southwest and joined the main line at Fremont. The Kansas City branch was greatly extended so that it went directly west to Denver and then north to Cheyenne. This change lost the connection of the St. Joseph line completely, and it ended with no connection at all. The Leavenworth branch was made much shorter, running directly south to join the Kansas City line, rather than west.

Probably more important even than the route of the newly chartered Union Pacific, were the provisions for its aid in land and money. It was given land to the extent of five odd sections per mile on each side of the road, and within ten miles. Monetary assistance was extended in the form of government bonds which were to be loaned at the rate of $16,000 per mile in the plains country, $32,000 in the foothills, and $48,000 in the mountains, and were to constitute a first mortgage on the property.

The charter also made provisions as to the financing of the enterprise. The stock was to be issued in $1000 shares, of which there were to be 100,000. Not more than

200 shares were to be held by any one person. Definite instructions were given as to the organization of the company and the composition of the board of directors. Final organization of the company could not take place unless at least 2000 shares of stock were represented.

The sale of stock was slow and the time provided in the chartering act for the organization of the company came and went. Finally in September of 1862 a meeting of the interested parties was held in New York. In spite of the absence of the requisite number of shares for a legal organization, the gathering proceeded to elect temporary officers. W. B. Ogden (Ill.) was elected president, H. V. Poor (N. Y.) secretary, and T. W. Alcott (N. Y.) treasurer. These men were all able and prominent, and designed to give the project prestige.

This September meeting was designed entirely to secure interest and arouse enthusiasm. In these aims it was successful to the extent that newspapers and public speakers all over the country described the Union Pacific as an epoch-making road, and pictured its future benefits in the most glowing of colors. In view of these favorable circumstances surveys were begun and preparations made to start construction.

Nationwide publicity and approbation did not necessarily mean subscriptions, and still the preliminary $2,000,000 was not forthcoming. While everyone was agreed as to the desirability of the project, capital was hard to secure. War prosperity had produced better paying investments for idle funds than that of a road which was not expected to pay dividends for many years.

The proponents of the Union Pacific largely overlooked the existence of peculiar economic conditions, and contended that the lack of funds was due to mistakes in the terms of the original charter. The thousand dollar bonds were too large for the smaller investor, who should be the backbone of the enterprise, while the first lien of the government was unfair in that it prevented the road from selling its own first mortgage bonds. The land grant was meagre because most of the land was in the uninhabited portions of the country and consequently unsalable. In fact it was contended, without any serious opposition, that most of the land was worthless for all time.

The first action of Congress in further encouraging the Union Pacific, was in rectifying the more or less minor mistake of gauge. The original act had given the President of the United States the power of determining the gauge. His decision rested on a comparison of the California 5' gauge and the Missouri 6' gauge, with the former finally receiving the preference. Congress changed it to the eastern standard of 4' 8½" in 1863.

The most important action of Congress came July 2, 1864, when it completely revamped the terms of the original bill. The land grant was doubled. The United States bonds were reduced to the rank of a second mortgage, and the road allowed to issue its own bonds. The number of shares was increased to 1,000,000 at a par value of $100, with no limit as to the amount that one individual could subscribe. The only limitation was that all stock had to be bought at par. Even the most radical Pacific railroad enthusiast had expected no more.

The activities of the company in securing this additional aid were not wholly above question. In spite of its dangerous financial condition it found itself able to spend almost half a million dollars in Washington in its "suspense account." One lawyer by the name of J. B.

Stewart received $30,000 for expending $200,000, and later refused to testify as to what he had done with the money. Whether or not this money was put to improper uses is a question for speculation.

The preliminary $2,000,000 was subscribed by October, 1863, before the additional aid was given. The formal organization of the company was consummated immediately, and the choice of General J. A. Dix for president gave the project a semi-military aspect. Work was begun, and in December, 1863, the first ground was broken at Omaha. The long dreamed-of project was actually under way.

The promoters of the Union Pacific soon found that enthusiasm was not the only factor necessary for constructing a railroad. Both capital and labor were scarce during the period of the war, and in consequence progress was very slow. Only forty miles were built during 1864 and 1865.

The Union Pacific had to meet an aggregation of all the usual difficulties that confronted the construction of a western road. It was hardly conceivable that traffic would be sufficiently heavy to pay operating expenses, to say nothing of dividends on the money invested. Through traffic would be light and local business would be almost non-existent because of a lack of population in the area traversed. It was conceivable that through traffic would increase, but the possibility of settling the line of the road sufficiently to make it profitable was rather remote. This situation meant that not only did the road have to provide for the expenses of construction, but also for the cost of operation for a considerable period.

The financial provisions of the charter also proved to be stumbling blocks. It was specified that the securities of the company had to be sold at par and for cash. Almost as soon as the capital stock was put on the market it fell below par. Private traders would hardly buy stock from the company at par when it could be obtained on the open market for considerably less. The sales of the company soon ceased and additional capital did not become available. As long as the road did not progress any further there would be no real demand for the stock at par, while at the same time the company could not finance any further construction unless it sold more stock. The horns of the dilemma seemed immovable.

Vice-president Durant found a solution for the financial problem in 1864. His proposal was in part the well worked idea that a small inside ring should take over the construction contracts and thereby secure a profit which could not be anticipated in operation. The significant part of the plan was its proposal for evading the financial arrangements of the charter. There was no objection to an outside corporation selling the capital stock of the Union Pacific at any figure it pleased, and so if the controlling members of the railroad voted construction contracts to themselves and indirectly paid for them with capital stock, that stock could be sold at the market price. When the contracts were made in that way the terms could be sufficiently high to recompense the construction company for any loss that it might incur in the sale of the securities.

The new organization which the inside ring of the Union Pacific used to take over construction contracts was the Credit Mobilier of America, which was a reorganization of the Pennsylvania corporation, the Fiscal Agency of America. A Pennsylvania company was used because of the leniency of the incorporation laws of that state.

The new company was privileged to engage in practically any kind of business and to establish branch offices at its own discretion. The New York branch soon took over the majority of the company's business, leaving the Philadelphia office as a figure-head.

The operations of the Credit Mobilier were based on the fact that its members also had control of the Union Pacific. Construction contracts were awarded to dummies, who then transferred them to the Credit Mobilier. Construction was paid by the Union Pacific in cash (check), which was then returned to the company for stocks and bonds, which in turn were sold in the open market for what they would bring. The terms of the contracts were made sufficiently high to allow for the depreciation of the railroad securities and to give a profit to the Credit Mobilier.

By means of the Credit Mobilier most of the pressing difficulties seemed to have been overcome. The securities of the Union Pacific were sold according to the terms of the law. Capital was raised and construction progressed. A profit was secured, at least by a portion of the stockholders. Liability was limited by the incorporation laws of the state of Pennsylvania. The only parties who had any complaint were the small stockholders and the government, and even in these cases it could be argued that at least the road was being built, which would have been impossible under any other conditions.

The chief engineer of the Union Pacific in 1864 was Peter A. Dey, one of the best informed of western railroad men. His estimate of the cost of the road was $30,000 a mile for the first hundred miles, and $27,000 a mile for the next hundred. Vice-president Durant, who was the active head of the company, objected to the grades of the proposed line and suggested that they be lessened and the estimate raised accordingly. This suggestion Dey followed reluctantly, raising the price to $50,000.

The first important contract was given to one Hoxie. The specifications followed the first recommendations of Dey, while the price was that of the amended plans. Whereupon Dey resigned, after a few pointed remarks about the practice of overcapitalizing roads, and its previous effect on the Chicago and Rock Island, for which both he and Durant had formerly worked. Dey's successor, two years later, was G. M. Dodge, who had also been formerly a Chicago and Rock Island man.

The affairs of the Union Pacific and the Credit Mobilier received a new turn in 1865 when Oakes and Oliver Ames began to be interested. Successful Massachusetts manufacturers, they were interested in the project as an investment, and stood in contrast to Durant, who was a speculator. The Ames brothers bought stock to retain, while Durant sold his interest as fast as he could.

The injection of the Ameses precipitated a quarrel with Durant, who was shortly later forced out of the management of the Credit Mobilier. His resentment was so great that he blocked any attempts to give construction contracts to the Credit Mobilier, even though he still retained a considerable interest in that organization. For almost two years the affairs of the company were deadlocked.

An agreement was reached in the summer of 1867, and the lucrative Ames contract was signed by both companies. Construction started in earnest, and the Union Pacific began to show signs of real life. The Credit

Mobilier declared its first dividend on December 12, 1867 —in round figures $2,500,000 in Union Pacific stock and a similar amount in bonds. With bonds selling at 80 and stock at 30, this meant a total of nearly $3,000,000, which was at least 100% on the capital invested.

Oakes Ames was also a member of the House of Representatives, and when he returned to Congress in 1867 with his pet project an assured success, his colleagues were eager to participate in the benefits. Many of them recalled former times in which Ames had offered them stock, or in some cases had promised to hold it for them. Now that the concern was paying large dividends, many members of Congress saw a chance to supplement their rather meagre salaries.

In spite of the fact that new capital was not necessary, Ames was perfectly willing to live up to his previous offers. He even went further and reminded Congressmen of his former conversations, and offered to sell a limited amount of Credit Mobilier stock at par, even though the market price at that time was considerably higher. According to his own memorandum his aim was to secure as wide a distribution as possible.

Undoubtedly Ames sought to secure prestige in his distribution of Credit Mobilier stock to members of Congress. Whether or not he expected to influence legislation is a matter of doubt. It seems probable that he was not adverse to lessening the possibility of hostile action on the part of Congress, but it is improbable that he expected to secure any positive favors.

The affairs of the Credit Mobilier were called to public attention during the campaign of 1872, when certain incriminating letters of Ames, hitherto unregarded, were given publicity. These letters concerned the distribution of Credit Mobilier stock to Congress, and seemed to give color to the charge that such sales were made for the purpose of influencing Congressional action.

The Ames letters were not important in their bearing on the campaign of 1872, particularly because at no time was there any suggestion that President Grant was involved. The resulting investigations, however, brought to light much that was questionable, and injured the political fortunes of quite a number of public men. Garfield, Wilson, Colfax and others were implicated. Senator Patterson was only saved from expulsion by the expiration of his term. Representatives Ames and Brooks were censured by the House.

In reality these men were the victims of an awakened public conscience. The practices in which they had indulged had been countenanced by preceding generations, and had carried with them no taint of wrong-doing. Oakes Ames, in particular, deserves sympathy. All through the investigations he was perfectly frank in his testimony and seemingly had no desire to conceal any of his actions. Up to the time of his death, shortly after the House vote of censure, he was unable to understand wherein he had erred.

There was no question but what the Credit Mobilier had been used to evade the letter of the law in dealing in Union Pacific securities. Such evasion might well have come from the purest of motives. The stock and bonds could not have been sold at par for cash, and unless some way out of the difficulty had been found, the building of the Union Pacific would have had to wait for future Congressional legislation.

The morality of letting construction contracts to stockholders was unquestioned at that time. A majority of western railroads were built under these conditions, and no condemnation ensued. The morals of a succeeding generation should not be held as a standard for earlier generations.

Undoubtedly the Credit Mobilier made excessive profits. A conservative estimate indicates approximately 370% before 1869, or 74% a year. This figure is based on the dividends declared by the Credit Mobilier, estimating Union Pacific stock at 30 and bonds at 85, on an original investment of $3,750,000; it also takes into account the depreciation of the Credit Mobilier stock. It is extremely conservative in that it does not take into account the bonus paid on part of the original Credit Mobilier stock, the later increased value of Union Pacific securities, or the fact that the most of the capital was not invested for the maximum period.

Excessive profits need not necessarily be considered an evidence of wrong-doing. In this particular case, however, they had a tendency to "milk" the Union Pacific. Union Pacific securities went down, capitalization went up, and the holdings of the government and of small stockholders were prejudiced. This phase of the matter was at least regrettable.

The question of bribing Congress still remains in dispute. Stock was sold to members of Congress at a time when capital could have been secured elsewhere upon better terms. Whether or not such action was intended to influence legislation favorably can not be answered with any assurance. The circumstances are sufficiently damaging to justify the vote of censure against Ames, even though he may very well have felt that he had done nothing to justify such action.

The awakening public conscience which viewed the

Credit Mobilier proceedings with distaste discovered similar situations throughout American public life. Most important in its relation to western railroads was Speaker Blaine's connection with the Little Rock and Fort Smith. It was claimed that the notorious "Mulligan Letters" gave evidence of improper financial relations between Blaine and the Union Pacific in regard to bonds of the Little Rock and Fort Smith, which it was alleged that the Union Pacific had bought from Blaine at an excessive figure in order to secure his influence in pending legislation.

Resulting investigations failed to produce any conclusive results, and finally Blaine was led to make a spectacular refutation of all charges from the floor of the House, reading the parts of the "Mulligan Letters" which he considered pertinent. His friends were convinced of his innocence, but others remained skeptical.

The Credit Mobilier and the Blaine investigations were portions of an accumulating mass of evidence of incompetence and corruption in American life. Exposures of this kind were so common in the period of the seventies that they have set the tone for the decade, and have led an eminent American historian to call it "The Nadir of National Disgrace."

CHAPTER VI

THE COMPLETION OF THE FIRST TRANSCONTINENTAL ROAD

Internal dissension between the Durant and Ames groups retarded the building of the Union Pacific until an agreement was reached in 1867. In spite of this disagreement work was not stopped entirely, but was at least kept nominally in progress. It was essential to keep the work going for political reasons, if for none other.

The labor problem was largely solved by the end of the war and the disbandment of the armies. High wages and the national reputation of the Union Pacific enterprise served to draw many of the discharged soldiers to the plains of Nebraska. The labor competition of the eastern manufacturing plants was lessened because of the depression which immediately followed the war, and many of the soldiers went west because there was no other opening for them.

These ex-soldiers were under the charge of a former army officer—Colonel Dodge, who had complete charge of construction. Dodge had been in railroad work before the war, taking part in the early surveys of Iowa. Just before the outbreak of the war he had helped to make a preliminary survey of the Union Pacific route. Then he had gone into the army, and he claimed that it was due to his advice that the terminus of the Union Pacific was placed at Omaha.

The military training of the chief of construction and

of many of his employees stood them in good stead during their work through the Indian country. Indian troubles were continuous throughout the period of the Civil War and immediately thereafter, particularly in the Nebraska country. The Indians had seen the gradual encroachment of the white man over a period of many years. The native tribes were pushed back further and further until it seemed only a matter of time until they would be pushed into the ocean. Then came the continuous stream across the plains to the Far West—Mormons, the miners, and the settlers, until the Indians were confined to the least valuable section of the country, with their game gradually disappearing.

It was little wonder that many Indians saw a final threat at their very existence when the steel rails began cutting through the very heart of the Indian country. Naturally they fought back. Fortunately for the railroad the Indians never discovered how to destroy rails or road bed.

Much of the Union Pacific construction was carried on under the protection of armed guards—sometimes United States troops. At times half of a construction crew would stand guard while the other half worked. Frequently the crew stacked its arms while it worked, ready at a moment's notice to ward off an Indian attack. This procedure was very reminiscent of the Biblical account of the building of Jerusalem—"everyone with one of his hands wrought in the work, and with the other hand held a weapon." Isolated workers were always in fear of an Indian raid, and frequently their fears were justified. For some time the entire work had the appearance of an Indian war.

The securing of supplies was a considerable problem

during the first years of construction. There were no railroad connections and supplies had to be hauled at least part of the way by boat or wagon, or both. The Chicago and Northwestern was completed to Omaha in 1867 and from that time had the contract of hauling all the Union Pacific materials. It was still necessary, however, to use wagon transportation to take much of this material to the scene of construction.

Construction was carried on in hundred mile stretches, with a fleet of wagons hauling the necessary supplies and materials. The whole stretch was graded and the bridge work completed before any rails were laid. This method of procedure made it necessary for the grading crews to be considerably in advance of the rest of the construction work.

Ties were taken from the surrounding country as much as possible. Great difficulty was experienced in securing wood on the treeless plains, and the expense was excessive. In the absence of hard wood, cotton-wood was "Burnetized," that is, dipped in a solution of zinc chloride. After the ties were in place, the placing and spiking of the rails occurred very rapidly, and the track was ready for use.

The semi-military organization of the employees of the Union Pacific was emphasized by the living quarters. By reason of the method of construction there were semi-permanent camps at each point at which the construction crews stopped. A tent colony was erected and was supplemented by a certain number of temporary frame houses for the more important officers and for the stores. Naturally all such construction was of the most temporary nature so that it could be removed at short notice and taken to the next location.

These camps attracted the usual camp following of land speculators, petty merchants, saloon-keepers, and prostitutes. The nature of the rough life made it inevitable that these groups were drawn from the lowest classes of society. Drunkenness, immorality, and personal violence were constant occurrences and gave the various stopping places the appropriate sobriquet of "Hell on wheels."

The most important of this kind of settlement came into existence at the place in which construction stopped for the winter. Here a large sized town would appear, property values would increase immensely, local vigilance committees would enforce a rough form of justice, and all the trappings of civilization would appear. The emphasis was on the amusement side of life, and saloons, dance halls, gambling halls, and houses of assignation occupied the most important position. Money flowed freely and blood was not an uncommon sight.

As soon as spring came and work on the railroad was resumed, the mushroom winter quarters disappeared over night. Every available piece of property was carried away, and the only remaining evidences of a former prosperity were the well worn streets and a few of the houses which were too cumbersome to be moved. A partial exception might be made in favor of Cheyenne, the winter quarters for 1867-68 (work was continued throughout the following winter). It followed the usual procedure, but was saved from ultimate annihilation by a succeeding mining boom.

Many attempts were made to divert the line of the Union Pacific to particular established communities. Among these the most important were Denver and Salt Lake City. Denver was afraid that if it did not secure the main line of the road its future growth would be badly stunted. It offered assistance to the extent of its ability if it could be placed on the main line. Whether the proffered aid was insufficient or the road would not have come on any terms does not appear, but at least the surveys were made considerably north of Denver. The Mormons were also exceedingly desirous of securing the main line of the Union Pacific. As the road was originally planned it would have gone through Salt Lake City and around the southern end of the lake. As it was finally built it missed the Mormon settlement completely, in spite of all the arguments and influence that Brigham Young and his followers could bring to bear. The Mormons supplied some of the labor for the road by subletting portions of the construction contracts.

Both the Denver and the Salt Lake City settlements found it necessary to encourage railroad systems of their own at a later time. Denver encouraged roads both to the north to connect with the Union Pacific, and south to draw business to Denver and to make connections with southern lines. The Mormons also were responsible for a railroad system which connected their settlements with the outside world.

The first forty miles of completed road was accepted by the President on January 24, 1866. By July of the same year the line had been completed 305 miles west of Omaha, and the first passenger tariff went into effect as far as Fort Kearney—ten cents per passenger per mile. The following year the Overland Mail was forced to move its eastern terminus to Fort Kearney, thus forecasting its early demise.

By the winter of 1867-68 the Union Pacific had reached Cheyenne and was engaged in a mad race with the Central Pacific to determine which road would build the furthest and receive the greater amount of government aid. Work was resumed early in the spring and rushed at the rate of from four to seven miles a day. In spite of the obstacles of winter work no halt was made in the cold period of 1868-69. By the spring of 1869 both companies were working in western Utah, and it looked as though the Union Pacific would build clear to the Pacific unless it were stopped.

The other end of the line was being built by the Central Pacific of California. The monopoly of the field by this road was due in large part to the foresight and enthusiasm of T. D. Judah. Judah was a graduate of Troy Polytechnic, and was a competent engineer as well as a railroad enthusiast. Coming to California in the fifties he was impressed with the desirability of eastern railroad connections, and worked long and earnestly to get other people interested. His project was for a private road to be built by a million hundred dollar subscriptions. Up to 1860 he had seemingly made little progress in imbuing other Californians with the idea of the practicability of his scheme.

The winter of 1860-61 saw an improvement in the chances for Congressional aid to a transcontinental road, and in consequence Judah succeeded in interesting four Sacramento merchants of moderate means—Leland Stanford, Collis P. Huntington, Mark Hopkins, and Charles Crocker. The Central Pacific Railroad Company was incorporated on June 28, 1861, and Judah was made chief engineer. During the summer Judah took a trip over the proposed route for the road and made preliminary observations on the subject.

The important scene of action in the winter of 1861-62 was Washington, where the Pacific railroad legislation was pending, and consequently Judah took himself hither to do what he could for the cause. His traveling companion on the long sea trip was a newly elected California representative, and Judah was able to impregnate him with the desirability of a transcontinental road, and in particular with the Central Pacific.

After some time in Washington Judah joined Peter Dey in a preliminary survey of the entire route. Dey was later put in charge of the construction of the Union Pacific, and so the trip of these two men made possible a closer agreement of the aims of the two companies than might otherwise have occurred.

The Congressional aid of the bill of 1862 naturally went to the Central Pacific because it was the only company in the field. In the same year one of the Central Pacific associates, Leland Stanford, became governor of California, and was thus able to throw the influence of his official position in favor of the road. No impropriety was seen in this combination of interests, because the Central Pacific was then the most important public enterprise confronting the citizens of California.

The Central Pacific had to meet exactly the same financial difficulties that confronted the Union Pacific, and it is not remarkable that they were met in a similar way. A subsidiary company was formed to take over construction contracts and to make the profit which was not promised by operation. As in the case of the Credit Mobilier it was used as the intermediary for the sale of the company's securities.

The first of the Central Pacific construction contracts were taken over by Crocker and Company, of which Charles Crocker was the head and the other associates were the members. For this purpose Crocker resigned from the management of the parent company and spent the majority of his time on the work of construction.

The connection between Crocker and Company and the Central Pacific was too close and obvious to be satisfactory. Outside investors saw the purpose of the scheme and were wary of the company's financial stability and its care for minor stockholders. To remedy this defect a new construction company was formed in 1867—the Contract and Finance Company, and it was under its auspices that most of the Central Pacific was built.

The chief advantage which the Contract and Finance Company had over the Credit Mobilier was that it was able to get its accounts into such shape that no one has ever quite been able to disentangle them. Huntington, Stanford, Crocker, and Hopkins subscribed to the capital stock, paying for it with their personal notes. Each man advanced the money necessary for construction as fast as he was able, and each one kept his own records. Profits were divided equally. If this method of finance was not sufficiently obtuse in itself, it was made absolutely hopeless by the "accidental" destruction of the company's books by fire in 1873.

The same comments might be made about the Contract and Finance Company as have previously been made about the Credit Mobilier. The four principal stockholders of the Central Pacific voted themselves excessive construction contracts and by this means secured control of the majority of the assets of the road. Regardless of the morality of this procedure, the interests of the remaining stockholders and of the government were jeopardized, to say nothing of the effect on the people of the state who later had to pay higher rates in order to support a weak road.

Initiative, courage, and indomitable perseverance constitute the more attractive side of the picture of the building of the Central Pacific. Climatic and engineering difficulties were seemingly insuperable at the outset of the work. The Sierras had to be crossed immediately, whereas the Union Pacific was able to build two-thirds of its road before encountering any appreciable engineering difficulties.

Both labor and capital were almost non-existent in the Far West. The rate for gold was practically prohibitive during the war period, and accumulations of fluid wealth could only be found in the East. Labor was even scarcer than in the East because every available man was seeking his fortune rather than a mere living. The labor problem was not finally solved until Chinese coolies were imported. This form of labor proved very desirable because of its cheapness and docility.

In spite of all difficulties the work on the Central Pacific was pushed energetically after 1865. As it began nearing completion a strong spirit of hostility grew up between the two companies, and in their competition to build more line and thus to secure a larger subsidy, the construction crews began to parallel each other. It is related that the Irish workers on the Union Pacific took the competition seriously and from their lower level exploded blasts under the Chinese of the Central Pacific, which the latter returned in kind, burying several Irishmen.

The meeting point of the two lines had not been definitely settled by Congress in its legislation. It had been assumed that the two roads would merely build until their tracks joined. Now it was discovered that a voluntary meeting point could not be agreed upon and unless further action was taken the roads would continue building indefinitely. In this extremity Congress finally set a definite point of junction at Promontory Point, Utah.

The formal junction of the rails took place on May 10, 1869, and the first American transcontinental railroad was completed. When the last spike was driven the blows of the sledge, as well as the speeches marking the occasion, were carried to the East by the telegraph. All over the country whistles were blown, bells were rung, guns were fired, processions were formed, and speeches became the order of the day. Congratulations were showered upon the officials of the successful companies. Editors joined in a pæan of praise. In truth, the completion of the first transcontinental road marked an epoch.

Not only was it true that for the first time the continent was spanned by iron rails, but also the time was one of general satisfaction with railroad achievements. The war was over, prosperity was returning, and the completion of the joint Union Pacific-Central Pacific project seemed a wonderful consummation of the hopes of years. The country looked forward to an unexcelled period of prosperity under the beneficent influence of the steam locomotive.

Under the superficial causes for rejoicing lay more ominous factors. Both the Pacific railroads had sold their capital stock at a large discount and were greatly overcapitalized. Both had incurred too heavy debts in construction. Both ran through sparsely settled sections of the country and could expect but little business. Both were built too rapidly and would soon need extensive repairs and improvements. The managements of both roads were aware of the real situation. Insiders were anxious to dispose of their holdings before their inevitable drop in price. Experts looked forward to the time when both lines would become the prey of speculators because of the drop in the value of their securities.

The original promoters of the Union Pacific, with the exception of Ames, disposed of their holdings as soon as possible. In 1871 Ames was replaced in the presidency by Thomas Scott, vice-president of the Pennsylvania Railroad and extensively interested in various western roads. After struggling for financial solvency for two years he disposed of his holdings to Jay Gould, who was interested in certain speculative possibilities. The only additional line constructed prior to 1873 was a branch from Kit Carson to Las Animas. This line was constructed to head off the Santa Fe and was later removed.

The Central Pacific associates also tried to dispose of their holdings during the latter sixties, but at the same time continued to add new properties to enhance the value of what they already had. They were unsuccessful in their attempted sales because the condition of the company was common knowledge, and no one cared to take over such a liability. There was little doubt in most people's minds that the Central Pacific was destined to be a losing proposition.

The economic prosperity of the early seventies and the failure of purchasers to appear led the associates to remodel their plans. As long as good times continued it might be possible for the Central Pacific to pay its own way, and if a monopoly of California overland business could be secured there was even a chance of continued profits in the future. In consequence the attention of the company was turned toward the control of all California railroad business.

The first attention of the Central Pacific was turned

toward the rich district tributary to San Francisco. Through good luck and the influence of Governor Stanford it secured extensive waterfront facilities in Oakland and San Francisco, amounting to a practical monopoly. Its own line to San Francisco was completed in 1869. The shorter Sacramento-San Francisco line of the California Pacific was forced out of business. Other central California lines were either purchased or built, so that by 1873 the Central Pacific had its desired monopoly.

With the control of central California secured the Central Pacific had only one other important potential danger. Congress had chartered a number of other transcontinental roads, and if any of them were built it would mean that they could seize a considerable portion of California traffic. The northern route made its California connection by means of the California and Oregon, a land grant road. Control of this line was secured by the Central Pacific, and construction started in order to fulfill the terms of the charter.

In the south the plans of the Central Pacific were immensely aided by the geography of the country. There were only two practical crossings of the Colorado River gorge, and their control meant the control of southern California. The crossings at the Needles and at Yuma thus became the objectives in the south, and there was every possibility that the Central Pacific would be able to occupy them before any other line would be able to build across the continent.

The southern extension of the Central Pacific was built by the Southern Pacific of California, not to be confused with the later Kentucky holding company of the same name. Work was started immediately and by 1873 the road was progressing satisfactorily. There was no doubt that unless some unusual catastrophe occurred it would win its objective. The southern transcontinental lines were hardly started by that time.

The character of both the Union Pacific and the Central Pacific led them to a monopoly of the territory through which they passed. Being the first lines and for many years the only lines in the regions they traversed, they had an exaggerated importance in both political and economic affairs. The Union Pacific, for instance, was practically supreme. It was influential in elections and in the appointment of non-elective officials, and frequently cast the deciding vote in economic matters. Particularly was this situation true in Wyoming, where the Union Pacific had a monopoly of transportation for many years. There is very little question that for a considerable period of time the Union Pacific was the power behind the throne in this region.

The Central Pacific built up a similar monopoly in California by 1873. As long as its original incorporators remained in control it continued to get stronger and stronger in both the economic and political life of the state. It was a common observation that the Southern Pacific controlled the state of California for over a quarter of a century. Its grip was lost around 1900 when Huntington died and his holdings were sold in the East.

Along with the railroad control went its usual associates of bribery and corruption. A feudal overlordship meant continual gifts to devoted followers. The prevalence of various forms of corruption was notorious, and long furnished one of the blackest pages of American life. Not until the turn of the century were the worst of the evils eradicated.

CHAPTER VII

The building of the Union Pacific was but one of the harbingers of prosperity in the period immediately following the Civil War. After the usual period of readjustment people began to turn their attention from the activities of war to those of peace. The important industries of the country began to revive, while the speculative fields of oil and gold received renewed attention. Both capital and labor became more plentiful.

The most important change in the West was the rapid growth of grain production west of the Mississippi. During the war period it doubled, with most of the increase in Minnesota, Iowa, and California. After the war it continued to grow by leaps and bounds. Additional grain necessitated more railroad facilities, and construction proceeded vigorously. The completion of the Union Pacific encouraged western settlement and hastened the process.

Universal prosperity and the growing needs of the expanding mining and agricultural sections of the West encouraged all western railroads to put their best efforts into construction and to try to occupy the important economic districts in advance of their competitors. In particular there was a rush to occupy the fertile farming sections of the grain-producing areas.

The most important lines in the field were the roads

centering in Chicago. These lines had reached the Mississippi during the fifties, and by the end of the war were in control of their western connections. Now they redoubled their efforts to reach the Missouri and to build up systems which would make them impregnable in their own territories.

The first railroad to be completed across the state of Iowa was the Chicago and Northwestern. It had reached a point on the Mississippi opposite Clinton, Iowa, in 1855, being the second eastern road to reach the river. The dominating figure in the road's future expansion was J. I. Blair, of Blairstown, New Jersey. It was largely due to his foresight and energy that future developments proceeded so rapidly.

The only possible western connecting line which had any track completed was the Lyons and Iowa Central, organized in 1853. This road was projected to run from Lyons (near Clinton) by way of Des Moines to Council Bluffs. Early in its history Boston capital was interested and the route of the road was changed to pass through Cedar Rapids; by 1859 this point had been reached. Blair sought to use this completed line in order both to save the expense of construction and to destroy a possible competitor. At first he bought a small interest, but as time went on he expanded it to give himself complete control. After certain legal complications were removed the remaining link between Clinton and Lyons was constructed, and the Northwestern had an all-rail route from Chicago to Cedar Rapids. The Lyons and Iowa Central was leased in perpetuity and its road became part of the main line of the Chicago and Northwestern.

The remaining distance between Cedar Rapids and Council Bluffs was occupied by the projected Iowa Central Air-Line. This road had been organized in 1853 by local capital, and was entirely dependent on government aid for any possible construction. Because of the absolute necessity of outside assistance the president had been sent to Washington with an absolutely free hand to do as he pleased. Whether or not it was due to the "pledges," which he said "were freely made," the act of 1856 gave the road everything which it had desired —a land grant from the Mississippi River to Council Bluffs.

Work on the Iowa Central Air-Line started immediately at the Mississippi, but came to a temporary stop with the panic of 1857, by which time but little had been done. During this period Blair had tried to secure control of the road but failed. With the cessation of construction he saw his opportunity. He immediately organized the Cedar Rapids and Missouri River, and started to build west from Cedar Rapids. As soon as the work was well under way he went to the Iowa legislature to convince it that the land grant should be transferred to the company that was ready and able to build the desired line. His arguments were convincing, and the land grant west of Cedar Rapids was transferred to the Blair company. The Iowa Central Air-Line was sold at auction, reorganized, and the route changed so that it eventually became a part of the Minneapolis-St. Louis line.

The building of the Cedar Rapids and Missouri River progressed steadily throughout the war. The bridge across the Mississippi at Clinton was completed in 1865, being the second one south of St. Paul. The road was completed to Council Bluffs in 1867, in time to secure the contract for hauling the majority of the Union Pacific supplies. The bridging of the Missouri, another important engineering feat, was successfully accomplished several years later.

While the Chicago and Northwestern had been beaten to the Missouri River by both the Hannibal and St. Jo. and the Pacific Railroad of Missouri, it had several advantages which they did not enjoy. It was the first of the Chicago roads to be finished, and had a complete line of rail, including the necessary bridges, of which neither of the Missouri roads could boast. Its terminus at Council Bluffs gave it a direct connection with the Union Pacific and an advantageous position in respect to all transcontinental traffic.

The advance of the Northwestern by no means stopped with the completion of the Council Bluffs line. Des Moines was entered through the control of the Des Moines and Minnesota. Extensions were made north and west from Council Bluffs under the name of the Sioux City and Pacific. Sioux City was reached in 1868, and from there lines were constructed to Fort Dodge, Iowa, and to Fremont, Nebraska. The latter branch was one of the connections of the Union Pacific which was provided for in the original incorporation of that road, and aided by a land grant. The main Nebraska extension of the Chicago and Northwestern was built west from Blair, and had reached Wisner by 1873.

Both the Sioux City and Pacific and its later subsidiary, the Fremont, Elkhorn and Missouri Valley, were Blair roads. They were built and operated in the interest of the Chicago and Northwestern, although they were not technically made an integral part of that system until the eighties.

The Minnesota extension of the Northwestern was made along the line of the Winona and St. Peter. This road, originally chartered as the Transit Railroad, was projected to run from Winona directly west across the state, and received both federal and state aid. In 1860 it was one of the roads that was foreclosed and bought by the state. Reorganized twice, it finally began building under the name of the Winona and St. Peter.

The resources of the Winona and St. Peter were very meagre and in consequence the construction company was paid in large part with the securities of the company. So far was this procedure carried that the control of the company finally passed to the construction company. In 1867 it disposed of its entire holdings to the Chicago and Northwestern, which, thereupon, took control of the line and started pushing the work vigorously. The road was completed straight across the state and as far west as Lake Kampeska, Dakota Territory, by 1873. The gap between the Chicago and Northwestern terminus at La Crosse and the Winona and St. Peter terminus at Winona was filled in by a line on the Wisconsin side of the river.

The second road to be completed to the Missouri was the Chicago and Rock Island, later the Chicago, Rock Island and Pacific. It was in advance of the Chicago and Northwestern when it reached the Mississippi at Rock Island in February, 1854, but lost its advantage in building across Iowa. The Rock Island did not leave its western connection to chance, but held a considerable interest in the Mississippi and Missouri River when it was chartered in 1852. This road bought out the franchises and property of the older Davenport and Iowa City railroad and projected its line to run across the state from Davenport to Council Bluffs.

The chief engineer of the Mississippi and Missouri

River was Peter A. Dey, formerly in the employ of the Chicago and Rock Island. He was assisted in his first surveys by G. M. Dodge, later of the Union Pacific. It is very probable that it was here that Dodge received his prejudice in favor of Omaha, which he later suggested to President Lincoln as the desirable terminus of the Union Pacific.

The work on the west bank of the Mississippi was begun in the fall of 1853, at which time the eastern line was nearing completion. Aided by a federal land grant the Mississippi and Missouri River was able to open the first completed Iowa railroad track, on July 19, 1855.

The Mississippi and Missouri River was also notable for the construction of the first bridge over the Mississippi south of St. Paul. Begun in 1853, it was completed two years later, and was the mechanical wonder of the West —comparing favorably in the public estimation with the J. A. Roebling Niagara suspension bridge, which was opened in 1854. For ten years it remained unchallenged. Then the Clinton bridge, the Burlington bridge, and the St. Louis bridge opened the way to numerous other similar structures.

Eulogies were by no means the only portion of the Rock Island bridge. All river men feared the new competition, and especially were the St. Louis merchants hostile. St. Louis was being seriously challenged by Chicago as a commercial center, and if trains were going to be able to cross the Mississippi without a stop it meant a further gain in prestige for the Lake Michigan city. It would then only be a question of time before the important river traffic of St. Louis would be relegated to the discard.

The opposition contended that a bridge across the Mis-

sissippi obstructed interstate traffic on the river, and was
a public nuisance. Furthermore, it was held that an
interstate bridge required a charter from Congress, which
had not been secured. The legal battle over the right of
the bridge to exist was postponed by its destruction by
fire when one of the steamers ran into it. Although the
river men claimed that the affair was an accident, the
court thought otherwise, and assessed damages. Among
the staff of railroad lawyers was Abraham Lincoln.

Immediately upon the restoration of the bridge a St.
Louis merchant secured a bill in chancery for its removal
on the grounds that it established an unwise precedent.
Although the Supreme Court overruled this action, the
whole matter was in litigation for many years. It was
finally found necessary to rebuild the bridge under the
separate authorizations of Illinois, of Iowa, and of the
United States.

The constant bridge litigation and the depression of
the latter fifties and early sixties, exhausted the funds of
the company. Money was loaned by the Chicago and
Rock Island, but the situation still remained unsatisfactory. Finally in 1866 the road was allowed to be foreclosed and sold. It was bought by the mother company,
which consolidated it with the main line under the name
of the Chicago, Rock Island and Pacific. Under this
name work was renewed with vigor, so that by the following year it was completed to Des Moines. It reached
Council Bluffs in June, 1869.

The Rock Island secured a second line across the state
in the Chicago and Southwestern, which was projected
from a point near Davenport to Leavenworth, Kansas.
Work was started at both ends as soon as the Council
Bluffs line had been completed. By 1873 it was finished

to Leavenworth, with a branch to Atchison. Not only did the Chicago, Rock Island and Pacific have two complete lines across the state of Iowa, but it was in a position to encroach on the territory of the Missouri roads and on the business of the Missouri river towns south of Omaha.

The Des Moines Valley Railroad was another strategic line that eventually became a part of the Rock Island system. This road was planned to run from Keokuk, near the mouth of the Des Moines River, up the river to the state capital. Work was started in the middle fifties, and the road was opened from Keokuk to Des Moines on August 29, 1866, being the first railroad to enter the state capital.

During the next four years the Des Moines Valley was completed to Fort Dodge. The panic of 1873 forced its foreclosure and sale, whereupon the portion from Keokuk to Des Moines was reorganized as the Keokuk and Des Moines and leased to the Chicago, Rock Island and Pacific in 1878. The portion from Des Moines to Fort Dodge remained independent.

The Chicago, Burlington and Quincy was the third road to reach Council Bluffs, arriving late in 1869. Its destinies were presided over by James F. Joy of Detroit, who was also president of the Michigan Central and had an interest in the New York Central. His were the first important dreams of western railroad empire, and they seemed to be well on the way to realization in the years preceding the panic of 1873.

The Chicago, Burlington and Quincy arrived at the Mississippi River during the same year (1856) that its logical western connection, the Burlington and Missouri River, received its federal land grant. The panic of 1857 gave Joy his opportunity to purchase the road, which he built as far as Ottumwa by the outbreak of the war. Work stopped at that point until the end of the war, but from 1867 to the end of 1869 construction reached its terminus at Council Bluffs. The bridge over the Mississippi River at Burlington was completed in 1868.

No sooner had the Iowa line been completed than the Burlington and Missouri River of Nebraska was chartered to continue the work further west. Aided by a federal land grant, it was able, by 1873, to build as far as a junction with the Union Pacific at Fort Kearney— 470 miles west of Burlington.

The building of the Burlington and Missouri River across Iowa brought it into competition with the Hannibal and St. Jo. for the business of southern Iowa and northern Missouri. To Joy this was undesired competition and so he sought a way to muzzle the Missouri road. During the war the Hannibal and St. Jo. had been extended eastward to a junction with the Burlington at Quincy, in order to provide a through route to the West. When the war was over this connection enabled the Chicago, Burlington and Quincy to dominate its smaller rival by threatening not to divide its through business, but to ship it all by way of its own line. The result was that the sale of the Hannibal and St. Jo. was forced, and it became a part of the Joy properties. The western termini of the two lines were connected in 1870 by the completion of the Kansas City, St. Jo. and Council Bluffs. Branches were also constructed to Atchison and Kansas City.

With the foregoing lines Joy had a complete road from New York via Chicago and Council Bluffs to Fort Kearney, thus affording excellent transcontinental connections, as well as offering a possibility of its ultimate completion to the coast. He also had a practical monopoly of southern Iowa and northern Missouri business, together with competitive lines to every Missouri River town of importance.

Besides his western connections, Joy was interested in a possible route to the Gulf. Backed by a group of Boston capitalists he bought the Kansas and Neosho Valley and reorganized it as the Missouri River, Fort Scott and Gulf. Work was started at Kansas City immediately after the close of the Civil War, and was pushed directly south. The construction soon developed into a race with the Missouri, Kansas and Texas to see which could reach the state border first.

Kansas had promised the federal land grant, carrying with it the right-of-way across Indian Territory, to the road that was first completed to the southern boundary of the state. Both roads were completed in 1870. The Missouri River, Fort Scott and Gulf arrived first, but the line of the road did not fulfill the specifications of the grant, which in consequence then went to the other line. Without this aid the loser had to stop construction at Baxter Springs.

While the Missouri River, Fort Scott and Gulf was building south Joy acquired another possible Gulf connection in the Leavenworth, Lawrence and Galveston. This road was the recipient of another portion of the Kansas land grant, and was projected to run from Leavenworth to Lawrence, and from there southwest to the state boundary in the direction of Galveston Bay. Under the Joy management it was constructed as far as Coffeyville, near the southern boundary of the state.

The "Joy system," as it came to be known, was the

first important western ownership group. Loosely-knit, over-capitalized, and over-built, it disintegrated rapidly with the panic of 1873. The Hannibal and St. Jo. became the football of contending forces and was lost for a decade. The Leavenworth, Lawrence and Galveston was soon absorbed by the Santa Fe. The Missouri River, Fort Scott and Gulf went to the same road for a brief period, but finally completed an independent line to the Gulf under the name of the Kansas City, Fort Scott and Memphis.

The breakdown of the Joy lines did not include the main line from Chicago to Fort Kearney. The Burlington and Missouri River lines of both Iowa and Nebraska remained. Future Burlington expansion was in the direction of completing this main line further west and of strengthening it with an extensive system of feeders. Instead of building toward the Gulf, the later development was more toward the north.

The fourth line to be completed to Council Bluffs, the Chicago, Milwaukee and St. Paul, did not reach that point until the latter seventies. Work progressed westward from McGregor very slowly, in large part because of the paucity of population in the northern part of Iowa, and the consequent lack of traffic. Even a federal land grant failed to hurry matters. The state finally became disgusted and transferred the western part of the grant to a new line, but any possible effects of this action were lost when the St. Paul immediately absorbed its possible competitor. By 1873 the main line was only two-thirds the way across the state.

Most of the new mileage of the Chicago, Milwaukee and St. Paul was acquired in Minnesota, and most of it was purchased rather than built. The Minnesota Central was built to a connection with the Iowa main line in 1867, thus furnishing the first all-rail route between St. Paul and Chicago. A more direct line was completed in 1872 by the building of the St. Paul and Chicago south to a connection with the Wisconsin main line of the St. Paul at La Crescent (opposite La Crosse). The western connection from La Crosse was over the Southern Minnesota, of which 173 miles had been completed by 1873. This road was not acquired until several years later, however.

The Illinois Central was the only other Chicago road to be completed across the state of Iowa before 1873. Its logical western connection at Dubuque was the Dubuque and Sioux City, which had been built as far as Iowa Falls by 1867. During that year it was acquired by the Illinois Central. Construction was not maintained, and in consequence the state transferred its land grant to the Iowa Falls and Sioux City. This new road was also acquired by the Illinois Central, which completed it across the state to Sioux City by 1870.

Further south, the Pacific Railroad of Missouri reached its Kansas City terminus in 1865, and was subsequently reorganized as the Missouri Pacific. Upon the return of prosperity it found itself in a very strategic position, running through the most populous portion of the state, and connecting two important commercial centers. It was hampered chiefly by its debt to the state, and by its lack of good connections with the East. Its gauge was not standard and there was no bridge across the Mississippi.

The St. Louis bridge was completed shortly after the end of the war, and in 1869 the track gauge of the whole line was made standard. The state lien was released in

1868 at a loss to the state of about $10,000,000. By the end of the sixties the financial condition of the Missouri Pacific was sufficiently strong to permit the payment of dividends.

During 1871 and 1872 there were rumors that the Missouri Pacific was being purchased in the interest of the "Joy lines." Instead of this, it went to the Atlantic and Pacific, a transcontinental land grant road newly chartered by Congress. After a brief period of activity this new system went to pieces with the panic of 1873.

One other line—the North Missouri, reached the Missouri River during the period. Its completion as far as the main line of the Hannibal and St. Jo. had given that road an entrance to St. Louis. Its own line to Kansas City was completed in 1869. Later its name was changed to the St. Louis, Kansas City and Northern, and finally in 1879 it was consolidated with several other roads to furnish the main line of the Wabash.

The completion of these more important main lines presumes also the building of shorter roads and of branch lines in the same district. Roads such as the Memphis and Little Rock and the Sioux City and St. Paul served to make connections between the larger towns untouched by the larger systems, while innumerable smaller roads acted as feeders, and served to control the business within a given area. Some of them were built by the parent road while others were acquired after they had been constructed. In fact, some roads were built merely to create undesired competition, and therefore to force the larger line to buy them at an attractive figure.

The building of east and west through lines was paralleled to some measure by the construction of north and south roads. Although Joy failed to build to the Gulf, two other lines succeeded during the period. In both cases the lines were built by more than one company, the northern roads making connection with lines from Texas.

The Missouri, Kansas and Texas, originally chartered as the Union Pacific Southern Branch, raced to the southern boundary of the state with the Missouri River, Fort Scott and Gulf in order to win the land grant offered by the state to the first road that should build to a particular point on the state boundary. It won the race, not by arriving first, but by reaching the correct point, and in consequence received the benefit of the Congressional land grant and the right-of-way across Indian Territory. With this victory safely assured it consolidated with a number of local lines in 1870 as the Missouri, Kansas and Texas, and two years later crossed the Red River into Texas.

The Terminus of the Katy (Missouri, Kansas and Texas) was at Denison, a town named in honor of one of the directors. Before the railroad was built the town was a cornfield. Traffic arrangements were made with the Missouri Pacific for the transportation of business to St. Louis and to points further east.

The Texas line to meet the Missouri, Kansas and Texas was the Houston and Texas Central, building north from Houston. About eighty miles were finished before the war, and work was immediately renewed upon the cessation of hostilities. Early in 1873 it joined its tracks to those of the Missouri, Kansas and Texas at Denison. Connections were made with Galveston over the Galveston, Houston and Henderson, completed in 1859, and the only railroad to enter Galveston until the late seventies.

The other northern line to make connections with the Gulf was the St. Louis and Iron Mountain. This road was in just as bad a financial condition as any road in the country, despite the fact that it had received state monetary aid upon which it had never paid any interest. After foreclosure and reorganization the state finally released its lien in despair. By 1870 southern connections were made with the Mobile and Ohio at Columbia, Kentucky, and two years later it reached the state line.

The Arkansas link of the road was built by the Cairo and Fulton, which was aided by a federal land grant and a small amount of monetary assistance from Missouri. It refused proffered Arkansas bond aid. Construction progressed rapidly after 1870, so that three years later the line had been completed from Cairo, by way of a junction with the St. Louis and Iron Mountain, to Texarkana, Texas. In 1874 these two roads were consolidated under the name of the St. Louis, Iron Mountain and Southern.

The southern portion of the line, with the exception of a small strip of Texas and Pacific track near Texarkana, was built by the International and Great Northern. This road was a consolidation (1873) of the Houston and Great Northern and the International, both local Texas lines. Their combined destinies were presided over by Galusha A. Grow, of homestead memory.

Aided by state money and land, the main line of the future International and Great Northern was completed late in 1872 from Houston to a junction with the Texas and Pacific. When the Cairo and Fulton was finished the following year, a second complete line from St. Louis to the Gulf was in operation. This line also used the Galveston, Houston and Henderson to effect an entrance to Galveston.

There were three outstanding groups of roads that carried on extensive building operations in the period prior to the panic of 1873. Two of these have been discussed in this chapter—the through east and west lines having their terminus in Chicago or St. Louis, and the north and south lines making connections with the Gulf. The third group, the transcontinental lines, are taken up at more length in the succeeding chapter. Certain concomitants of their construction, however, deserve notice here.

The construction of the transcontinental roads brought about the construction of other roads in the more populous portions of the West, so that there soon grew up complete systems in the more important commercial and agricultural regions. While the railroad net was expanding into Kansas and Nebraska, and was being built up in California, various intervening sections began to be significant.

Colorado began to be important, largely because of the growth of her mining industries. Vice versa, the mining was encouraged by the completion of the railroads. Cities such as Denver, Pueblo, and Colorado Springs began to build up for themselves the control of the area round about by the encouragement of railroads to the outlying mining districts.

The Mormons also found it desirable to lay the foundations of an adequate transportational system of their own. Under the leadership of Brigham Young various lines were chartered and work started. The necessary experience for their construction came in large part from

the earlier contacts which the Mormons had had with
the building of the Union Pacific.

The one and only purpose of the Mormon railroads
was to furnish adequate transportation. Both profits
and the control of the roads were entirely subsidiary.
Naturally the most important lines were built north and
south from Salt Lake City, although east and west connections were also begun. When these roads were sufficiently completed in the early seventies, they were sold
to the Union Pacific.

CHAPTER VIII

Within two years of the completion of the Union Pacific all of the transcontinental routes that were then considered possible had been occupied by Congressionally chartered land grant railroads. These roads were the only ones able to start construction prior to the panic of 1873.

When the Union Pacific had been chartered, provision had been made for branch line connections in the east. By far the most important of these subsidiary roads was the Leavenworth, Pawnee and Western. Its ultimate expansion was sufficient to make it a serious competitor for the business which it was expected that the mother company would monopolize. Its final construction made it more of a through line in itself than a branch of the Union Pacific.

The Leavenworth, Pawnee and Western had been chartered by the state of Kansas as early as 1855, although but little work had been done on it at that time. When the Union Pacific was chartered the Kansas road was given the portion of the grant from the mouth of the Kansas River northeast to a junction with a main line of the Union Pacific at the hundredth meridian. In the first blush of enthusiasm the Union Pacific acquired the stock of the Leavenworth, Pawnee and Western, and

112

started work near Kansas City (Wyandotte) in September, 1863, even before the main line was begun. In January, 1864, the Kansas legislature adjourned for four days in order that the members might have the opportunity of riding over the newly opened line between Wyandotte and Lawrence.

The funds of the new company were soon exhausted, and in consequence work came to a stop. The mother company had no additional capital to spend for branch lines and so was glad to find purchasers in J. C. Fremont and Sam Hallett. Under the new direction the name of the line was changed to that of Union Pacific Eastern Division in order to convey more immediately the connection with the main line of the Union Pacific.

The aspirations of the road were immensely widened in 1866 when, due to the pressure of the people of Colorado, and particularly those of Denver, the route was extended so that connection might be made with the Union Pacific at a point not more than fifty miles west of the meridian of Denver. Three years later the land grant was extended for the whole distance of the road, but no bond aid was given. During 1866 the road also improved its position by making connections with the Missouri Pacific at Kansas City.

With these changes and additions the Eastern Division became a vastly more appealing proposition to eastern capital. An excursion of eastern capitalists in the spring of 1866 surveyed the property with a view toward investment. Later in the year many of them were led by the example of J. Edgar Thompson of the Pennsylvania Railroad to make investments. The prestige of such assistance, as well as the money itself, was a valuable asset.

The success of the excursion of 1866 led the company
to use the same idea the following year in order to secure
publicity and additional funds. This time the party was
headed by Simon Cameron of Pennsylvania and was composed for the most part of newspaper men. It went as
far west as Fort Harker, which in June, 1867, was the
end of the road. At this time Adna Anderson was the
general superintendent, having succeeded W. W. Wright.
Both men had been connected with the federal operation
of southern railroads during the war, and show in a
specific way how many similar individuals naturally
gravitated toward the new railroads of the West.

A further change in the charter of the company occurred in 1869 when it was permitted to change its name
to the Kansas Pacific and to assign the portion of its
land grant and its construction from Denver to Cheyenne to the Denver Pacific. This last change was again
made to appeal to Denver sentiment. The Denver Pacific was a local road designed to make connections with
the Union Pacific, and already partially built. Actually
the change made little difference. The Kansas Pacific
absorbed the Denver Pacific and constructed a good share
of its line. The Denver-Cheyenne line was completed
in the spring of 1870, and the Kansas City-Denver line
a few months later, so that through trains were running
over the entire length of the road early in 1871.

The Kansas Pacific-Denver Pacific line was extremely
important from a strategic point of view. It paralleled
two-thirds of the Union Pacific, and was a more direct
line, at least for business from St. Louis and the South.
In case of any trouble it could be used by the Chicago
lines, and the charter of the Union Pacific forbade discriminations against any connecting road. If the worst

came to the worst it was always possible to extend the Kansas Pacific to a direct connection with the Central Pacific. Finally, it ran through a more populous portion of the country and was in a more favorable position to secure a large share of the western grain and mining production.

There were certain offsetting disadvantages, however. While the charter of the Union Pacific forbade discriminations against connecting lines the practice did not always carry out the theory. Actually the Kansas Pacific did not get a fair division of the traffic or of rates. Then, too, the line was poorly built and greatly overcapitalized. For many years it was continually on the verge of bankruptcy because of the large amount of "water" in its stock.

The one other Kansas road with transcontinental aspirations was the Atchison, Topeka and Santa Fe. It was begun as a purely local enterprise, chartered by the state, and was never quite in the position of the land grant roads aided by Congress. In after years it became notable for being one of the strongest roads in the West.

The utmost for which the original incorporators hoped was that some day the road might extend as far as the old Spanish town of Santa Fe, one of the most important of the Spanish colonial trading centers. The interest of the United States in the trade of this community dates from about the time of the revolution of 1821. With the breaking of direct connections with Spain and with the lifting of the Spanish colonial restrictions the people of the Southwest began to look more and more to the United States for their connection with the outside world.

Adventurous American traders immediately began to make periodic trips to Santa Fe in order to participate in its large and lucrative business. There soon came into existence a well marked trail, which antedated those to California and Oregon by nearly twenty years. Pack horses were succeeded by Conestoga wagons as the trade became well established. Some of the larger trains were even guarded by United States troops as far as the border. What the trip lost in adventure and romance it gained in larger profits to the trader.

When the Mexican War added the whole of the Southwest to the territory of the Union, there were not lacking those men who looked forward to binding the new territory more closely to the older communities with the steel bands of the railroad. Among these speculators was one Cyrus Holliday of Kansas, whose dreams were eventually to take form in one of the most important of the western railroad projects.

When Cyrus Holliday began speculating on railroads to the Southwest his friends told him that his usual good sense was waning, and that the idea of such a road was so remote as to be ridiculous. In view of their skepticism he confined himself to the chartering of the Atchison and Topeka (1859), to run between the two towns named; but in the back of his mind he still retained his old ideas.

The new road encountered the usual financial difficulties, and in spite of all efforts was unable to start construction. When Congress gave Kansas a land grant for railroad use in 1863 the route of the Atchison and Topeka was included, and expanded to continue to the western boundary of the state. Provision was also made for a southern branch. The company immediately avowed its extended purpose by being rechartered as the Atchison, Topeka and Santa Fe. The branch was acquired and constructed in the interest of the Joy lines, but eventually found its way back to the parent company.

The land grant gave but little immediate encouragement, for there were but few people making war time purchases of Kansas land. Holliday went to New York, but was unsuccessful in interesting eastern capital. A construction company was finally persuaded to undertake the first part of the building, but when it came to look over the project at first hand it refused to live up to the terms of the contract.

Not until 1868 was anyone found who would assume the burdens of construction. In that year, T. J. Peters of Cincinnati was persuaded to risk his financial reputation and solvency in the venture. He was paid in large part with the securities of the company, which he in turn disposed of as fast as possible. The process was carried on so fast that by 1869 the control of the road had passed into New England hands and Henry Keyes of Newbury, Vermont, became president.

With the new control and more adequate financial backing, work proceeded steadily. Construction had originally started at Topeka, which lay on the Kansas Pacific, but in 1870 the road was finished east to Atchison. Three years later western construction had advanced to Granada, Colorado, and during the depression of the seventies the Santa Fe was one of the few western roads which continued to expand.

Success was not due in any great measure to the hoped for Santa Fe trade. It was caused in most part by the very fortunate increase in the cattle business. The road crossed all of the north and south cattle trails further south than its nearest competitor, and as more and more cattle were shipped east from Colorado and Kansas the Santa Fe prospered accordingly.

The Atchison, Topeka and Santa Fe early proved a thorn in the side of Denver, which was just beginning to recover its temper from its experiences with the Union Pacific. As soon as the Santa Fe reached Colorado it nullified the advantages which Denver had so laboriously acquired by securing the Kansas and Pacific. All southern Colorado business found the Santa Fe a great deal more advantageous than the route through Denver.

To retain its prestige Denver organized (1870) the narrow-gauge Denver and Rio Grande to build south and head off the Santa Fe. The moving figure of the new road was the energetic and dominating General W. J. Palmer. By dint of unceasing activity he succeeded in interesting Philadelphia capital and in starting construction. By 1873 he had completed his road as far as Pueblo, and the next year he started building west from that point. For the time being it looked as though the Rio Grande might accomplish its object. Unfortunately it suffered from the depression of the seventies more than did the Santa Fe, and in consequence lost a large share of its favorable position.

The Atchison, Topeka and Santa Fe was the only southern road with transcontinental aspirations to be aided by Congress during the progress of the war. As soon as the South returned to the Union, however, the way was opened for the assistance of the lines further south. The war time animosity played but little part in the chartering of railroads to the Southwest.

The Atlantic and Pacific was chartered in 1866 to run over the 35th parallel route—from Springfield, Missouri, by way of Albuquerque and the Needles to the coast. It also had the right to construct a branch from the Canadian River to Van Buren, Arkansas. With the proper connections the road could therefore have a direct line to the coast from either St. Louis or Memphis, or both. As in the case of the Union Pacific, such connections were left to separate private companies.

The dominating figure of the new company was J. C. Fremont, under whose control was purchased the Southwest Branch of the Pacific Railroad, which had already built half-way across the state in the direction of Springfield. This purchase made it fairly certain that the Atlantic and Pacific would be primarily a St. Louis road. Between St. Louis and Pacific Junction, which was the eastern terminus of the Southwest Branch, the tracks of the Missouri Pacific were used. By 1873 the main line of the new system had progressed as far as a junction with the Missouri, Kansas and Texas at Vinita, Indian Territory.

The Atlantic and Pacific took a radical step when it leased the whole Missouri Pacific system in order to secure its entrance to St. Louis and to build up a monopoly of Missouri business. This purchase proved to be extremely unfortunate when the greatly over-capitalized system was overtaken by the panic of 1873. The lease of the Missouri Pacific was set aside and work on the main line came to a halt. No further progress was possible until both new management and new backing had been secured.

The most southerly project aided by Congress was the Texas and Pacific, chartered to run from Marshall, Texas, along the 32nd parallel and by way of the Yuma crossing of the Colorado River to San Diego, California. The part of the line which went through Texas was aided by state land donations, while the remainder participated in the usual Congressional assistance.

Various earlier Texas roads had attempted to build along this same general route, but had only succeeded in getting as far west as Longview, on the International and Great Northern. Under the presidency of Thomas Scott, who was also vice-president of the Pennsylvania Railroad, the Texas and Pacific bought up its predecessors and started work. It was completed to Dallas in 1873 and to Fort Worth three years later. The Marshall-Texarkana line, completed in 1873, produced through north and south connections. The panic of the same year proved disastrous. After fighting several years for additional Congressional aid, Scott sold out his interest and retired from the control.

Further south than the Texas and Pacific, the future line of the Southern Pacific was being built. Its original name of the Buffalo Bayou, Brazos and Colorado was changed in 1870 to the Galveston, Harrisburg and San Antonio, and the scope of the project increased. Construction was not renewed until 1873, but from that time the work proceeded steadily until a junction with the Southern Pacific was effected.

These southern roads were paralleled in the North by the beginning of the Northern Pacific. The northern route had not been injured by the outbreak of the Civil War, and so on the same day that the Union Pacific had its aid increased, the Northern Pacific was chartered and given a land grant. It was projected to run from Lake Superior by the most available route to Portland, Oregon.

This route did not present exceptional engineering difficulties, and was superior in relation to trade with the

Far East. Its disadvantages were that it was longer, did not have important terminals, ran through a meagerly settled portion of the country, and had a climate which many people feared was too cold for successful railroading.

The best known exponent of the northern route, Asa Whitney, died in obscurity before the road was chartered. His most prominent successor was Josiah Perham, the originator of the excursion idea and a firm believer in advertising. His first love had been the central route, but he had transferred his affections further north when the Union Pacific was brought into being without his participation.

Perham's original scheme was the same as that of T. D. Judah—the building of a road with capital obtained from a million hundred dollar subscriptions. With this idea in mind he chartered the People's Pacific Railroad in Maine and started to raise money. Many people were interested, but before any definite action could be taken the whole aspect of the venture was changed by the rumor that Congress was about to charter a similar line. The plans of the company were remolded and Perham and his followers went to Washington to use their influence in favor of the prospective legislation.

As soon as the Northern Pacific was chartered, Perham and his group bought stock to the limit of their ability, and Perham was elected the first president. The resources of the group were limited, however, and new stock purchases soon caused Perham to be outvoted, whereupon he resigned from the presidency.

About the time that Perham withdrew from the presidency, money was secured for the first survey by an "Original Interests Agreement," subscribed to by a number of important eastern railroad men. Each of these men contributed a portion of the cost of this survey, and under these auspices it was completed during 1867-68. The main problem of raising funds for construction still remained intact.

The incorporators of the Northern Pacific knew, as did everyone else, that the future of the road rested largely on its financial management. Every effort was made to secure the best possible agency for the disposal of the securities of the company. There was little doubt as to which banking house was preferable, and as early as 1865 Perham had approached the house of Jay Cooke and Company for aid. This banking firm was at the time one of the most important and influential in the United States. It had close relations with the government in the financing of the Civil War, and had emerged from the episode with a greatly enhanced reputation. No one doubted but that if Cooke took hold of the project its success was assured.

Jay Cooke was skeptical about the affairs of the Northern Pacific when he was first approached by Perham, and consequently refused to give it his support. At the same time he did not entirely put the idea out of his mind. After the war was over he felt the need of some large problem to occupy his mind, and when he was approached again on the subject of the Northern Pacific his answer was not entirely unfavorable.

By no stretch of the imagination could Cooke have been called a novice in western affairs. Among other things he had floated bonds for the North Missouri railroad and for the Lake Superior and Duluth, and the applications of both these and other lines had led him to look into western railroad affairs quite extensively.

Probably Cooke was influenced in his final decision by his holdings of western lands as much as by anything else. He had bought widely in Iowa and later in Minnesota, of both agricultural properties and town sites. In 1868 he visited his Minnesota properties at a time when Duluth had only a few frame houses, a school, and a land office, while Superior could boast of only some three hundred inhabitants. He was so pleased with the future possibilities of Duluth that he increased his holdings largely.

When Cooke began to consider the Northern Pacific project seriously he collected all the available material on the subject, and for a long time his desk was a clutter of books, maps, and letters. To be sure of the value of the land grant he equipped two expeditions at his own expense. Their reports were so favorable that at a later time when they were circulated for advertising purposes, the region came to be known popularly as "Jay Cooke's Banana Belt."

The favorable reports on the Northern Pacific from all sources satisfied Cooke that the project was desirable and so in 1869 he contracted to sell the securities of the company and to act as financial agent. Once the decision was made his earlier skepticism seemed to disappear entirely and he threw himself whole-heartedly into the venture. Everyone was satisfied. The success of the project seemed assured.

Construction was started at Pacific Junction early in 1870. Three years later the road had been completed as far as Bismarck, North Dakota, which was named after the great German Chancellor, then in favor in the United States. The Lake Superior and Mississippi was leased to give a Duluth-St. Paul connection, while an agreement with the St. Paul and Pacific offered a more direct route between St. Paul and the main line of the Northern Pacific. The St. Paul and Sioux City was leased, making direct connections with the Union Pacific, while in the Far West an interest was secured in the Oregon Steam Navigation Company.

The agreement by which Cooke agreed to back the railroad provided for the disposition of $100,000,000 of stock and a similar amount of bonds. The stock was divided into eighteen shares, of which six were held by Cooke, and these were subdivided to meet the needs of investors. A part payment plan was used whereby the money was received as the road was completed, thus securing a steady flow of capital until the line's completion. Enough stock was reserved to give Cooke a stock bonus of $200 for each $1000 of bonds sold. The $100,000,000 of first mortgage bonds promised 7.3% and were to be sold at 88. Besides their ordinary sale they were to be used to pay off prior issues of stock at fifty cents on the dollar, and were to be the security for an immediate advance of $500,000 by Jay Cooke and Company.

This generous agreement was modified still more in the favor of Cooke the following year. The eighteen shares were increased to twenty-four, and the payments changed accordingly. Cooke received also a half interest in town lots and land in the vicinity of Duluth. Provision was made for the immediate raising of a $5,000,000 pool for the prosecution of the work to the Red River. The pool money, plus $600,000 to retire the outstanding stock, was raised immediately by means of a liberal land bonus on all subscriptions.

The bonus paid to members of the original pool, the

rate of the bond issue, and the commission given to
Cooke all helped to raise the capitalization of the company to an excessive figure. Every effort was made to
get prominent men interested in the pool—from Vice-
President Colfax down, and particularly to interest newspaper men. The resulting influence and advertising not
only prevented adverse action, but finally resulted in
the passage by Congress of a bill for a branch, which
in reality changed the route of the road in the Far West.

An extensive advertising campaign was opened in the
United States in order to sell the stocks and bonds.
Pamphlets were printed, newspapers and magazines used,
and speakers encouraged. In 1871 an excursion of newspaper men to the Red River valley was financed. Bay-
ard Taylor, C. A. Dana, William Bross, Samuel Bowles,
and other prominent journalists took the trip. In spite
of all that could be done, subscriptions came in slowly.
Rumors of corruption, extravagance, and mismanagement
were hard to advertise out of existence. Land would not
sell, and the greatest sinecure on the line was the position of land agent.

The first serious setback of the company came in Europe. As soon as Cooke took hold an attempt was made
to interest the Rothschilds, but the effort failed because
of the conservatism of the English firm. Immediately
thereafter a branch office was opened in London, and
money was spent freely for advertising purposes. Dutch
and German merchants were offered large commissions,
and some of them espoused the cause of the Northern
Pacific. The hopes of the company were crushed by the
Franco-German War of 1870. German merchants refused for the time being to engage in outside activities,
while the rest of Europe was fearful of a monetary de-

pression and withdrew as much as possible from unnecessary engagements. The foreign sales of the securities of the company were practically stopped.

The closing European market and the small number of sales in the United States had their bad effect increased by the faulty management of the road. President Smith and his Vermont Central clique, who were in control, had very little first hand knowledge of the situation. Their first interest was in the East, which they did not leave. It mattered little whether or not the current rumors of fraud and corruption were true. Management from a distance of 1500 miles was bound to produce an immense amount of delay and unnecessary confusion. The road suffered greatly from a lack of competent oversight.

An improvement was made in October, 1870, when W. Milnor Roberts was made chief engineer. At least the work was done adequately under his direction. The reform, however, was too limited. The general management and the purchasing activities still remained untouched. Lavish expenditures for equipment and supplies were supplemented by a salary of $20,000 a year which President Smith voted himself, in spite of the fact that he never left Vermont.

Jay Cooke gradually lost patience with the way in which the funds that he collected with such difficulty disappeared. Finally in 1872 he forced the resignation of President Smith, whose place was taken by General G. W. Cass, former president of the Pittsburg, Chicago and Fort Wayne, a Pennsylvania Railroad subsidiary. Economies were enforced, but in spite of them the condition of the road did not improve. Bond sales failed to pay current expenses and so Jay Cooke and Company continually had to advance money to meet current needs. Labor frequently had to be paid in vouchers instead of cash. It was freely predicted in the fall of 1872 that work would not be resumed the following spring.

A final attempt to rehabilitate the fortunes of the company occurred in April, 1873, when Jay Cooke tried to secure additional capital by forming a syndicate which would give a stock bonus of 50% on subscriptions to the bonds. At the same time he pressed upon Congress the need of additional legislation.

All of Cooke's plans failed. A bad winter and tight money killed the syndicate. The Credit Mobilier and other similar scandals made Congress look askance at any additional railroad aid. Even Cooke himself could no longer make further advances to the company because he was overloaded with non-negotiable paper. After futile attempts to meet the situation, Jay Cooke and Company had to bow to the inevitable—the doors of the most important banking house in America were closed on September 18, 1873.

The failure of Jay Cooke and Company pricked the prosperity bubble and precipitated one of the worst financial panics in the history of the United States. Stocks and bonds fell rapidly. Other overloaded banking houses failed, carrying with them industrial securities of all kinds. Ready money became non-existent, and the entire credit system of the country collapsed.

The Northern Pacific and its subsidiary lines managed to maintain solvency for a year before they went along in the general smash. In January, 1875, the Northern Pacific defaulted the interest on its bonds. The following year it was foreclosed and sold, while its subsidiary lines were lost. The only rainbow in the storm was the increasing amount of wheat production in the Red River valley, which forecast the eventual financial success of the project.

The St. Paul and Pacific, eventually destined to become the Great Northern, was also foreclosed and sold. At this time it consisted of two main lines. The first went north to a connection with the main line of the Northern Pacific at Brainerd, but was not as yet completed. The second division was building west toward the Dakotas, and was completed as far as Breckenridge, in the extreme western part of Minnesota.

The Lake Superior and Mississippi was reorganized in 1877 as the St. Paul and Duluth. It had been completed from St. Paul to Duluth in 1870 and had been acquired by the Northern Pacific two years later. The St. Paul and Sioux City, acquired in 1870 and completed in 1872, eventually became a part of the Chicago and Northwestern.

Cooke's interest in the Oregon Steam Navigation Company had been in the nature of the ownership of $5,000,-000 of the stock, which had been bought at 40 and paid for half in cash and half in Northern Pacific bonds at 90. This stock was sold to pay off some of the obligations of Jay Cooke and Company, and was bought in behalf of the Portland directors. By a process of consolidation (1879) the company became the Oregon Railroad and Navigation Company.

CHAPTER IX

Western railroad speculation was one of the outstanding causes of the panic of 1873. The situation in which Jay Cooke and Company found itself was paralleled in the case of numerous other banking houses. The excessive holding of poor grade railroad securities was not a situation which could last forever, and when a major disaster occurred, such as the failure of Cooke, the credit structure of the country was severely shaken by the train of ruin which it carried in its wake.

Mistakes, fraud, misrepresentation, and over-development could all secure a certain amount of immunity during a period of economic prosperity, but when the good times were succeeded by depression, such evils received an accumulated amount of criticism and opposition. The same westerner who had enthused most heartily over prospective advantages might well be the first to blame the railroads for not bringing the economic prosperity for which he had hoped. The result was that when depression occurred during the seventies it was the occasion for searching analysis, frequently wrong, and bitter opposition.

The Santa Fe sums up the underlying trouble of the railroads in its report for 1888—"The history of western railroad construction for the past quarter of a century has demonstrated that successful results can only be attained by occupying territory promptly, and often in advance of actual needs." Practically every road was over-built, which meant that excessive inducements had to be given to secure new capital, upon which dividends might not be paid for many years.

Western enthusiasm was ordinarily adequate only for the chartering and advertising of the prospective road. At the most, local capital very seldom exceeded the price of the necessary surveying. At this point the affairs of the company languished until aid could be secured elsewhere. Every western railroad promoter eventually had to look to the East or to Europe for the capital to realize his dreams.

The western railroad promoter was not only handicapped by the lack of ready capital in the West, but even more by the number of other roads which were bidding for public support. All of them were weak, and in consequence they were forced to make the proffered returns on their securities high enough to be very attractive. The situation was such that stock soon became of little value to raise money, and even bonds were discounted in liberal fashion, depending on the importance and stability of the road concerned.

The use of state and local bond aid was a favorite means of enticing eastern capital. These bonds were issued either as a subscription to the capital stock of the company or as a direct loan, guaranteed by a mortgage. The whole procedure really amounted to a loan of government credit, for the only advantage to the railroad lay in the difference between the selling price of the government bonds and that of the railroad bonds. In cases such as the Cairo and Fulton, the railroad found it more advantageous to sell its own securities than those of the state. All such state and local aid bonds found their sale in the East. There was little more market for them in the West than there was for the original securities of the railroad. The absence of investments did not indicate a lack of confidence on the part of the western public, but only a lack of capital.

The position of the federal bond aid to the Union Pacific was exactly that of state and local aid. The situation was changed somewhat when the government allowed its holdings to be reduced to a second lien, for then the road could issue its own first mortgage bonds, and the government aid was more nearly a complete addition to the funds of the company. In any event, however, the value still depended on the salability of the issue in the East, and the difference between its selling price and that of a similar railroad security.

Even federal land grants were in large part valuable only in their power of attracting eastern capital. As far as the West was concerned land had little value because everyone had as much as he wanted. Most western farmers were "land poor," and even if they hoped for a boundless domain their circumstances would not permit additional purchases. In addition, much of the land granted was in the arid sections of the West and had little value to anyone at any time.

Three possibilities confronted the railroads in the disposition of their land grants. They might be held for future profit after settlement had occurred, they might be sold in small tracts to eastern settlers, or they might be sold in large parcels to eastern land companies for either grazing or speculative purposes. One or all of these methods were usually tried, depending on the circumstances of the company and the location of the land. In any event, the capital which was invested came eventually from the East. Even if the land were held and mortgaged, the bonds had to be sold in the East.

Federal and state aid, after all, were given to but a comparatively small number of roads. The remainder had to depend upon the sale of their own securities. Ordinarily these stocks and bonds were only salable in times of prosperity. They were almost purely speculative in character, seldom being listed in the New York stock exchange. A vast number of miscellaneous issues were held in all important banking houses and also in the hands of private investors, particularly in New England.

The speculative nature of western railroad securities was reflected in their price. As strong a road as the Union Pacific sold for many years around 20, and other roads were of course lower. Bonds, being better secured, sold at a higher figure, but it was a rare issue that was not discounted ten to twenty percent, even in spite of the high rate of interest normally paid.

High interest and a low market price were no deterrents to western railroads. Feeling confident of eventual prosperity they issued stock and bonds as long as they were absorbed, regardless of the capitalization. Everything possible was mortgaged, even including very improbable future business. The outstanding indebtedness of many lines reached staggering proportions.

The low price of stock and the general difficulties attending its sale led it to be used in other ways than in trying to interest investors. Many times it was given as a bonus on bond purchases. The most general use was to give it in part payment of construction contracts. If this sort of arrangement could be made it was easy to issue additional paper, and the cash resources of the company could be husbanded. As much as three-quarters of the cost of construction was sometimes paid in the securities of the company. While the road always preferred to use stock for this purpose, it sometimes made partial payment in bonds. Naturally these securities had to be sold by the construction companies in the East.

This opportunistic use of capital stock had very unfortunate results. The construction company always placed its prices sufficiently high to cover any possible depreciation of the company's securities, and also to pay it for doing business in this manner. Further than that, the construction was usually as poor as would be accepted. The ballasting was inadequate, the track was poor, and the equipment was as light as possible. Accidents and delays were innumerable and costly, and the succeeding decade usually saw the practical rebuilding of the road.

When the principal stockholders of a road formed their own construction company the procedure was just the same. If the road returned large immediate profits on construction it made little difference whether or not the railroad would be able to pay dividends in the future. The controlling interests received all that they had any expectation of making and were then satisfied with whatever fate might hold in store.

Obviously the majority of western railroads were overcapitalized, but that fact in itself did not cause anyone immediate worry. Railroad building was promoted on the assumption that railroads were an economic panacea, and would create wealth through their mere existence.

It was expected that the rise in property values would in itself be sufficient to pay for the road, while the reduction in the cost of transportation would make everyone wealthy.

The country's optimistic hopes were the occasion of a vast amount of both waste and corruption. Even with the most honest of railroad men there was an immense amount of waste and inefficiency because of a desire to occupy territory in advance of their competitors. On the other hand there were plenty of dishonest promoters, who used all the tricks of free and unregulated competition to amass wealth for themselves at the expense of more simple minded or less experienced individuals.

The history of the Atchison, Topeka and Santa Fe illustrates very well the evils inherent in the situation. Projected at a time when building would have meant economic suicide, it exhausted its funds in a little surveying. Progress stopped while the president sought vainly to sell the securities of the company in the East. Even a federal land grant and county aid did not produce immediate construction.

The prosperity of the post-Civil War period gave the Santa Fe its start. The construction was let to contractors who were paid in part with the securities of the company. These securities were sold in the East, with the result that control soon passed to that district. The entire road bed, track, and equipment were of such a nature that they had to be replaced within fifteen years. The only peculiarity of the Santa Fe was that it avoided financial insolvency during the middle seventies, due in large part to the growing cattle business, which the original incorporators could hardly be accused of foreseeing.

The bad results of financial practices such as those of the Santa Fe, and this road is not in the least extreme, were bound to be evident sooner or later. Careful observers were not unaware of the excess of speculative, unnegotiable paper, and of the poor financial condition of the majority of western roads. They were not entirely surprised when the failure of Jay Cooke and Company was succeeded by the failure of other similar houses and a period of universal depression.

The collapse of eastern business meant the failure of western railroads. Loans were called, further capital was impossible to obtain, and both government and company securities fell to an impossible figure. Construction ceased and many of the roads went into the hands of receivers. Not until the end of the decade did conditions become normal and allow further expansion.

The "Joy system" was one of the first casualties, succeeded shortly later by the Atlantic and Pacific. Other roads followed—The Northern Pacific, the Memphis and Little Rock, the Kansas Pacific, the International and Great Northern, the Arkansas Central, the Burlington, Cedar Rapids and Northern, the Burlington and Southwestern, and the Missouri Pacific, to mention only some of the most important. The group of roads having their eastern termini at Chicago were the most important ones to maintain financial solvency.

The panic had one of its most serious effects in the change of opinion all over the country concerning railroads. In the West the failure of the railroads was a particularly wide-spread phenomenon, and in consequence the criticism of them was equally wide-spread. For the time being their benefits were obscured; instead of bringing the millennium they had only brought a panic and hard times. The advantages for which the westerner had dreamed, prayed, and worked, turned into a machinery of oppression before his very eyes.

The farmer who had worked for one or more railroads and had invested a little capital in them, saw his hopes disappear. Prices went down so that his holdings were worth almost nothing. Many times the line in which he was interested stopped work before it was available for his use. Even if it were completed, prosperity was still not visible. Higher property values and lower transportation prices meant very little when the price of grain continued to drop while outside prices continued to rise. The net result was that the comparative position of the farmer was much the same, except that he still owed money on his railroad stock subscription.

Not only was each individual burdened with his own debt, but also he was responsible in part for the state, local, and federal assistance. Many towns and villages had been playing for high stakes and had drawn blanks. Others had hoped to become railroad and commercial centers and still remained on some insignificant branch line. States had hoped to build up important railroad systems and had succeeded only in securing a few fragmentary lines.

State bonds had for the most part been sold cheaply, and their use had entailed a considerable amount of waste and fraud. The money disappeared and no railroads came. The state was then compelled either to lift its lien or to foreclose a valueless road. Nothing remained but the state debt and the taxes necessary for its payment. The incident rankled in the minds of the hard-pressed taxpayers, who frequently had had no part in the creation of the original debt.

The various county and town debts were even more objectionable because they were more immediate and were frequently larger in proportion to the total wealth. Then, too, the states could and did, in case of necessity, repudiate their bond issues, while local political subdivisions, not being sovereign, could not follow this procedure. A few made an effort in this direction, but with no success.

Large numbers of towns and counties tried to avoid payment of their railroad bond issues—usually by pleading an irregularity of issue. Without exception the Supreme Court upheld the rights of the innocent purchaser, even if some slight irregularities could be proved. Gross irregularities or fraud sometimes voided the issue. These decisions served to further embitter the West. It felt that such decisions were obviously unfair and that, therefore, there must be some kind of an unholy alliance between the railroads and the courts. The majority of this feeling descended upon the railroads, from which so much was expected and so little seemingly accomplished. The railroads were present and tangible, and could be hated successfully.

These local bond issues often did prove an actual hardship to the taxpayers. The difficulty of payment was frequently aggravated by the fact that many of the bonds were issued in the fifties to run twenty years, and consequently matured during the depression of the seventies. Usually the population and property values had not grown as fast as was expected, and many times it was new settlers or the second generation of the old who had to suffer for the mistakes of their predecessors. It is not amazing that they resented the necessity of paying the bad debts of a bygone time.

Local resentment was increased by the rapid change of railroad control from the West to the East. The whole financial process looked in this direction, since all securities eventually found their final resting places in the safes of eastern investors and banking houses. With the exception of the Central Pacific, all of the transcontinental lines were controlled from the East. By 1873 the majority of important western lines were owned by eastern capital. Control became vested in groups of capitalists in Chicago, New York, Philadelphia, and Boston.

The very development of the roads served to lose for them a measure of local support. The enthusiasm for a new and struggling road rapidly disappeared when that line became long and important. It no longer needed help, and could not appeal so much to the sympathies and desires of the people. It began to be judged on the basis of unrealized hopes rather than of dreams which might still be fulfilled.

Even externally the appearance of the road changed. Local western roads were absorbed by more important eastern lines, or run by eastern capital. The management lost its touch with local sentiment and was inclined to give it but little consideration. Trains began running through the less important towns, all the general offices were combined and moved east, while rates were made without respect to local sentiment. Employees were brought in from the outside and local officials were either replaced or moved elsewhere.

There is little wonder that the change in management and character of western railroads lost the sympathy of the local communities. All that they could see was that their long worked for projects were taken over by outside people, who were apparently making money at the expense of the original incorporators and of the people along the line of the road. No longer was there any close contact between the management and the users, and each lost sight of the other's viewpoint. The growing lack of sympathy was frequently increased to a bitter antagonism by the sharp dealing and fraud to which the roads descended. Bond aid obtained on false pretenses, fraudulent construction contracts, supposed through lines which remained only branches, the "squeezing out" of minority stockholders, and similar practices were enough to fan the growing flame of discontent to a white heat. As time went on these practices came to be condemned more and more by the general public, who saw in them evidences of their own betrayal.

Eastern control was bad enough, but was not quite as objectionable as foreign manipulations. Foreign holdings were largely in bonds, and were found particularly in England, Germany, and Holland. For instance, Dutch interests were very large in the Missouri, Kansas and Texas, the California Pacific, the St. Paul and Pacific, the Chicago and Northwestern, the Central Pacific, the Union Pacific, the Denver Pacific, the Missouri Pacific, the Oregon and California, the Kansas and Pacific, the Denver and Rio Grande, the Cairo and Fulton, and the Atchison, Topeka and Santa Fe, to mention some of the more important roads.

When Jay Cooke controlled the destinies of the Northern Pacific, he established a London office, and also had extensive relations with Dutch and German merchants. The Gould properties were later backed largely by English capital, and Gould had a London office. Naturally the

West objected to foreign holdings just as much if not more than it did to those of the East.

It must not be thought that the West was alone in its revulsion of feeling toward the railroads. The same sentiment existed in the East, and with practically the same causes. It was slightly less virulent, partly because the abuses were less in evidence, but more because of the more emotional spirit of the West. The West tended to be either on the heights or in the depths. When it lost its virgin railroad enthusiasm, it reversed its sentiments and became actively and bitterly hostile.

The attitude of the West resulted in both negative and positive action. Further aid to the railroads was stopped and frequently prohibited for the future, while at the same time a beginning was made in the regulation of the railroad system then in existence. Combined with the development of eastern feeling it was able to stop federal aid, but was not sufficiently strong to start positive regulation.

Federal government railroad aid came to an abrupt end. The one experiment in loaning government credit was never repeated, but the next thirty-five years were spent in trying to collect the amount which had been loaned. The last important land grant was that to the Texas and Pacific in 1871. Subsequent developments were in the direction of the repeal of such grants as had been made, rather than in their extension and supplementation.

State aid disappeared with equal rapidity. One experience was enough for each state to learn its lesson, and future state constitutions universally prohibited the loan of state credit to a private corporation (with the exception of poor farms). There were no experiments in state railroad aid after the seventies. The succeeding constitutions also quite generally contained stricter provisions concerning discriminations, connections, pools, capitalization, consolidation, and similar matters. Local aid was affected in the same manner, but to some extent each community had to have its own experience. The panic of 1857 gave the first set-back to local aid, and the three constitutions of that year prohibited it—Minnesota, Iowa, and Oregon; Nevada took the same action in 1864.

The post-Civil War period witnessed a reaction in favor of the railroads. Starting with the new state of Kansas in 1862, the new constitutions of the older states favored local aid—Missouri (1865), Arkansas (1868), Nebraska (1869), California (1870), Minnesota (1871), and Texas (1871). The effects of earlier ventures had not been entirely lost, however, and such aid was generally restricted. A definite limit was often fixed, based on the value of the taxable property. Usually a popular vote, and frequently a two-thirds majority, was required to make the bond issue valid.

The early seventies saw an end of local aid. With the exception of Nebraska (1875) all the constitutions of the period prohibited it—California (1872 and 1874), Arkansas (1873 and 1874), Kansas (1874), Missouri (1875), Texas (1876), Colorado (1876). This policy was continued into the future, with the exceptions of North Dakota (1889), and Utah (1895). In both these cases, however, the surrounding restrictions amounted practically to a prohibition.

The other side of this negative legislation was the movement toward positive regulation, as shown in both state legislation and the trend toward national action. The Congressional agitation took its first significant form in the Windom report of 1874. This report upheld the right of Congress to pass regulatory legislation, and recommended a law compelling the public filing of rates, the separate management of competing lines, greater rates for long than for short hauls to lake ports, and the establishment of a Bureau of Commerce, which was to have supervisory powers, and was to advise Congress concerning the need of further legislation.

The report spent a great deal of space on the discussion of the various possible types of regulation. While it proposed a certain amount of direct control, it placed its chief reliance on the good effects of competition. It realized that competition was decreasing, and so in order to halt this tendency it proposed that the government improve waterways, build canals, and connect them with a government owned railroad. It was held that such enforced government competition would be sufficient to force all rates to a reasonable basis.

The Windom report failed of adoption both because anti-railroad agitation was not sufficiently strong and because it was divided. Many individuals opposed the particular plan proposed by the committee, while others were in favor of leaving all action to the states. Some of the ideas were eventually enacted into law, while others were abandoned. The significant feature of the report was its mere existence. The movement for government regulation was well under way.

Four years later came the Reagan report, which also asserted the right of Congress to regulate interstate traffic. It dropped the idea of federal competition, however, and turned to more direct supervision. It submitted a bill prohibiting personal discrimination, rebates, combinations, and charging a larger amount for a short than a long haul, and requiring the publication of rates. Again no action was taken. The majority of Congress felt that railroad regulation was a state matter, and in this opinion it was backed by the attitude of the Supreme Court.

The real heart of the anti-railroad, or "granger movement" as it is usually known, came in the state regulatory laws of the Middle West. The first of the group was that of Illinois, which was based on a similar Massachusetts act. These two laws, together with that of Wisconsin, formed the basis of most of the western legislation. The most important single influence was the work of the Massachusetts commission, and the writings of its chairman, Charles Francis Adams, Jr.

The Illinois act was followed in the states west of the Mississippi by Minnesota (1871 and 1874), Missouri (1875), California (1876), and Iowa (1878). All but California provided a schedule of maximum rates. Outside of the rate schedules the main feature of all the laws was the provision for a commission to supervise the railroads, gather information, prosecute law breakers, and recommend additional legislation. Missouri was the only state to give its commission real power by allowing it to adjust the state schedule of rates.

The legal theory underlying such regulatory acts was that of the common law, which held that certain services were semi-public in nature, and, therefore, subject to regulation by the government. The Supreme Court accepted this theory and held the acts to be constitutional. The main difficulty of this form of regulation was discovered by the Minnesota commission in its first report, when it said that "it is clear that State lines have been obliterated." Interstate traffic was continually increasing in size and importance, and according to the

Constitution was subject only to the jurisdiction of Congress.

These laws were bitterly opposed by the railroad interests, who held them to be an unjustifiable interference with private business, and animated by harmful intent. The roads in general stayed within the letter of the law, but strove to make their rates ridiculous in order to discredit the legislation and encourage opposition. Every effort, both fair and unfair, was made to have the laws repealed, even to blaming the lack of construction during the middle seventies on them, and threatening not to build further until they were taken off the statute books.

Probably the real danger that the roads saw was the possibility of more stringent regulation in the future; the laws which then existed were neither very severe nor very well enforced. The only really bad feature was the conflict between the various state measures. In cases where a road touched half a dozen states the varying local requirements frequently proved embarrassing, and were a serious obstacle both to efficient operation and to intelligent bookkeeping.

Possibly the most interesting feature of the period of anti-railroad agitation was its vast difference from the feeling of a few short years before. The early attitude was well expressed by the Dakota Railroad Commission, when it said (1885)—"The whistle of a locomotive would be the sweetest music a resident of the broad prairies of Dakota could hear, and the mere rumor that a party of railroad surveyors had been seen in a particular locality was enough to fill the hearts of every settler with joy, and cause visions of townsite and county seat speculation to color with all the beauteous hues of the rainbow his dreams at night."

Changing economic conditions, speculation, over-building, and corruption reversed the feeling over night. The vigorous spirit of the protest has been expressed more forcefully than poetically in "An Indignant Taxpayer's Sentiment on the County Debt"—

"We will come out upon our farms,
We will not pay this debt,
We'll get out an injunction quick,
Let the bondholders sweat.

"We will not pay one cent of tax,
We have no dollars to spare,
To be mixed up in such a deal,
Would make an angel swear.

"We'll hang the first official up,
To the nearest wagon tongue;
Who dares to make a levy or tax
By a neck-tie will be strung."

CHAPTER X

The depression of the seventies included within itself the seeds of future prosperity. The whole country was in the process of an economic transformation which was to produce a period of prosperity greater than anything that had gone before. Even more than anywhere else, the West was in the grip of changing conditions, which were destined to produce an entirely new era.

One of the earliest attractions to the Far West was gold, and thousands of embryo miners were enticed into a search for the more easily available deposits. Placer mining soon took the richest cream in California, Colorado, and elsewhere. By the latter seventies the succession of gold booms had seemingly come to an end, and it looked as though the West might suffer. Then it was discovered that while the most available gold had been removed, it still existed in large quantities if mined more intensively. It was also found that the ores which had been rejected in the search for gold were frequently rich in other metals such as silver and lead. By 1880 the single town of Leadville, Colorado, with a population of 15,000, was shipping a million dollars worth of gold, silver, and lead every month.

This new development in mining led to the use of improved methods, and made the business more comparable to manufacturing in its stability. When a mine was

146

opened it could be expected that production would at least continue for several years. The value of these products was vastly increased by the immense expansion of industry in the United States, and the consequent increase in the use of metal. The Michigan iron and copper fields, which had been discovered before the Civil War, began to be exploited.

It was also during the seventies that the West became the granary of the nation. The "great American desert" was converted into fields of wheat and corn. Prior to the Civil War the only trans-Mississippi states to produce any considerable amount of grain were Minnesota, Iowa, and Missouri. During the latter sixties and the seventies production was increased with startling rapidity, particularly in the Dakotas, Nebraska, and Kansas. Other minor grains and farm products also received an impetus.

The majority of the growing grain production of the West was shipped East immediately. Shipping centers such as the towns along the Missouri River, the Mississippi, and the Great Lakes expanded to take care of the new business. St. Paul and Minneapolis became important as milling centers for the wheat of the Northwest. The growing industrialism of the East made it more and more dependent on the western grain, so that the market expanded with as great rapidity as did the production.

Much of the surplus grain was shipped abroad, the amount exported doubling in the four years between 1876 and 1880. The exportation of corn in this period increased from forty to ninety-one million bushels, and wheat from seventy to one hundred and fifty million bushels. This increasing demand on the part of Europe had the effect of lessening the isolation of the West. It was becoming true that the price of grain was regulated by the Liverpool market, and no intelligent western farmer could afford to be negligent of European conditions.

Even more spectacular than the rapidly increasing grain production was the development of the cattle business. High meat prices during the Civil War led to experimentation with the long-horned, stringy breed of cattle which ran wild in the West—particularly in Texas. It was found that if this semi-wild stock were crossed with Hereford, that a fat but sturdy combination could be evolved.

The new combination stock could easily be produced in Texas, but at that point it was entirely unavailable for the markets of the North and East. Railroads as yet had not reached the region, and refrigeration was not known. It then became evident that the only practical method of procedure was to drive the cattle north, feeding them on the way on the free grass of the public domain, to eventually ship them East on the newly built line of the Union Pacific or some similar northern road. The final discovery was that it was possible to winter the cattle on the plains of the North and have them in good shape for market in the spring.

As the western cattle business developed it became customary to gather the cattle together in Texas in the spring and to drive them slowly throughout the summer on the "long drive" to the North, tended by cowboys, and consuming the grass on the public land. In the winter they were herded on the plains of Wyoming, Montana, or Idaho, and from there they were shipped East the following spring. By this procedure the only cost was that of the few cowboys who did the herding, and the transportation charges to the East. The cattle ran wild, and the grass and land were free. The rapid development of the business during the seventies is well illustrated by the experience of Wyoming. During the decade it had an increase of cattle population from 11,000 to 211,000. Other states and territories had similar experiences.

Each of the new western railroads dipped into this business at some point along the "long drive," and served to lessen the number of cattle which finally reached the far North. Ogallala on the Union Pacific was one of the earliest of such shipping points, but was soon rivalled by Baxter Springs on the Missouri River, Fort Scott and Gulf, Coffeyville on the Leavenworth, Lawrence and Galveston, Denison on the Missouri, Kansas and Texas, Abilene on the Missouri Pacific, Dodge City on the Atchison, Topeka and Santa Fe, Glendive and Miles City on the Northern Pacific, and other similar centers. Many of these towns were more important during this period than ever again in their histories.

Cattle raising on a large scale meant the development of slaughtering and packing centers, and the practical disappearance of the local slaughtering house. Chicago and Kansas City soon obtained preëminence in this field, and were able to drive out local competition. At first their area of control was comparatively small, but with the development of refrigerator cars and the use of the tin can they were finally able during the eighties to secure a practical monopoly throughout the entire United States.

The growth of the cattle business, as that of grain, led to an increase in the amount of exportation. At first it was only dried and salted meats which were sent, but soon fresh products were added. The use of refrigeration developed a great deal more rapidly on water than it did on land, so that by the latter seventies there was a real beginning of the exportation of fresh beef and other meat products. The reverse action was the importation of various foreign stocks such as Percheron horses, Jersey cows, and Poland China hogs, for breeding purposes.

The lucrative returns from cattle soon led to the glutting of the market by overproduction. Local cattle men were joined by foreign groups, particularly British and Scotch. Land was bought from settlers, from the railroads, or illegally "borrowed" from the public domain. Soon it became necessary to erect fences in order to prevent extensive thefts, and this necessity led to the introduction of barbed wire. The fences also became necessary to hold the cattle until the price rose, for with the monopoly control of the packing industry and the increase of cattle raising the market price tended to go down.

The fencing of the cattle ranges was also hastened by the encroaching line of settlement. Individual settlers pushed further and further west, entering the land which had formerly been held sacred to the use of the "long drive." These pioneers fenced their land and were willing to resist the depredations of the large herds by force if necessary. Skirmishes between the settlers and the cattlemen became more and more frequent. Naturally the permanent inhabitants were the ones to secure government backing, and as early as 1872 Missouri prohibited the entry of cattle into the state because of "Spanish fever." This particular law was held unconstitutional by the courts on the ground that it regulated interstate traffic.

Encroaching settlement soon forecast the end of the "long drive" during the latter seventies. The large herds

were driven further and further west until they reached
the semi-arid plains. In 1884 the cattlemen held a convention in St. Louis, at which they considered the whole
situation, and finally petitioned Congress that it establish a national cattle trail at least six miles wide, from
Texas to Manitoba.

The following year Kansas passed a strict quarantine
law against "Texas fever," which accomplished its real
purpose of excluding Texas herds en route to the North.
The cattle trail was moved further west, but Colorado
immediately passed a similar law, and the "long drive"
was at an end. The project of a national cattle trail
did not prove interesting to a Congress which was just
then engaged in restoring to the public domain some of
the land which it had formerly given the railroads.

The end of the "long drive" did not ruin the cattle
business, but merely changed its form. Cattle ranches
became the recognized method of doing business, and the
fencing of the land proceeded even more rapidly than
before. All in all the change was a benefit to the railroads, which were able to dispose of some of their less
valuable land and to be assured of a stable traffic.

The cattle business soon found an additional check
from another quarter. The sheep business, which had
been in its experimental stage during the seventies, became important during the eighties. The inferior Spanish strain of the West was crossed with Merino to produce
a hardy animal with a good crop of wool, and wool
production increased five fold during the decade of the
seventies.

Sheep were potential users of the same pasture land
which was suitable for cattle. The cattle had the advantage of being the first on the ground, but the sheep had

the advantage of being less particular in their diet; cattle would not graze on the same land which had been used for sheep, while the sheep had no such dainty preferences. The encroachment of the newcomers was, therefore, doubly objectionable to the cattlemen, who had formerly monopolized all the available land, and who considered the lowly, unarmed sheepman a disgrace to the human stock. There were many bitter and bloody incidents before each group was finally satisfied as to its correct niche in the life of the West.

Mining, cattle and sheep raising, more grain, and a general increase in settlement all brought additional business to the railroads, and made them respectable, dividend paying investments. Each line did its best to expand and to secure its share of the rapidly growing business of the West. The isolated splendor of the Union Pacific did not last for long.

The roads quite naturally came to be concentrated in the districts which produced the most business. Chicago and St. Louis lines pushed to the Missouri River and across into the grain country of Kansas and Nebraska. St. Louis and Missouri River lines built south to control Texas business. Chicago and Milwaukee roads built to the twin cities of St. Paul and Minneapolis and west into Minnesota and the Dakotas. The mining districts of Colorado, Idaho, and Utah received their share of the new construction, as well as California.

The result of all this building was competition in its most virulent form, which was accepted by the public as being the only desirable means of regulating rates. Most people agreed that "competition is the life of trade." Regulatory legislation was only an unfortunate necessity in cases where competition did not exist or was stifled.

In one way the railroad business lent itself very well
to the competitive theory. The cost of operating a railroad varied but little with the amount of traffic carried,
because the fixed charges were so nearly stationary. In
most cases additional tonnage meant so much additional
profit. In consequence it was profitable to reduce rates
considerably, if thereby any large increase of traffic could
be secured.

On the other hand there were numerous offsetting disadvantages. The permanence of both fixed and operating
charges proved a drawback in times of depression. If
business slumped because of the excess of outside competition, the cost continued practically the same. A fac-
tory could at least stop production at such a time, but
a railroad had no such option. Besides popular resentment and the possibility of government action, such stop-
page would be uneconomic because of the rapid deterioration of materials and equipment and the dispersion
of labor.

It was really only a question of time until railroad
competion would become sufficiently severe to call forth
collective action. Its obvious advantages made agreement imperative as competition increased. During the
seventies this competition increased to such an extent
that the time was ripe for some kind of coöperation
between parallel lines, and as might have been expected,
the coöperation emerged.

The main difficulty which confronted any group agreement was that of enforcement. If rates were to be maintained and services standardized it was necessary that an
organization be created which would have power to
equalize rates or distribute traffic. Such action could
only be binding if coupled with the power of disciplining

refractory members, and it was well nigh impossible to induce the individual roads to cede power which might be used to their own disadvantage. The individual initiative which made western railroads possible made common action more difficult.

The first common action concerned minor elements, avoiding the principal problems of rates, traffic, and labor. Groups of skilled employees, such as car builders, master mechanics, and train masters began to meet together to discuss the common problems of their various professions. Such groups, even though lacking the power of binding action, tended to produce a greater uniformity of service in the United States than had hitherto been the case.

A similar problem was that of uniform time, and of train connections between the various roads. Hundreds of time standards in the United States, combined with independent train schedules, produced very awkward train connections for the traveling and shipping public as well as for the railroads themselves. A long series of conferences between traffic officials, which finally resulted in the General Time Convention, at first alleviated and finally corrected the situation.

In the more important item of coöperation in rate making and traffic distribution the railroads followed the precedent of the manufacturers. Even before the Civil War the manufacturers had made efforts to avoid competitive troubles by pooling all prospective business and dividing it according to the strength of the respective companies. In the manufacturing world these agreements were never very successful because they depended too much on the good faith of the participating parties.

Railroads were in a somewhat more favorable position. They had to be operated continuously. The large original cost prevented unexpected competition. The large number of stockholders and the semi-public nature of the undertaking made the accounts more available. Traffic could not so easily be falsified or concealed.

The first traffic agreements were informal understandings in respect to some one locality or to a particular type of business. In the first case, the traffic agents of the two or more roads that entered a town would gather together and agree upon the rates to and from that point. Such an understanding would be based on good faith between people who knew each other, and on the common knowledge which everyone might have of the other fellow's business.

The second variety of agreement is illustrated very well in the West by the cattle industry. Early in the seventies the various interested roads began meeting together to determine upon an equitable charge to be made from all competing points. A flat rate per car was agreed upon for live cattle from such points as Baxter Springs, Chetopa, and Vinita, to Chicago and St. Louis. Again, this was merely a "gentlemen's agreement," not backed by force.

Somewhat anomalously, rate agreements and pools did not have their origin in the East and spread from there to the West. The first important permanent agreement was western and additional agreements appeared all over the country practically simultaneously. The reasons for this situation are not far to seek. Most of the eastern roads had been built through a comparatively well settled country, and for the immediate present there was enough traffic for all. Western roads, on the contrary, were built in less settled districts, and any competition at all was dangerous. In consequence the railroads all over the country began to see the worst effects of unregulated competition at about the same time, and met it in a similar way.

The first permanent and well organized traffic division scheme was introduced in the West in the Chicago-Omaha territory. The building of the Union Pacific had made Omaha the most attractive terminus for the "granger roads," and by 1870 three of them had reached that point. Traffic was prospective rather than present, and the equality of the roads in length and financial stability made competition suicidal. Nothing seemed more desirable than that the three roads agree peacefully on a division of the existing business.

The idea of coöperation germinated in the "Omaha pool" of 1870. The roads agreed to divide the receipts from all Chicago-Omaha business equally, after deducting half to cover operating expenses. The agreement was informal and oral, depending for its success upon good faith and the ability to see each other's books. Very little division of receipts actually took place, because the eastern connections adopted the practice of delivering all business to each one of the roads in succession for a week at a time.

The "Omaha pool" was not only the first important recorded organization of its kind, but also one of the most successful. Its frictionless operation throughout the seventies served as a monument to the good faith of the parties concerned. When a new competitor appeared in 1879 in the Chicago, Milwaukee and St. Paul, it was taken into the pool on a basis of equality. Not until 1882 did the affairs of the association become sufficiently complex to require a written agreement and definite machinery for enforcement.

Other Missouri River points besides Omaha soon received their quota of eastern connections, and competition became important in the making of rates. Not only was each of these towns a competitive point in itself, but also each one sought to secure the business of its neighbors. Any one of them would serve almost equally well for a shipping point for the products from further west. The nature of the competition to and from Missouri River points was of such a sort that it was soon evident that it could not be regulated by pools of the business of each town, as in the case of the "Omaha pool." Some larger organization was necessary in order to make all the rates harmonious and to prevent the competition of one town with another. By the middle seventies sufficient lines participated in the business from the Missouri River so that action became imperative.

Representatives of the interested roads met in August, 1876, to try to work out some kind of satisfactory traffic arrangement. It was early decided that only the roads to the southern part of the Missouri River should be included, as it was there that the greater portion of lines terminated, and as it was also there that the greatest amount of homogeneity of interests existed. Omaha was excluded because the lines of the "Omaha pool" were not willing to set aside that very successful organization.

The comparative complexity of the new group led to its organization as the Southwestern Railway Rate Association, along the lines of the recently organized Southern Railway and Steamship Association (1875), rather than along the lines of the "Omaha pool." The controlling body was a Board of Directors, composed of the general managers of the roads concerned. R. S. Stevens of the Hannibal and St. Jo. was elected president, and J. W.

Midgley, formerly secretary to the president of the Chicago and Northwestern, secretary.

The Board of Directors was to decide upon the rates to be charged on competitive traffic, and to apportion the proceeds. The accounts were to be balanced monthly and the roads having a business in excess of their apportionment were to divide such excess among the other lines according to their apportionment. Fifty percent of the receipts were to be deducted before this division occurred, in order to pay for the cost of transportation.

It was expected that in practice the amount of traffic on each road would tend to become stabilized, as in the case of the "Omaha pool," and practically do away with the necessity of monthly payments. No such happy consummation occurred, and the traffic varied greatly from month to month. In fact, all the affairs of the pool proved a great deal more complex than were at first expected.

Complexity was not the only unexpected bad feature which the southwestern pool had to meet. The percentage allowed for operating expenses proved too high. Competition was not stifled, since it was found to be profitable to carry business even at the reduced rate, and particularly with the hope that a larger share of business might mean a more favorable consideration the next time that percentages were allotted. The main trouble, however, lay in the Board of Directors. Each member was primarily interested in the affairs of his own road, and in consequence neglected the best interests of the association.

The most outstanding of these difficulties were remedied by the early eighties. The management was centralized and made effective by giving complete control to the secretary, or commissioner, as he became known. The Board of Directors remained only as a reviewing body. The percentage allowed for operating expenses was reduced. Other minor defects were remedied from time to time.

These two pools were the only important formal bodies organized in the West during the seventies. Neither had assumed final form by the end of the decade, but both were recognizable. The absence of other similar organizations was due entirely to the lack of important competition. Railroad pools only became widespread in the West when the railroad net became sufficiently well advanced to create undesired competition.

Pooling and rate agreements were immediately advantageous to the railroads, even though they did not entirely do away with the growing evils of the period. In spite of all modifications and exceptions, fair rates and an equitable division of the traffic were more possible. At least the periods between actual open rate warfare were lengthened.

The existence of pools played no part in the anti-railroad feeling of the seventies. As yet they were too new to be considered as either an advantage or a drawback. People did not know what they were, or what their effect would be. In consequence there was little attempt to conceal their operations. A decade later the situation had changed, and they were quite universally condemned by the consuming public.

Pooling agreements were undoubtedly one of the hopeful signs to the railroads when prosperity began to return in the latter seventies. With the increase of business of all kinds the future began to look brighter. An equitable division of traffic at remunerative rates seemed to point to a new era of prosperity for the western railroads, and the opening of the decade of the eighties was viewed with optimism and confidence.

CHAPTER XI

Jay Gould was undoubtedly the best known railroad manipulator of the seventies and eighties. Starting as a poor boy he had worked himself up to a position of affluence and power by the use of his exceptional energy, keen intellect, and lack of moral scruples. His imagination, astuteness, and power of making quick decisions were matched only by his willingness to take advantage of any situation, regardless of the effect on others.

Gould was also notable for his inventiveness and versatility. No project was too large or complicated for his grasp. If the particular idea which he first conceived did not work out satisfactorily, he changed it to something more profitable. He never waged a long and desperate struggle. If people did not fit with his plans he changed the plans. Many of his most important and lucrative deals came from the failure of some other project.

Most of Gould's earlier interests lay in the East. He was brought into the public eye by his attempt with Fisk to corner the gold market in 1869. His specialties were the New York City street railways, the telegraph lines, and the Pacific Mail Steamship Company. The last two of these interests had a close connection with his later dealings in western railroads.

The entrance of Gould into the field of western railroads was in large part accidental. He saw the speculative opportunities in the depression of Union Pacific securities in the period shortly after the road's completion. In his subsequent manipulations he became interested in a large number of western lines, which he then proceeded to use for his own advantage. His control was always exercised from the East, and it is probable that he never saw some of his properties, owing to his infrequent western trips.

The whole interest of Gould lay in the manipulation of the securities of his various companies. The development of the roads was an entirely minor concern. In all cases the property was used to aid his financial transactions. This process meant the gradual deterioration of the Gould lines until they became a synonym for bad management and poor equipment. In spite of these conditions Gould retired with a fortune, and his influence was such that a certain group of western roads still carries his name.

Gould's entrance into western railroad affairs came with his purchase of the control of the Union Pacific at a nominal figure from Thomas Scott in the early seventies. He hoped to get Grant to favor the establishment of a sinking fund, which would advance the price of the securities of the road and produce a net profit on the transaction. The whole scheme rested on the attitude of Grant, and particularly on the terms of his address to Congress.

President Grant was at first in favor of the idea, but at the last minute he heard that the scheme was planned entirely to make a speculative profit on the company's securities, and so he dropped the recommendation from his message to Congress. The Union Pacific immediately stopped trying to pay the government, and Gould's plan had failed. The subsequent increase in the value of the company's securities finally made their sale profitable, and Gould disposed of his holdings. He did not, however, receive the profit for which he had originally hoped, and must have had a feeling of frustration at the failure of his plans. At any rate he did not lose interest in the affairs of the Union Pacific, but waited for his opportunity to turn his knowledge into account.

With the return of prosperity in the latter seventies, Gould saw an opportunity to profit from his insight into the affairs of the Union Pacific. He saw the potential threat of the Kansas Pacific-Denver Pacific line to the Union Pacific, and planned to utilize this fact for his own advantage. His idea was that if he bought the almost worthless stock of the Kansas road he could threaten the business of the parent company and force a consolidation, which would have the effect of raising the price of Kansas Pacific and Denver Pacific securities.

As soon as Gould had disposed of his Union Pacific holdings he invested in the stock of the Denver Pacific and Kansas Pacific. Then he proposed to the Union Pacific that the three roads be consolidated, each receiving stock in the consolidated company to the value of its original holdings. Such a proposition of course was to the disadvantage of the Union Pacific, whose securities were selling at a much higher rate than those of its proposed new lines. The merger would have had the effect of raising the value of the securities of the weaker roads at the expense of the stronger.

Unfortunately for Gould, the Union Pacific had the situation well under control and refused to take seriously the possible competition of the Kansas Pacific. It refused to overburden itself further. In consequence Gould found himself with two profitless companies on his hands, and little prospect of any improvement in the situation. Instead of pocketing his loss, he came to the conclusion that the only trouble with his plan was that it did not carry a sufficient threat. If he could really provide a potential danger to the Union Pacific, there was no reason why the scheme should not be successful.

The expansion of the original plan occurred in one of Gould's infrequent trips to the West. He purchased control of enough western roads to provide a line from the East along the whole route of the Union Pacific. To the Wabash, which he had obtained at an earlier time, he added the Missouri Pacific, the St. Jo. and Denver, the Kansas Central, the Central Branch Union Pacific, the Missouri, Kansas and Texas, the Texas and Pacific, the Denver and Rio Grande, and the Denver, South Park and Pacific. The whole group was in close touch with the Vanderbilt New York Central system.

Gould's purchases gave him a through line which was longer than that of the Union Pacific. Starting east of the Mississippi it competed all the way to Cheyenne, with the possibility of being completed the entire distance to the coast. It also had connections with the Gulf, and a large number of feeders. The acquired franchises made it possible to build parallel to the Union Pacific, practically mile by mile. There was no option left for the Union Pacific, and it had to give in to Gould on his own terms—the consolidation of the Union Pacific, Kansas Pacific, and Denver Pacific on equal terms. Gould also seized the occasion to unload some of his less valuable western securities on the Union Pacific.

The price of the consolidated stock was greater than that of Gould's former holdings, so he gradually disposed of his Kansas Pacific and Denver Pacific stock. But what should be done with the rest of the properties? There would be no benefit in disposing of them on the open market, since the profit would not be at all commensurate to the investment. On the other hand, there was some question as to whether or not their retention would be anything but a bad investment.

Gould was influenced in his final decision by his clear view of the possible profits from western railroads. He saw that for the time being the only large return lay in either the manipulation of the securities or in securing a monopoly of the business of some particular territory. Furthermore, Gould was the type of man who would not have been content in the development of his properties and the waiting for dividends. He wanted more action and larger returns.

The net result of Gould's view was a concentration on his southwestern holdings. They were particularly available for stock speculation because they were all weak and poorly managed. They were equally as available for the control of the business of the Southwest, because they constituted nearly all the important lines of that district. If they were handled rightly there was no reason why they might not be made to furnish large returns.

The Colorado roads were sold immediately, and no doubt in part because of the vigorous opposition of the Colorado security holders. Their strategic advantages in the control of the Southwest was very small, and did not warrant the expenditure of any great amount of time or money to keep control. The Kansas lines were in a somewhat similar position, but here it was easier to hold them than to sell them at the current market price.

The Missouri Pacific was used as the cornerstone of

the new Gould railroad system. If control were to be centralized it was necessary to have one road which was strong, and could act as leasor of subsidiary lines. The Missouri Pacific occupied a strategic position and had excellent prospects of financial strength. It could also be held with a very small investment, because when it had been reorganized after the Civil War only a small amount of its capital stock had been issued.

Eastern connections were made over the Wabash, St. Louis and Pacific, a consolidation (1879) of the Wabash Railway of Ohio and the St. Louis, Kansas City and Northern of Missouri (formerly the North Missouri). A policy of rapid expansion had been immediately adopted. The main line from Toledo was completed across northern Missouri to Kansas City and St. Jo. by the acquisition and construction of the Quincy, Missouri and Pacific. The old North Missouri line was continued northwest toward Council Bluffs. The Chicago and Paducah was acquired to give an entrance to Chicago. A contract with the Delaware, Lackawanna and Western called for the building and equipping of a Buffalo connection.

These developments of the Wabash made it an extremely dangerous road in a competitive sense. A through line from Buffalo to Kansas City and Omaha was a new departure in railroad management. It was the only line to enter into the competitive fields of both the eastern trunk lines and the "granger roads." In either of these fields it was especially dangerous because it had connections further east or further west, as the case might be. It also entered the field of the "Omaha pool" as well as that of the Southwestern Railway Rate Association, and in the latter case was included both in the roads having their eastern termini at Chicago and those beginning at St. Louis. Its very existence was anomalous and destroyed the effectiveness of the ordinary division of roads into groups for rate-making purposes. The road most immediately affected by the Wabash was the Chicago, Burlington and Quincy. The main lines of the two were nearly parallel, having the same termini and entering the same territory. The line of the Wabash to Council Bluffs was designed in part as a blow to the Burlington, while the Burlington threatened retaliation by projecting a line to Denver, which would give it an advantage in the hauling of Colorado and through business. In turn the Wabash threatened to build branch lines into Nebraska to encroach upon the territory of its rival.

The trouble between the two companies was compromised by a formal understanding in 1880. The Wabash agreed not to invade the Nebraska territory of the Chicago, Burlington and Quincy, and also not to compete further in southern Iowa except for the joint completion by both roads of the line to Council Bluffs. In return the Burlington agreed not to complete its line to Denver. Superficially the agreement seemed to favor the Burlington. Actually Gould never expected to live up to its terms, but only negotiated it in order to give himself time to strengthen his position.

The Council Bluffs connection was finished at once, but the "Omaha pool" hesitated to admit it, because the more circuitous route seemed to make an equality with the more favorable lines an injustice. Judicious rate cuts by the Wabash soon illustrated sufficiently the dangers of non-admittance, and so it was allowed to enter late in 1881 on a basis of equality.

The admission of the Wabash marked the beginning of a new era for the "Omaha pool." The Chicago, Milwaukee and St. Paul was nearing completion and the Missouri Pacific had started building northward. The old verbal agreement was becoming antiquated in the light of the increasing complexity of new conditions. In January, 1882, a new written agreement was finally adopted under the name of the Iowa Trunk Lines Association, and G. H. Daniels was given charge as commissioner. Shortly later the territory was expanded to include competitive points in Nebraska—the conflict being between the Union Pacific, the Chicago and Northwestern, and the Chicago, Burlington and Quincy. In the next few years other roads were admitted and a complicated system of rates and percentage returns was evolved.

The effect of the Wabash on the southwestern pool was even more serious. It had been given recognition as early as 1877, at which time it was given special rates on traffic to Toledo, although it was not admitted to the organization proper. These rates were formulated on the basis of similar rates to Chicago and St. Louis. At the same time the pool was expanded to include all earnings, so that no road would be tempted to increase its traffic in order to secure the 50% given for operating expenses.

Early in 1878 the admission of the Wabash and the extension of the pool to cover competitive points in Kansas and Nebraska was discussed, but no action was taken. At the same time there was a noticeable tendency toward an increase of the amounts of grain shipped down the Mississippi River. The St. Louis roads, which handled this business, demanded a larger proportion of the proceeds of the pool, but their demand was refused by the

Chicago lines. As a result, the St. Louis members withdrew from the pool, and in this action they were backed by the Wabash, which resented its exclusion from the benefits of the organization.

The breakdown of the pool meant war, and each group of roads organized for its own protection. With the aid of the Wabash the St. Louis roads secured a partial victory, but the final agreement represented a compromise. The Wabash was admitted to the pool, receiving, together with the Hannibal and St. Jo., 10% of the total traffic, while the Chicago and St. Louis groups each received 45%. The Chicago rate was made 5¢ higher than the St. Louis rate, and the Toledo rate 5¢ higher than that of Chicago. Competitive Kansas and Nebraska business was included. Secretary Midgley was given complete control of rates and traffic distribution.

Scarcely a year elapsed before war broke out afresh. The Chicago and Alton entered the competitive field and demanded a share of the business. Its demands were refused by the Chicago lines and by the Wabash; the pool ceased to function, and rates were cut from two-thirds to nine-tenths. The Chicago roads continued the pool organization, while the St. Louis lines worked in comparative harmony, and the Wabash stood aloof for the time being.

The Chicago lines immediately took the offensive, and aided by their longer haul cut the rates to such a point that the St. Louis roads would have had to haul their Kansas City business free of charge in order to meet them. Then the Wabash entered the fight and proceeded to make joint rates that would place the Chicago lines in the same position that they had placed the St. Louis lines.

The action of the Wabash immediately spread the war into the territory of the eastern trunk lines and forced them to take a hand. At first they attempted to equalize rates to the Mississippi, but the Chicago roads refused to support the attempt. Then they threatened to route all business via St. Louis, but the Chicago lines could not be bluffed any more easily than cajoled. The trunk lines were finally forced to manipulate their rates so that they produced an equality to the Missouri River. The result was weird but effective, and conditions began to improve. The association was finally restored, with the Chicago and Alton winning its objective of one-third of the St. Louis business, and the Wabash getting an additional 1% of the total business of the pool.

The next difficulty of the pool came with the entrance of the Wabash into Chicago, which would mean its participation in both St. Louis and Chicago business. The Chicago roads at first tried to impose legal obstacles to the entrance into Chicago, but when the Wabash reached its temporary 23rd Street station it began to cut passenger rates; at one time the far from Chicago to the Misrouri River (500 miles) was as low as fifty cents. The inevitable result was that the Wabash won its contentions without conditions.

Just as affairs began to become normal, the Wabash again lowered rates because it felt it was not securing its fair share of local Chicago-St. Louis business as handled by the Chicago-St. Louis pool. In spite of the local character of the contention, rate demoralization spread over most of the West. Again the Wabash won its contention, but the bad rate conditions were not remedied for several years.

During the entire period of the troubles of the southwestern pool the enmity of the Wabash, St. Louis and Pacific and the Chicago, Burlington and Quincy never ceased. In spite of the agreement of 1880, Gould invaded the territory to the north by building a branch to Des Moines. The Burlington protested, but did nothing. Shortly thereafter the Missouri Pacific began building into Nebraska territory, while Vanderbilt, with whom Gould was connected, began buying into the Burlington. At this point the situation began to look critical for the Iowa line.

The Chicago, Burlington and Quincy was now in such a position that it either had to undertake vigorous expansion or resign itself to becoming a minor project. The Gould lines had expanded until they competed at every important point, and at the same time had better eastern connections. The only hope of the Burlington was to expand westward, and to gain an advantage in this field which it did not have elsewhere. Its difficulties in such a program were the self-limiting provisions of the agreement of 1880 and the inevitable competition of the Union Pacific and of the Atchison, Topeka and Santa Fe.

The decision of the Burlington was to expand. Gould's position that the Nebraska line was built by the Missouri Pacific and not by the Wabash was declared a subterfuge, and the directors voted unanimously for the continuation of the main line to a junction with the Denver and Rio Grande at Denver. The line was finished in the spring of 1882. Gould tried to stop the extension by threatening to build parallel roads to both Denver and Chicago, but he failed to frighten the Burlington, which was now engaged in what it knew to be a life and death struggle.

Gould's next move was the purchase of the Hannibal

and St. Jo., which had remained unattached since the breakdown of the Joy system. Obviously the purchase was made only to embarrass the Chicago, Burlington and Quincy by the control of a direct competitor, for the road added but little to the position of the Gould lines. President Perkins of the Chicago, Burlington and Quincy tried to buy the property from Gould, but the deal fell through because the price could not be made satisfactory to both parties.

Upon the failure of peaceful attempts at purchase, the Chicago, Burlington and Quincy tried its hand at bluffing, and threatened to build to Kansas City. By this time Gould's position was weak. He had failed to stop the Denver extension, and the Wabash was threatened by financial insolvency because of over-building and rate troubles. In consequence he abruptly changed his plans, sold the Hannibal and St. Jo. to Perkins on his own terms, leased the Wabash to the St. Louis, Iron Mountain and Southern, and retired to the southern field where by this time he was in complete control. The Hannibal and St. Jo. became an integral and permanent part of the Burlington.

In the Southwest Gould was more successful than in the North. The roads in that district were all weak financially and offered but little opposition. To his original purchases of the Missouri Pacific, the Texas and Pacific, and the Missouri, Kansas and Texas, he added the St. Louis, Iron Mountain and Southern and the International and Great Northern. With these two additional roads he had complete control of the routes to the Gulf. as well as a monopoly of most of Missouri, Arkansas, Indian Territory, and parts of Texas and Kansas. The last of them carried with itself the lease of the

Galveston, Houston and Henderson, and the consequent control of Galveston.

The only important western connection which Gould lacked was to the Pacific coast. Four lines existed which would have made up that deficiency—the Southern Pacific, the Atchison, Topeka and Santa Fe, the Atlantic and Pacific, and the Texas and Pacific. The first two were strongly independent and could not be acquired. The third was in a hopeless financial condition, and its completion to the coast would have meant a financial outlay which Gould was not prepared to make. In consequence the Texas and Pacific was the only remaining possibility.

The destinies of the Texas and Pacific were controlled during the seventies by Thomas Scott, who was anxious to complete his line to the Pacific. Scott's principal difficulty was the lack of capital, and so he appealed to Congress for additional aid. In his efforts he was opposed by the Southern Pacific, which was willing and ready to build if it could secure federal authorization, preferably with a land grant. The struggle between the two roads took place in Congress, but the strong anti-railroad feeling of the time blocked any action. Congress was unwilling to extend any further aid to the Texas and Pacific, and was equally unwilling to encourage a monopoly of transcontinental transportation by transferring the land grant to the Southern Pacific.

The Southern Pacific solved the difficulty by securing territorial charters and starting to build east on its own capital. By the latter seventies Scott knew that he was beaten, and was more than willing to unload his holdings on Gould. Gould's first action was to declare a truce with the Huntington group and to make an agreement whereby the roads were to be brought to a junction, the traffic divided, and the land grant transferred to the Southern Pacific (later ruled illegal). The resulting transcontinental connection, while not entirely satisfactory, was made to serve.

The most serious danger which threatened the Southern Pacific-Texas and Pacific line was the possibility of competition by the Atchison, Topeka and Santa Fe. In 1880 this road had secured from the St. Louis and San Francisco (which held possession of the Atlantic and Pacific) a half interest in the Atlantic and Pacific, which it proposed building to the coast. If this plan were consummated it would mean a shorter line than that of its southern competitor, with better connections.

Huntington and Gould came together in the face of this common danger and bought control of the St. Louis and San Francisco, which gave them the other half interest in the Atlantic and Pacific, and halted the Santa Fe. The Southern Pacific had also by this time gained control of all the available crossings of the Colorado River, so that for the time being the plans of the Santa Fe were brought to a halt.

Along with the growth of the Gould system came a centralization of control. Minor roads were consolidated with the larger companies, which in turn were consolidated with, or leased to, others. The St. Louis, Iron Mountain and Southern and the Missouri, Kansas and Texas were connected by an interchange of stock, and both were then leased to the Missouri Pacific. The Wabash was leased to the Iron Mountain. The Galveston, Houston and Henderson was leased to the International and Great Northern, which in turn was attached to the Missouri, Kansas and Texas by a stock exchange. Rumors of the approaching consolidation of the Texas and Pacific were continually in the air.

As the various roads were leased, Gould was able to dispose of his holdings at a profitable figure, while still retaining control. The leased lines still remained under his direction and could be used for his profit without any risk. If hard times came Gould could retire without difficulty and without pecuniary loss. By the correct manipulation of rates the properties still held by Gould could take complete advantage of the monopoly control of the Southwest.

Gould was not becoming conservative in his policies of the early eighties. He knew the condition of his properties and realized that a crash was inevitable some time, and when that time came, he wanted to be somewhere else. The Wabash had the worst symptoms. Over-built and with insufficient traffic, it had been engaged in rate wars almost continuously. On the other hand its financial mismanagement and manipulation were notorious. Its dividend for November, 1881, for example, had been paid in the face of an empty treasury, and the price of its stock had been maintained by loans from the directors, frequently without security. As soon as it was leased to the St. Louis, Iron Mountain and Southern, the insiders began to unload.

When the crash finally came in June, 1884, and the Wabash went into the hands of the receiver, it was found that Gould's only remaining interest was in bonds and in certain cash advances. During the next two years practically all the branch lines were lost. The reorganization of 1886 divided the road into two parts—that east and that west of the Mississippi. Gould gradually lost interest, so that when the entire line was reunited a few years later, his name had disappeared completely from the list of stockholders. The effects of his management, however, never wore off entirely.

The collapse of the Wabash was spectacular, but was by no means a hard blow to Gould. He had merely made all he could out of it, and turned his attention elsewhere. The Central Railroad of New Jersey was acquired, and then Gould and Vanderbilt tried to purchase the Baltimore and Ohio to form a connecting link to the West. The final aim of their plans may possibly be seen in the effort of Jay's son George, twenty years later, to secure a road from ocean to ocean. In the West the Omaha extension was opened in 1882, and in 1887 a line was opened to Pueblo, at which point it made connections with the Denver and Rio Grande to Denver.

While expansion still continued to occur, the position of the Gould lines became increasingly weak. Overbuilding, over-capitalization, and speculation could not go on forever. It was possible only during the unusually good times of the early eighties. The financial stringency of 1884, besides causing the failure of the Wabash, was responsible for the collapse of the Texas and Pacific, and the weakening of all the roads. Extensive labor troubles in the succeeding years aided the process. More and more the new construction was carried on by the strongest of the Gould lines—the Missouri Pacific.

The failure of the Texas and Pacific occurred about the same time as that of the Wabash, and for the same general reasons. The only difference was that Gould had finished with the Wabash, but still wanted to retain the Texas and Pacific. The bondholders had grown restless because they felt that their interests were being prejudiced by the construction contracts which Gould was making with himself. Finally they demanded control of the road, and when Gould refused, they petitioned the court for the appointment of a receiver. A compromise was finally effected whereby each side elected eight directors and the seventeenth was appointed jointly.

The compromise failed to produce satisfactory results, and again the bondholders petitioned for a receiver, and this time their petition was granted. Gould was now in serious trouble, because the last thing that he wanted was a foreclosure sale, which would mean the end of his control. At just this time there appeared rumors, source unknown, to the effect that the financial affairs of the Texas and Pacific would not bear scrutiny; the securities of the company declined in value, and the bondholders were brought to terms. An assessment was levied on the stock, the receiver was discharged, and Gould maintained control.

The Missouri, Kansas and Texas also grew somewhat restive as time went on. Gould disposed of his holdings as soon as the road was safely leased to the Missouri Pacific, and the new anti-Gould directors felt very strongly that the line was being run to their loss and to the advantage of the Missouri Pacific. A compromise commission investigated the matter and returned the same verdict; thereupon the directors petitioned for a receiver and the setting aside of the lease. The contention of the Missouri Pacific was that the Missouri, Kansas and Texas had never been a paying investment, and that it was entirely dependent upon its connections.

The court accepted the view of the stockholders; a receiver was appointed and the lease was set aside. When the road was reorganized in 1891 a part interest was held by the Standard Oil people. It soon expanded to both St. Louis and Houston, thus becoming entirely independent of the Missouri Pacific.

The International and Great Northern was closely connected with the Missouri, Kansas and Texas and defaulted its bond issue in 1888. Both the Missouri, Kansas and Texas and the Missouri Pacific fought for its control, because to both of them it was a vital link in their connections with the Gulf. A compromise was finally effected whereby the control was divided equally, with the Central Trust Company acting as arbiter with a control of 1000 shares, and the road was reorganized. The same two roads were also interested in the Galveston, Houston and Henderson, another vital connection. After the Missouri, Kansas and Texas had completed its own line to Houston, it used the Galveston road jointly with the Missouri Pacific.

By the latter eighties the Gould properties had dwindled to the Missouri Pacific, with its satellite, the St. Louis, Iron Mountain and Southern, and the Texas and Pacific. Even the Missouri Pacific began to show signs of strain. Dividends were only possible in 1889 and 1890 because of the curtailment of necessary repairs and replacements. During the latter year the stockholders voted an increase of $10,000,000 in stock and a similar amount in collateral trust bonds, while in 1891 a $2,000,000 deficit had to be paid from the accumulated surplus.

In 1892 there was a similar deficit and during the following year still another deficit. The road managed to stay out of the receiver's hands by a rapid increase of the floating debt, which was finally funded in 1895 by the issue of gold funding notes to the extent of $13,000,000.

After 1897 the road again began to show a profit, even with the additional capitalization.

It must not be thought that the breakdown of the Gould system was injurious to Gould himself. In practically every case he had made his profit and retired from the management before the crash came. His thoughts were turning elsewhere, and during the early nineties he began to buy back into the Union Pacific. His prospective plans will probably forever remain a secret, for he died in 1892, before they were launched. His son George took control of his properties, and the Missouri Pacific fast became a family tradition.

The Gould system was a monument to one man—Jay Gould. Its conception, its progress, and its final dissolution were all due to him. One must of necessity admire the courage, shrewdness, and intense activity that made it possible. On the other hand it must be recognized that the whole episode was one of monopolization and stock speculation. There was never any effort to build up a strong, soundly managed group of roads. From the time that he bought the Missouri Pacific until his death in 1892 the one dominant note was speculation. Both in prosperity and depression he pursued his aim shrewdly and relentlessly. Absolutely dominating, he let no idea of business morality or personal charity deflect him from his purpose.

The result was a monopolistic system founded on financial mismanagement and speculation. Gould made a fortune, but the roads that he touched never quite recovered from his lack of knowledge and interest in sound railroading. In spite of a certain element of romance and beauty of manipulation, the effects of Gould's interest in the field of western railroads must be deplored.

CHAPTER XII

Undoubtedly the most outstanding achievement of the
early eighties was the completion of a considerable number of the transcontinental roads. Their completion
made the western railroad net assume a permanent form,
and finished the railroad conquest of the Far West, begun
by the Union Pacific twenty years before.

On the Pacific coast the strongest road was the Central
Pacific. Aided by both ability and energy, its unbroken
line of success was continued at least until the middle
eighties. Its two objectives were to secure and maintain
its control of California business, and to monopolize the
transcontinental entrances to the state. These two ideas
were inseparable, and reacted upon each other.

The southern extension of the Central Pacific was built
under the name of the Southern Pacific of California. It
was projected to secure the business of southern California
and to head off the two southern transcontinental lines
chartered by Congress—the Atlantic and Pacific and the
Texas and Pacific. Its objectives were Yuma and the
Needles, the only two available crossings of the Colorado
River. These two places were the strategic points in the
control of southern California.

The Texas and Pacific proved to be the first of the
eastern roads to provide a real menace. During the early

seventies Scott steadily pushed his line over the plains of Texas. At the other end, the Southern Pacific rushed its line to Yuma, where it arrived in 1877. At about this time the work on both roads was brought to a halt. The Texas and Pacific could find no more funds for construction, while the Southern Pacific lacked authority to build outside the boundaries of California.

Both roads found it desirable to transfer their activities to Congress. Scott tried to secure additional aid, while the Southern Pacific tried to secure a right-of-way, preferably with a land grant. Naturally the two projects were antagonistic and the whole affair soon became a struggle for personal advantage. Both plans felt the retardation of the growing anti-railroad movement. Congress was hardly willing to give further aid at the time that it was beginning to look forward to the withdrawal of much of the assistance made at an earlier date. On the other hand, it was equally loath to assist the Southern Pacific, thus producing both a central and southern route under the control of one company. Monopoly was not a desirable quality in the seventies.

The Huntington group tried to cover up the monopoly phase as much as possible by separating the managements of the Central Pacific and Southern Pacific. Huntington, who was president of both roads, resigned from the Southern Pacific in favor of Colton. The Contract and Finance Company, which had been too closely connected with the Central Pacific, was succeeded by the Western Development Company. These changes were made more for the sake of the attitude of the public than to deceive railroad men, because the insiders were quite aware that the real situation had not been changed.

Both the Texas and Pacific and the Southern Pacific

probably exceeded strict morality in their attempts to influence Congress. Huntington wrote to Colton that in his opinion "more work [has been] done since Congress adjourned for the Texas and Pacific than was ever done before in the whole history of this country," and asserted that Scott was spending money freely. About a particular act he said, "it costs money to fix things," and estimated that "with $200,000 I can pass our bill." It may be said to his credit (?) that he did not invest this $200,000 because he did not feel that the bill was worth it.

The efforts of both Scott and Huntington finally proved gainless because of the opposition in Congress, and neither received the desired legislation. When this situation was thoroughly evident, the Southern Pacific decided to proceed without the authorization of Congress. A Southern Pacific was chartered in both Arizona and New Mexico, and preparations were made to build without outside assistance.

The one remaining obstacle was the existence of a government Indian reservation at Yuma. The tracks of the Southern Pacific could not be laid, or a bridge built, until authority had been received from the War Department. The Texas and Pacific saw the advantage of the possession of this strategic point and in 1876, although the end of the main line was still 1200 miles distant, it applied for permission to break ground at Yuma. This permission was granted by General McDowell, in whose department the Yuma reservation lay, but within a month he revoked his order until he could hear directly from the War Department.

The scene of action was next transferred to the office of the Secretary of War. In April, 1877, he granted permission to the Southern Pacific to build across the reservation, on the condition that such tracks were to be removed if his action was not confirmed by Congress in the next session. Four months later the same permission was given to the Texas and Pacific, but almost immediately thereafter the Secretary of War revoked both permissions until the cases of both roads could be heard more fully. Apparently he was being strongly buffeted by the two forces.

During the time that the Secretary of War was making up his mind as to his correct method of procedure, the Southern Pacific took advantage of the situation and erected a permanent bridge and built its track most of the way across the reservation. The succeeding restraining order was relaxed enough to allow repairs on the existing track, and under this authority the Southern Pacific proceeded without more ado to continue to build until it was completed across the reservation.

The construction crew of the Southern Pacific had now done its work, so it only remained for Huntington to fix the situation in Washington. He was favored by a unanimous protest on the part of the people around Yuma when the military forced the trains to stop running. By his tact in his interviews with the Secretary of War, several Cabinet members, and the President he finally secured an executive order from the President, dated October 9, 1877, which allowed the operation of the Southern Pacific.

With the success of the Southern Pacific in crossing the Yuma reservation it started to build east, and Scott knew that he was beaten. In these circumstances he was glad to dispose of his holdings to Gould, who just at this time was building up his western railroad system. Gould and Huntington immediately came to an agreement, November 26, 1881, by which the two lines were to be joined near El Paso, traffic was to be pro-rated, and the land grant of the Texas and Pacific was to be released to the Southern Pacific. The junction of the two lines occurred in 1882 a short distance east of El Paso, but Congress refused to accept the transfer of the land grant, and eventually restored it to the public domain.

The Southern Pacific was not content with a joint line with the Texas and Pacific, and the following year it completed its own through line by a junction with the Galveston, Harrisburg and San Antonio, which had steadily been building west. The acquisition and building of this and other lines soon produced a through Southern Pacific route from San Francisco to New Orleans. The control of a steamship line gave it its own connections with New York.

The building and control of a large number of independent lines by the Central Pacific-Southern Pacific was not entirely satisfactory from the point of view of operation, and so the controlling interests looked for a way to consolidate the properties. A satisfactory plan was found in the chartering of the Southern Pacific Company of Kentucky in 1884. The advantages of incorporating in this state were many and diverse. The company had practically unlimited powers except to operate Kentucky railroads. Its capital could be increased at will, the liability of the stockholders was narrowly limited, and the company did not need to even have an office in Kentucky.

Within the next year the Southern Pacific Company leased all the properties of the Central Pacific, practically all controlled roads north of Goshen, and the entire route from San Francisco to New Orleans. The only important line not included was the San Francisco and North Pacific, which was building north from San Francisco under independent management. By this time the Huntington group had been in control of some 85% of the California roads for half a dozen years, and the Southern Pacific Company welded them together in a single highly unified system.

The most important competition which the Southern Pacific received came from the Atchison, Topeka and Santa Fe, one of the strongest of the transcontinental roads. Its destinies were controlled for the most part by Thomas Nickerson, who was president from 1874 to 1880, and W. B. Strong, who was vice-president and general manager from 1877 on, and president from 1881 to 1889. T. Jefferson Coolidge was president during the intervening year of 1880-1881. These men were responsible for making the Santa Fe strong and significant, and for retaining its independence. Strong, who had the longest connection, received his training on the Chicago, Burlington and Quincy.

The chief competitor of the Santa Fe during the seventies was the Denver and Rio Grande, organized by Denver capital to head off the Kansas road and to secure the control of southern Colorado for Denver. At first it gave every indication of success. 1871 saw it as far south as Colorado Springs and by 1872 it had reached Pueblo, while the Santa Fe did not enter Colorado until the summer of 1873. Both roads were slowed down by the panic of 1873, and during the succeeding depression the Santa Fe finished its main line to Pueblo, while the Rio Grande tapped some of the mining country west of that point.

The economic revival of the latter seventies saw both roads looking south toward Santa Fe. The one good entry into New Mexico was the Raton pass, and so both lines prepared to rush engineering crews to take possession and start work. The Santa Fe arrived there first, located its line, and was able to maintain its position. During 1878 and 1879 it made sure of its victory by building from La Junta through Trinidad into New Mexico.

Having beaten the Denver and Rio Grande to the south the Santa Fe turned its attention to cutting it off in the west. The Rio Grande had been completed from Pueblo to Canon City, but seemingly could get no further because of the lack of funds. Right above Canon City was a pass in the mountains which had room for only one railroad and which controlled the entrance to the Leadville mining district. The town in this region at first tried to get the Denver and Rio Grande to build, but failing that, it began offering inducements to the Atchison, Topeka and Santa Fe.

When the real Leadville boom started in 1878 both roads were more than willing to exert every possible effort to occupy the essential pass. As in the case of the Raton pass, the Santa Fe crew arrived first and took possession. It was aided in holding its position by a body of citizens, who were incensed because the Rio Grande had not built earlier. When the Denver and Rio Grande group arrived they found themselves confronted by the Santa Fe crew, backed by a mob of armed citizens. There was nothing left but to withdraw.

Work was started immediately in the cañon, in order to insure its permanent possession, and the Denver and Rio Grande was enjoined from interfering. All the materials for construction had to be hauled by wagon from Pueblo, since the Denver and Rio Grande would hardly permit the use of its own tracks for its defeat.

The Rio Grande sought relief in the courts, on the plea that the charter of the Atchison, Topeka and Santa Fe did not give authority for the new construction. The Denver Circuit Court decided in favor of the Santa Fe, and conceded it the prior right to build. The Santa Fe immediately followed up this advantage by threatening to parallel the whole line of the Denver and Rio Grande. The result was that the Rio Grande seemed hopelessly defeated and made the best terms possible.

The complete victory of the Santa Fe led it to go further than it had at first intended and to lease the entire line of the Rio Grande. This action immediately made the more northerly lines—the Union Pacific, the Kansas Pacific, and the Colorado Central feel the threat of Santa Fe competition. The Kansas road used its new branch entirely to draw business to its main line, and the northern lines retaliated by boycotting Santa Fe business—a magnificent gesture with little potential threat.

The lease of the Denver and Rio Grande did not at all stop the fight and the old management continued the struggle. Both companies kept crews in the disputed cañon, and there were continual quarrels and fights. The Denver and Rio Grande party renewed its hope in the spring of 1879, when additional capital was secured. More men were put into the field, the line north of the pass was occupied, and the Attorney-General of Colorado was persuaded to bring *quo warranto* proceedings to determine the right by which a Kansas corporation built in the state of Colorado.

The seemingly secure position of the Santa Fe was

entirely destroyed during the year of 1879. In April
the Supreme Court reversed the Circuit Court and gave
the Denver and Rio Grande the prior right to build in
the Leadville cañon; the *quo warranto* suit succeeded
and the Santa Fe was enjoined from operating the Denver and Rio Grande. The Santa Fe referred the matter
to the United States court on a motion to quash the proceedings, but the Denver and Rio Grande took the bull
by the horns and resumed the control of its line by
force. The resulting riots were so severe that Governor
Pitkin threatened to call out the state troops.

The Denver and Rio Grande was finally placed in the
hands of a receiver; the lease was cancelled upon its
promise to pay for all the construction done on its line
up to that time. The Circuit Court upheld this action
in January, 1880, and during the following month the
roads came to an amicable agreement. The lease was
repudiated; the Rio Grande was to pay $1,800,000 for
all franchises and for the work done, and was not to
continue its line south into New Mexico; the Santa Fe
was not to parallel any of the track of the Rio Grande;
half of the Denver and Rio Grande business, including
a quarter of the Denver business, was to be shipped by
way of the Santa Fe, while the other half was to go over
the Kansas Pacific. A traffic agreement was formulated
in 1882, which gave the Santa Fe the right of running
its own trains to Denver.

The long standing dispute between the Santa Fe on
one hand and the Union Pacific and Kansas Pacific on
the other, was also settled during 1879. The Colorado
Railways' Association was formed in order to establish uniform rates over the field of Colorado competitive traffic. The Denver and Rio Grande was

admitted as soon as it came out of the hands of the receiver.

The conclusion of the "Rio Grande War" was a good thing for both companies. The Rio Grande was left to expand in Colorado, while the Santa Fe was free to turn its attention to the transcontinental field. While the Rio Grande was left largely as a local road, the superior financial resources of the Santa Fe made it on the whole desirable that it should be the road to be in a position to build to the coast.

In the midst of the troubles of the Rio Grande (1879), Jay Gould bought a half interest as a part of his western railroad speculation, but he soon sold out his holdings when he turned his attention to the development of his southwestern system. The road's receiver was discharged in 1880, and the line was completed to the southern boundary of Colorado. The western branch was completed to the state line in 1882. A year later its continuation in Utah was completed to Ogden by the Denver and Rio Grande Western, a subsidiary corporation. This construction produced a new and competitive line for the whole haul of the Union Pacific.

In the meantime the Santa Fe continued its construction south and west. It missed the city of Santa Fe by a few miles, and constructed a stub to that point (1880). Notable during this same year was the election to the presidency of T. Jefferson Coolidge. He was also a large stockholder in the Chicago, Burlington and Quincy, and although his incumbency was only for a year, it was an evidence of the continued friendly feeling between the two lines.

The Santa Fe finished the first transcontinental line to be completed after the Union Pacific when it joined its tracks to those of the Southern Pacific at Deming, New Mexico, in March, 1881. The whole line, however, was built too rapidly and practically had to be rebuilt during the next few years. The completion of connections with the coast was not the final object of the Santa Fe. It still remained in an unsatisfactory position because it was dependent for both its eastern and western connections on independent lines. In the uncontrolled competition of the early eighties such a situation was little less than disastrous, and in consequence the principal aim of the road became the securing of its own lines to the principal termini of both east and west.

The most available connection both east and west lay in the old Atlantic and Pacific, which had been sold under foreclosure and reorganized in 1876 as a part of the St. Louis and San Francisco. Its main line ran from St. Louis to Vinita, Indian Territory, and its franchises included a land grant from Congress along the 35th parallel to the coast. A short connecting line between the two roads would give the Santa Fe an entrance to St. Louis, while the western rights would give it transcontinental connections and a land grant.

The St. Louis and San Francisco was hard pressed for cash, and was willing to dispose of a half interest in the Atlantic and Pacific in order to secure its completion. By an agreement made in 1880 the Santa Fe secured this half interest, and the two companies jointly guaranteed its completion. The main lines of the Santa Fe and the St. Louis and San Francisco were to be connected by a branch from Pierce City to Wichita. For thirty years all westbound traffic was to go via the Santa Fe, while eastbound traffic was to be divided—that for

Chicago going from Wichita over the Santa Fe, and that to St. Louis going from Wichita over the St. Louis and San Francisco. The settlement of disputes was provided for by a system of trustees. One man was elected by each company and the third was elected jointly; they held the stock of the Atlantic and Pacific and had final authority in the case of any trouble which might arise.

The connecting link between the Santa Fe and the Frisco was completed in 1880, and three years later the latter road completed its own line from Pacific Junction to St. Louis, whereas hitherto it had been dependent upon the use of the tracks of the Missouri Pacific. By these additions the Santa Fe attained a fairly adequate entrance to St. Louis for at least thirty years. It was during the same general period that the entrance to Denver over the tracks of the Denver and Rio Grande was secured.

The interest of the Santa Fe in the Atlantic and Pacific and its agreement with the Frisco produced an immediate threat to the Gould lines and to the Southern Pacific. As long as it had remained an intermediate line it was dependent on its connections, and its competition was not dangerous. Once it entered St. Louis and built to the coast it would become an active competitor for all the business of the whole territory traversed.

At this time the Gould and Huntington lines were in close agreement. Gould had renounced all hope of building to the coast, and in consequence the two systems were largely complementary. Gould's lines acted as feeders for the Southern Pacific transcontinental business, while at the same time they were benefited by having satisfactory connections with the coast. The more advantageous route of the Santa Fe offered direct competition to both groups of roads.

The first move of the Southern Pacific was to cut off the Atlantic and Pacific just as it had done the Texas and Pacific. A branch of the Southern Pacific of California was built to the Needles, which was the only available crossing of the Colorado River. With this point secured the Atlantic and Pacific could never hope to enter California except over the tracks of its rival.

The defensive action of the Southern Pacific was soon supplemented by offense. Acting jointly, Huntington and Gould purchased control of the St. Louis and San Francisco, thus giving them the other half interest in the Atlantic and Pacific, and effectually stopping the plans of the Santa Fe to have an entirely independent line. Incidentally it completed the Gould control of the Southwest, and left the Southern Pacific in control of every transcontinental route except that of the Northern Pacific.

The Santa Fe seemingly accepted the inevitable and restricted its plans. An agreement with the Southern Pacific allowed the completion of the Atlantic and Pacific to the Colorado River, at which point the tracks of the two roads were to be joined. The complete line was opened in August, 1883, although the bridge over the Colorado River was not completed until the following year. At this point the Santa Fe had to admit defeat for the time being, and to content itself with somewhat unsatisfactory traffic arrangements.

The Santa Fe was not a road to long admit defeat, and so when it found itself checked at the Colorado River it turned its attention further south. It conceived the idea of securing an outlet in Mexico on the Gulf of California, and thus be in a position to ship its traffic to the coast over its own line. While such a connection would not be entirely satisfactory from a commercial point of view, it would produce active competition and possibly be a sufficient threat to secure better arrangements on California business.

The road which was involved in the new plan of the Santa Fe was the Sonora Railway, projected to run north from Guaymas on the Gulf of California. It had been acquired by Nickerson in 1879 mainly to secure the subsidy offered by the Mexican government, and its construction had been carried on very leisurely. Now in 1882, when the fight with the Huntington-Gould group was at its climax, the Santa Fe took over the Sonora Railway formally and rushed it to completion. It then was in a position to ship directly to the coast over its own lines, and threatened to reduce rates. The completion of the Mexican Central in 1884 gave a direct line to Mexico City.

The threat of the new connection of the Santa Fe was sufficient to bring the Southern Pacific to terms. In 1884 the Southern Pacific sold a controlling interest in the Atlantic and Pacific to the Santa Fe, as well as a half interest and a lease of the branch from Mojave to the Colorado River. The Santa Fe also secured trackage rights to San Francisco and soon began the operation of its own trains to that city. Its victory was complete.

Further expansion in California was mostly in the direction of building up a control of the southern part of the state. Roads were built, purchased, and consolidated to give the Santa Fe adequate connections with the coast at Los Angeles and San Diego. All the California lines were consolidated in 1889 as the Southern

California and brought into the system proper. The Santa Fe's own line to San Francisco was not built until the latter nineties.

The completion of the Santa Fe to the Pacific coast gave it time to turn its attention elsewhere. Outside of its own line to Denver, which was completed in 1887, it had two main objectives—the control of a road to Chicago and of one to the Gulf. Both of these aims were important if the Santa Fe were to build up an effective control of the territory which it had already occupied.

The Gulf connection was secured by the purchase of the Gulf, Colorado and Santa Fe in 1886. This road had been chartered in the seventies by the citizens of Galveston in order to have a road free from Houston domination. Until it was built there was only one road entering Galveston. Work was started immediately, and when the line was purchased by the Santa Fe it had succeeded in building into Indian Territory. Immediately thereafter it was completed to a junction with the Southern Kansas at Purcell, Indian Territory (1887).

No such easy method existed for gaining an entrance to Chicago, and so an entirely new line had to be constructed under the name of the Chicago, Santa Fe and California Railway. It practically paralleled the line of the Chicago, Burlington and Quincy across Illinois and southern Iowa, and was opened to use on May 1, 1888. A project to secure an independent line to St. Louis was begun by the purchase of the St. Louis, Kansas City and Colorado, but the road was never built because of the financial depression of the latter eighties.

By 1888 the Santa Fe was one of the most strategically important roads in the West, and rumors were on foot that it was trying to buy the Erie in order to secure a line to the Atlantic coast. Without this prospective expansion it had a complete line of its own from Chicago to the Pacific coast, being the only line in this position. It also had connections with most of the important Missouri River towns, with Denver, with the principal cities of Texas, and with the Gulf. It also had adequate traffic arrangements for entering St. Louis and San Francisco. The only insuperable obstacle which it encountered was the depression of the latter eighties, which made it stop all expansion and embark on a severe policy of retrenchment.

CHAPTER XIII

THE COMPLETION OF THE NORTHERN TRANS-
CONTINENTAL ROADS

The most important of the northern transcontinental lines was the Union Pacific, partly because of its early construction and partly because of its central route. The main difficulty of the Union Pacific was financial. Built before the traffic was large enough to make it pay, its excessive construction expenses produced obligations which were almost impossible to meet. The original owners sold out immediately. Thomas Scott tried his hand and failed. Jay Gould made an effort to stabilize the finances, but finally injured them still further.

The most troublesome obligation of the Union Pacific was the $65,000,000 bond issue of the government, with interest at 6%, which was due thirty years after the road's completion. The original act had provided that all payments by the government for transportation should be applied to the debt, and that after the completion of the road at least 5% of the net income should be used to pay off the advances of the government. (It is understood, unless otherwise stated, that this discussion applies equally to all roads in the debt of the government.)

It was presumed by most people that as soon as the Union Pacific was finished the repayment of the loan would be begun, but such did not prove to be the case.

The meaning of practically every phase of the act was called into question—the date of completion, the time of payment, what constituted "net earnings," and other similar questions. While these matters were being threshed out in court, payments of any kind were held in abeyance. In some cases the company was undoubtedly merely blocking payment, but in other cases there was a legitimate question as to what the phraseology of the act implied.

During the time in which the meaning of the Congressional act was being determined in the courts the railroad either made insufficient payments or refused to make any at all, and in consequence the sum total of the debt continued to increase. At the same time, the affairs of both the company and of the government seemed to make settlement desirable. The company was vitally interested in the stabilizing of the value of its securities, while the federal treasury was embarrassed by the greenback situation. In 1873 Congress prohibited further issues of securities by the company except to retire or refund its existing debt, but the law was not obeyed.

During the middle seventies the company tried to secure a sinking fund arrangement, but the anti-railroad feeling of the time was unfavorable to such a project. In 1876 the House passed a bill making a sinking fund unlawful, as well as the paying of dividends when the road was in default on its bonds, but the measure failed to pass the Senate. Under the existing circumstances it might have been possible to foreclose the road, but it was hard to see in what way the government would benefit by such action.

The supposedly final solution of the whole affair came

with the passage of the Thurman Act in 1878, which bowed to the railroad point of view to the extent of being based on the sinking fund idea. A sinking fund was to be created by putting aside 25% of the net earnings. Deductions were to be made from this fund if the remaining 75% did not prove adequate to pay the interest on the company's bonds. The scheme applied only to the Union Pacific and the Central Pacific. An auditor of railroad accounts was created a month later in order to assure the correctness of the railroad's accounts.

By the time of the passage of the Thurman Act the roads were in a fairly open state of hostility, and sought in every possible way to make the operation of the act ineffective. They continued their fight in the courts, and sought to have the new act set aside on the plea that it was a violation of the contract of the first act. The Supreme Court, in a divided opinion, decided against the railroad's contention.

Once the legal battle had been lost, the most available method of making the act ineffective was to cut the amount of "net earnings," either by the interpretation of the word, or by manipulating the properties. The interpretation of the term "net earnings" was fought out in the courts, with but partial success to the railroads. The Central Pacific attained its object by diverting much of its profitable business to branch lines, while the Union Pacific secured the same result by an issue of collateral trust bonds.

The evasions of the railroads made the Thurman Act fail, and instead of the debt growing smaller it gradually increased. By the middle of the eighties its eventual payment looked impossible, and a Congressional committee so reported in 1887. No one had any hope that more than a portion of it would ever be met, and the only remaining question was as to the extent of the loss by the government. In the meantime, no action of any sort was undertaken.

The Union Pacific did not find it necessary to stop expansion, even though it was unable to pay its debt to the government. After its consolidation with the Denver Pacific and the Kansas Pacific in 1880 it had two main objectives—(1) to secure the necessary feeders to make its main line profitable; (2) to make itself secure against competition either by agreement or by securing its own outlet to the ocean.

The Union Pacific was fairly secure in its position during the seventies, but conditions began to change during the early eighties. The building of the Texas and Pacific, the Santa Fe, the Denver and Rio Grande, the Northern Pacific, and the Southern Pacific began to create competition in the field of transcontinental business. The Southern Pacific in particular was a thorn in the flesh of the Union Pacific. When it completed its own southern line it tended to ship all business by that route, with the double purpose of avoiding the payments required by the Thurman Act and of obviating the necessity of dividing the proceeds of the business with the Union Pacific.

Conditions were also becoming troublesome in the east. The roads which at first had only give eastern connections began to expand further west and to take a portion of the Nebraska business. Some of them, such as the Chicago, Burlington and Quincy, expanded west as far as Colorado. Other Colorado roads, as well as the Santa Fe, began to secure a share of the business from the mountain states. The receipts of the Union Pacific began to show a corresponding decline.

The breakdown of the Iowa Trunk Lines Association in 1883 offered the Union Pacific a chance to make its position in the east more secure. The dissatisfied lines were the Chicago, Milwaukee and St. Paul, and the Chicago, Rock Island and Pacific, both of which had no branch lines west of the Missouri River. They resented the superiority of the Chicago and Northwestern and the Chicago, Burlington and Quincy, both of which roads were able to carry their own business to Kansas and Nebraska in addition to their share of the pool. No quarrel could have been more opportune for the purposes of the Union Pacific.

The resulting agreement between the dissatisfied members—the St. Paul, the Rock Island, and the Union Pacific, is usually known as the "Tripartite agreement." The Chicago roads were to be considered as equal and were to make all through westbound rates, while the Union Pacific was to make all eastbound rates. The division of proceeds was roughly on the basis of mileage, but the Union Pacific was able to secure the better of the bargain by a judicious handling of the situation.

The "Tripartite agreement" placed the dissatisfied members in the saddle, and the other lines were forced to make concessions. The Western Trunk Line Association was formed to succeed the Iowa Trunk Lines Association, and was based on the principles of the "Tripartite agreement." The only line not to accept this solution was the Chicago, Burlington and Quincy, which was buoyed up by its recent victory over the Wabash, and refused to enter the new association because the Union Pacific would not agree to divide its Nebraska business.

The new organization was only partially successful. The Burlington was outside it; the broadening of the agreement had also increased the danger of outside competition, particularly in Colorado. Trouble came in March, 1884, when the St. Louis and San Francisco, lowered the rates to Colorado. Secretary Vining immediately retaliated by lowering the association rates, but instead of ending the trouble, his action only broadened its scope. The Santa Fe backed the St. Louis and San Francisco, in which it was closely interested, while the Chicago, Burlington and Quincy and the Chicago and Alton met the cut. Gradually the war spread over the entire West.

The rate war of 1884 had at least one good effect. It led the Chicago, Burlington and Quincy to come to an agreement with the Union Pacific, the latter road conceding a portion of the Nebraska business. The main issue in the trouble was finally compromised and the pool reconstituted. Succeeding developments gradually expanded its area and increased the number of participants. The Chicago and Northwestern and the Chicago, Burlington and Quincy, with their Nebraska connections and branches, continued to be the important disturbing elements.

The troubles of the Iowa pool were vitally important to the Union Pacific, which depended on its eastern connections for a large share of its business. At a time when other roads were expanding west of the Missouri and new transcontinental routes were being opened, it was essential that good relations be maintained with the more easterly lines. The "Tripartite agreement" secured a satisfactory status with its non-competitive connections, but other roads were an increasing annoyance. The Nebraska branches, although growing in number and extent, found an ever increasing amount of competition.

Further west, the Union Pacific was finding keen competition in Colorado. The acquisition of the Denver Pacific and the Kansas Pacific had given a Denver connection and a partial hold over Colorado business. Neither of these results was entirely satisfactory, however, and particularly in view of the excessive cost of the new lines. The line of the Denver and Rio Grande south from Denver soon became important, and the Santa Fe was finished to a junction at Pueblo as early as 1876, with later a line of its own to Denver. While the Santa Fe and the Denver and Rio Grande did not have the most amicable of relations, still a traffic agreement between them was sufficient to create considerable competition for the Union Pacific.

Additional competition for Colorado business came with the building of several Chicago and St. Louis lines. The Chicago, Burlington and Quincy was opened to Denver in 1883, while the Missouri Pacific was finished to Pueblo in 1887, and the Rock Island to Colorado Springs in 1890. In all three cases additional competition was created, and particularly because the newer roads could afford better eastern connections, with a single haul to either St. Louis or Chicago.

The Union Pacific attempted to cement its position in Colorado by the formation of a traffic agreement in 1879 under the name of the Colorado Railways' Association, and including the Union Pacific, the Kansas Pacific, and the Santa Fe. The consolidation of the first two was followed shortly later by the admission of the Denver and Rio Grande, and then by the admission of the Chicago, Burlington and Quincy. The Union

Pacific received the lion's share of the proceeds, and consequently was in continual trouble with the Santa Fe. Internal troubles were irritating, but the downfall of the organization in 1886 was caused by the continued encroachments of other similar organizations, until little real power remained to it. In consequence of this dissolution, the position of the Union Pacific was that much weakened.

The Union Pacific had better luck in Utah. The Mormons, who had built its connecting links, were interested only in securing railroad connections and did not much care in whom the management vested. The three lines making the southern connection from Ogden were acquired by the Union Pacific, and consolidated in 1881 as the Utah Central, with Sidney Dillon, president of the Union Pacific, as president. The Oregon Short Line was chartered in the same year to build north.

In the Far West the Union Pacific was most seriously hampered by the lack of its own line to the coast. Dependent in the east, it was still more unfortunate in the west, where it had only one possible connection— the Central Pacific. As time went on and the Huntington group secured an alternate route in their Southern Pacific, conditions kept getting worse. Twenty-five percent of the net income of the Central Pacific went to the government, while over half of the through rate went to the Union Pacific. In consequence every effort was made to use the southern line as much as possible, and particularly when the control of a steamship line made it possible to haul freight all the way to New York. This trouble with the Central Pacific reached periodic crises throughout the eighties, and served to increase the interest of the Union Pacific in an outlet of its own.

The most promising independent route was that to the northwest, following in general the line of the old Oregon Trail. It would pass through the mining districts of Idaho and tap the rich country of Oregon and Washington. It would not be quite as direct as the line of the Northern Pacific, then building, but would be sufficiently strong to create effective competition and thus to threaten the other transcontinental roads.

The northern end of such a route would presumably be Portland, to which the Oregon Steam Navigation Company gave the easiest entrance. This company had been organized in the sixties to afford communication along the Columbia River. Its steamship line, punctuated by railroads around the unnavigable portions of the stream, had soon built up a monopoly of the territory. As time went on the steamships were supplemented by a complete line of railroad.

When Jay Cooke was the guiding light in the affairs of the Northern Pacific, he looked to the Oregon Steam Navigation Company for his western connections. In 1871 he bought three-quarters of the $5,000,000 of capital stock at 40, paying for it half in cash and half in Northern Pacific bonds at 90. When Jay Cooke and Company failed this stock was sold to settle some of its obligations, and repurchased by the Portland directors.

The Oregon Steam Navigation Company was badly affected by the panic of 1873. Its bonds were held in large part in Germany, and these bondholders soon became restless concerning the condition of their property. A group of those interested in various Oregon railroads banded together and sent to America one Henry Villard to look after their interests. Villard soon became interested in western railroad possibilities, and was particularly impressed by the strategic importance of the Oregon Steam Navigation Company. Little by little he began to acquire control of the lines in which he was interested, although he was continually hampered by his lack of ready capital for investment.

To get capital, Villard approached Jay Gould, who in the latter seventies was the dominating figure in the western railroad world, and particularly in the Union Pacific. An agreement was reached whereby Villard was to be enabled to buy the Oregon Steam Navigation Company, and in conjunction with the Union Pacific was to build the connecting link between the two roads. Before anything could be done along this line Gould had sold his interest in the Union Pacific and refused to back Villard any further. At the same time the German bondholders whom Villard represented became dissatisfied and clamored for action.

In this extremity Villard formed his own company, bought out the holdings of the German bondholders, and in 1879 combined the Oregon Steamship Company with the Oregon Steam Navigation Company to form the Oregon Railway and Navigation Company. A short time later the Union Pacific, which held some of the stock of the Oregon company, started building north. An agreement was made by which the tracks of the two companies were joined at Huntington in 1884 and operated as a through line. The Union Pacific had achieved its object of an independent line to the coast.

Villard's agreement with the Union Pacific in the Northwest was part of his plan to secure control of that section of the country. His chief possible competitor lay in the Northern Pacific, which would be able to handle the majority of the transcontinental business because of its more direct line—that is, if it were ever built. After the panic of 1873, however, it seemed completely crushed, and Villard did not worry much about its eventual completion.

Unfortunately for Villard the Northern Pacific began to show signs of life with the business expansion which came around 1880, and President Billings began to push the work west. Villard tried to get Billings to promise to use the Oregon Railway and Navigation Company for the western connection, but the best offer he could secure was the promise to use it until the line of the Northern Pacific was completed. The threat was real, and again Villard was hampered by his lack of funds.

The result of Villard's cogitations on his new difficulty was the formation of his "blind pool." His idea was the creation of a holding company which would control both the Northern Pacific and the Oregon Railway and Navigation Company, and operate them in harmony. For this purpose he needed the immediate control of a large sum of money in order to secure control of the Northern Pacific, while at the same time he feared to broach his plan to others because its publication might well advance the stock to a prohibitive price.

Because of these considerations Villard offered speculative investors a chance to enter a "blind pool"—backed only by the security of his personal reputation. Whether it was the security which he offered or the optimism of the time, the $8,000,000 was oversubscribed at once, no one knowing for what purpose the money was to be used. The Oregon and Transcontinental Company was at once organized, and control of the Northern Pacific was secured. The stability of Villard's position was assured.

As soon as the desired control was acquired, a new bond issue was floated and the work on the Northern Pacific was pushed toward completion. The last spike was finally driven in September, 1883, amid universal eulogies. The Oregon and California was leased the same year; when completed it would afford a direct line from Portland to San Francisco. The St. Paul and Northern Pacific was acquired in order to have a direct line to St. Paul.

The Northern Pacific completed its main line to Seattle in 1887, and as a result the Portland branch lost some of its significance. The interest of the Union Pacific was recognized in a joint lease of the Oregon Railway and Navigation Company. In 1889 a direct line to Milwaukee was secured by a contract with the Wisconsin Central, and this agreement was the precursor of a lease. In the same year the Union Pacific failed in an attempt to purchase control of the Oregon and Transcontinental.

The completion of the Northern Pacific was followed shortly later by that of the Canadian Pacific. The latter road proved a very disturbing element to the roads further south, particularly after it secured control of lines entering the United States. It was especially dangerous after the formation of the Interstate Commerce Commission, because it was under no necessity of following the rulings of that body.

The most continuous trouble which all transcontinental lines had to face was water competition. The route around the Horn had been in use for many years, but it never was a very dangerous competitor because the trip took too much time to make it usable for most products. The real danger lay in the Panama route, which was controlled by a combination of the Pacific Mail Steamship Company and the Panama Railroad.

The Pacific Mail Steamship Company was a Gould property and when Gould secured control of the Union Pacific there was a virtual certainty that the two companies would be operated in harmony. The agreement finally resolved upon was designed to cut down the net income of the Union Pacific and to increase that of the steamship company. The Pacific Mail was guaranteed a monthly gross business of $60,000 (made $110,000 in 1880) on condition that it would not cut rates. In practice this meant that the Union Pacific paid a monthly subsidy of between $60,000 and $75,000 to prevent the competition of the steamship company.

When Gould withdrew from the control of the Union Pacific that company objected to paying the subsidy and notified the steamship company that when the existing contract expired on January 1, 1882 it would not be renewed. President Dillon's position was that he wanted to reduce the subsidy to a minimum and to establish his own oriental steamship company. Apparently the action of the Union Pacific was taken largely as a threat, for a new contract was drawn which called for $95,000 a month.

Up to this point the transcontinental situation was fairly simple, since the Central Pacific-Union Pacific line had a monopoly of its field. Between 1881 and 1883, however, the number of complete transcontinental lines increased immensely, and every one of these roads was a possible competitor with every other one. Traffic did not increase as fast as the facilities for its handling, and was frequently insufficient for profitable operation. As in the case of the roads farther east, the only reasonable solution of the problem seemed to be an equitable division of the existing business.

An attempt was made to meet the situation by the formation of the Transcontinental Traffic Association in September, 1883. Its membership furnishes a good summary of the roads interested in transcontinental business—the Union Pacific, the Central Pacific, the Southern Pacific, the Texas and Pacific, the Galveston, Houston and San Antonio, the Denver and Rio Grande, the Chicago, Burlington and Quincy, the Atchison, Topeka and Santa Fe, the Atlantic and Pacific, the Northern Pacific, and the Oregon Railway and Navigation Company.

The general form of the contract was a rate agreement, to be enforced by fines, and with a commissioner (G. W. Ristine) in charge. The important competitive points of San Francisco and Portland were given the same rate, regardless of route, although the Northern Pacific was given an advantage with respect to smaller points in the Northwest and the Southern Pacific was given a similar advantage to smaller points in California. The subsidy to the Pacific Mail Steamship Company was taken over by the association.

Eastern connections objected immediately to a system which would permit Portland goods to be shipped via San Francisco, and vice versa. The original plan was therefore dropped and each road given a monopoly of its own territory. Continual trouble came from the Northern Pacific and the Oregon Railway and Navigation Company, both of which were willing to cut their steamship rates from Portland to San Francisco so that they would be able to secure a part of the California business. To stop this practice the association began subsidizing them with a percentage of the total California revenue.

The Transcontinental Traffic Association never worked with entire satisfaction to all parties. Various types and strengths of roads, widely different routes, different connections, and outside competition were some of the factors which prevented complete success. An effort was made to improve the situation by proposing to include all the roads which made any of the haul from Chicago or St. Louis. This plan failed, largely because it was too important and radical a change to secure the approval of all parties. At one time the Union Pacific and the Texas and Pacific threatened to withdraw because of the non-inclusion of the St. Louis and San Francisco, but were placated by the promise of the Santa Fe to see that rates were maintained.

Early in 1884 an attempt was made to create a money pool, but the Santa Fe refused to join any such association as long as the Union Pacific was bound by the "Tripartite agreement" and did not have control over its own westbound rates. In this attitude it was backed by the Chicago, Burlington and Quincy, a road which was usually friendly to the Santa Fe, and was also influenced by its fight with the Union Pacific over Nebraska business.

The objections of the Santa Fe and the Burlington were overcome in the latter part of 1884, and Commissioner Bogue decided on the percentage for each road of the business between the Missouri River and the coast. The Northern Pacific was given a monopoly of Oregon business as well as a subsidy of 7% of the San Francisco traffic, to prevent its competition. During the following year separate pools were created for the northern and southern lines.

In spite of the new organization, the position of the Southern Pacific still remained a very disturbing factor. With its southern line from San Francisco to New Orleans and its steamship service from the latter place to New York, it held a favorable position which it utilized to the utmost. It soon was carrying a great deal more than its share of the business of the pool, and objected strenuously when its percentage was not raised. The other lines refused to make any concessions, basing their action on the ground that the Southern Pacific was using its steamship line to cut the through rate, and that such competition was unfair and should not be recognized.

Other difficulties appeared in the subsidy to the Pacific Mail Steamship Company, and in the completion of the Canadian Pacific in 1886. The northern lines, and particularly the Union Pacific, felt that with the steamship line of the Southern Pacific they were receiving no commensurate advantage for their subsidy to the Pacific Mail. Then, too, the completion of the Canadian Pacific meant further competition and loss of traffic.

All these misunderstandings and disagreements finally led to a breakdown of the association early in 1886. A bad rate war succeeded, and it was two years before its effects wore off. Along with this breakdown of the transcontinental association went the dissolution of the Pacific Coast Association, a pool of the Pacific coast business of the lines east of the Missouri River. Voluntary railroad coöperation seemed to have broken down completely in the Far West.

When the Transcontinental Traffic Association was

restored in December, 1887, the Canadian Pacific was included and given a differential on San Francisco business. The Pacific Mail subsidy was continued, but at a reduced figure. The position of the Southern Pacific remained approximately the same. The whole procedure represented a compromise. While it settled the difficulties for the time being, even the most optimistic of its partisans could not contend that affairs were settled for all time. The transcontinental field had proven even more complicated than those further east.

CHAPTER XIV

The completion of the transcontinental lines was paralleled by the building of an immense number of smaller lines and feeders, which by the latter eighties had given the western railroad net the form which it retains today. The total western railroad mileage increased by over 40,000 miles during the decade, or considerably in excess of the amount which had hitherto been in existence. Some of the states such as Kansas, Nebraska, and Texas, practically tripled their mileage, while those to start construction at a later period increased their mileage from ten to twenty times.

Notable among the roads that have not been heretofore discussed, and that were completed during the latter part of this period, was the Great Northern. This road was originally known as the St. Paul and Pacific, and was involved in the early plans of the Northern Pacific, as its proposed connection with St. Paul. The line was never completed under these auspices, and when the panic of 1873 occurred the road found itself with two incomplete main lines—one from St. Paul north in the direction of the Northern Pacific, and the other west from St. Paul to a point near the Dakota boundary.

James J. Hill became the dominant figure during the seventies. Entering the employ of the road toward the end of the Civil War, he had gradually advanced himself to a position of power. When the road's connection with the Northern Pacific came to an end he saw his opportunity to acquire it himself. Not having sufficient funds in his own name he interested outside capital, and when the line was reorganized in 1879 as the St. Paul, Minneapolis and Manitoba, George Stephens of Montreal was president, and J. J. Hill was general manager.

Because of the Canadian capital the road directed its energies toward building north to a connection with the Canadian Pacific, then being constructed. At the same time the western line was not neglected, and after making connections with Fargo and Grand Forks, was pushed across Dakota. Its completion to the coast was problematical, particularly because most of its line would parallel that of the Northern Pacific.

Naturally Hill was not content with the position of general manager, and continued to buy the stock of the company as fast as he could raise the funds. 1883 found him in control, and the same year saw him assume the presidency of the company. At that time the road's two northern lines had reached the Canadian boundary, and the western division had advanced as far as Devil's Lake, Dakota.

Hill's principal ambition was to complete his road to transcontinental connections, but in the meantime he did not slight his northern branches, which were completed to junctions with the Canadian Pacific. In spite of the depression of the latter eighties work was continued on the western division. In 1890 other roads were consolidated and the company's name was changed to the Great Northern, and in June, 1893, the through line was completed to Seattle. A traffic agreement with the Oregon

Railway and Navigation Company gave it a Portland connection the following year.

In spite of the great effort which was necessary for the construction of a transcontinental road during a period of depression, Hill found time for the development of feeders. During the latter eighties a branch was completed to Ellendale, Dakota (North Dakota), and another to Huron, Dakota (South Dakota). The Montana Central was acquired and extended to Butte and Anaconda. The Eastern Railway Company gave a line from St. Paul to Duluth.

The activity of the Great Northern served to arouse the Northern Pacific, which had lain almost dormant since its completion in 1883. It made a strenuous effort to cut off the Great Northern and to remedy its dependence on the Oregon Railway and Navigation Company by building its own lines to Portland and Seattle. It also entered Winnipeg, and was able to run its own trains to Chicago by means of an operating contract. In these ways it improved its position to such an extent that it was able to offer extremely dangerous competition to the Great Northern by 1893.

The northern transcontinental situation was further complicated by the building of the "Soo"—the Minneapolis, St. Paul and Sault St. Marie, a Canadian Pacific line. This road was the product of the consolidation of local lines, and by 1893 was completed from Sault St. Marie via St. Paul to Portal on the Canadian Pacific. It gave the latter a line of ingress to Michigan, Wisconsin, and Minnesota, and served to complicate the efforts of the United States roads to maintain rates.

The Chicago Great Western was another comparatively new line, formed by taking over roads already par-

tially built. In 1892 it took over its Chicago-St. Paul
line, which had been completed five years earlier, and at
the same time acquired a line from Chicago to St.
Joseph, which it immediately finished to Kansas City. With
these two acquisitions it became an active competitor
for both St. Paul and Missouri River business.

The Chicago, Milwaukee and St. Paul did most of its
building and consolidating during the early eighties, at
which time it finished its lines across Minnesota and Iowa.
It stopped its building program entirely at the time of
the small panic of 1884, but revived it enough during
1886-87 to complete its road via Ottumwa to Kansas
City. Immediately thereafter work again slowed down,
so that it had stopped entirely by the end of the decade.

The Chicago and Northwestern covered somewhat the
same territory as the St. Paul, but was more active in
its operations. The early eighties found it in the Dakotas,
Kansas, and Nebraska. Its largest single acquisition was
the St. Paul, Minneapolis and Omaha in 1882. This line
had been formed in 1880 by a consolidation, of which the
St. Paul and Sioux City was the most important part.

The western extension of the Northwestern was built
by the Fremont, Elkhorn and Missouri Valley and the
Sioux City and Pacific, these two roads being operated
together after 1884. Construction was started late in the
sixties, but little work was done until the eighties; during
that decade the road reached Granger, Wyoming, Dead-
wood, Dakota Territory, and Superior, near the southern
boundary of Kansas. These extensions gave the Northwestern a strategic position in the West.

The Chicago, Burlington and Quincy consolidated
practically all of its branches into the parent system
during the years 1883-85—the Burlington and Missouri

River of both Iowa and Nebraska, the St. Louis, Keokuk and Northwestern, the Council Bluffs and Kansas City, the Hannibal and St. Jo., and the St. Jo. and Council Bluffs. During the same period it made connections with St. Louis. Most of its building was done further west, where it completed lines to Cheyenne, Wyoming, and to Billings, Montana, as well as numerous branches.

The only important connection which the Chicago, Rock Island and Pacific made during the early eighties was that to Kansas City. Later in the decade the road became more active and built as far west as Colorado Springs, at which point it made transcontinental connections by way of the Denver and Rio Grande. It also had dreams of a Gulf connection, and for that purpose started building south from Herington, Kansas. The Texas part of the road was to be built by the Chicago, Rock Island and Texas, which also started work. Unfortunately the panic of 1893 brought construction to an end at Fort Worth.

With these roads, a summary of the achievements of the important western roads by the latter eighties has been completed. Besides the larger and more significant portions of their lines, their branches and the numerous small independent lines which were built during the same period must not be forgotten. The majority of such enterprises were conducted in the first two tiers of trans-Mississippi states and in Colorado and the coast states. While they do not have the intrinsic interest of the longer lines, they were the real source of profit, both in the business they carried themselves and in the amount they drew to the main through lines.

While the completion of the trunk lines was the most spectacular feature of the eighties, the change in the character of railroading during the same period was just as important, if not more so. The emphasis was changing from the construction of new road to the efficient operation of that already built, and the manipulation of systems already constructed and in operation. For instance, the only important connection of the Southern Pacific which was finished after 1884 was the California and Oregon, from Sacramento to Portland. The generation of railroad builders was being rapidly depleted by death.

The competitive areas of the West became well defined during the eighties. The first, and possibly the most important, was the region which is bounded roughly on the east by a line drawn from Chicago to St. Louis, and on the west by the Missouri River. It was in this district that the first two western pools were formed—the "Omaha pool" and the Southwestern Railway Rate Association. Both continued in operation throughout the eighties.

The Southwestern Railway Rate Association was probably the most stable organization of its kind in the West. During the early eighties it had its share of trouble caused by the building of new lines and the ever-increasing demands of the old ones. Its form changed somewhat during the period, but still retained the outstanding characteristics of a division of traffic, supplemented by a money settlement of balances at the end of each month. Its most disturbing element was the Wabash, which made connections further east than the rest of the lines, and was consequently in a very favorable position in the event of any disturbance. The financial difficulties of the Wabash during the middle of the decade put an end to that source of trouble.

The "Omaha pool" finally proved too simple an organization to cope with the increasing competition, and so in 1882 it was put into a more definite and stable form as the Iowa Trunk Lines Association, with G. H. Daniels as commissioner. Both the plan of the organization and its troubles were very similar to those of the southwestern pool. The situation in both cases has already been discussed in Chapter XI.

The most noteworthy change in the two pools was their continued expansion because of the ever-widening field of competition. At a comparatively early date both groups expanded to include the competitive business of Kansas and Nebraska. It soon became necessary to make a disposition of the business that went to points further west, and particularly that which was destined for points in Colorado, Utah, and the Pacific coast.

Further expansion was carried on by means of subsidiary pools, and this form was adopted largely to simplify the bookkeeping and the rate-making. Colorado business was given into the control of the Colorado Traffic Association, formed in 1882, and Pacific coast business was given to the Pacific Coast Association, formed in 1884. Both of these groups were brought together under the control of the Southwestern Railway Rate Association, although the first was finally transferred to the control of the Omaha organization. The second ultimately went to pieces upon the failure of the transcontinental pool, since it could not maintain the integrity of its rates without stable transcontinental conditions.

The Colorado association was taken over by the "Omaha pool" upon its reorganization in 1884, after the trouble which led to the formation of the "Tripartite agreement." At this time all Colorado and Utah business was included within the domain of the association. After several changes in name the mother pool became known as the Western Traffic Association by 1887. In spite of its limited field the organization had continued to grow more important because of its strategic position, so that by the latter eighties it was the dominant western organization.

The competitive field of Colorado tended to come more and more under the control of the more eastern group of roads, as their members continued to expand toward the west. As early as 1879 the roads which actually entered Colorado had formed the Colorado Railways' Association, but by the middle eighties the encroachments of the more eastern groups had proceeded to such an extent that the Colorado organization went out of existence.

The roads competing for the carriage of transcontinental business were grouped in the Transcontinental Traffic Association, which has been discussed before. The organization was always weak, and upon its frequent failures the entire western rate structure was badly damaged. One of these failures was directly responsible for the breakdown of the Pacific Coast Association.

Competitive areas also existed in the upper Mississippi valley, particularly in regard to the corn of Iowa and the wheat of Minnesota and the Dakotas. These fields were covered respectively by the Central Iowa Traffic Association and the Northwestern Traffic Association, both created in 1882 and headed by the same commissioner. Both were rate agreements, enforceable by fines, and both worked with a moderate degree of success.

Texas competition was somewhat slower to develop than that elsewhere. A local pool was formed in 1882, but not until 1885 was it succeeded by the Texas Traffic Association, covering both local and through business. Water competition was especially dangerous, and so the railroads tried to control it by admitting certain steamship lines to the pool and giving them all the business in return for the maintenance of rates.

Besides the larger organizations there were innumerable smaller pools. Possibly the most important of these was the Chicago-St. Louis pool formed in 1882 to include the local traffic between these two points. In many cases where two or three roads entered a particular place, either a rate agreement was made or the traffic pooled.

Along with the freight agreements went similar passenger organizations. Sometimes, as in the case of the Chicago-St. Louis pool, they were lumped together. At other times they paralleled each other. The rate agreement, enforced by penalties for violation, was more common in the passenger than in the freight field. Naturally the passenger agreements were less important than the freight, because of the lesser value of the traffic included. Frequently rate wars spread from one field to the other.

As time went on the various pools began to overlap and to afford parallel competition. Numerous attempts were made to combine them into one large organization, but up to the time of the passage of the Interstate Commerce Act in 1887 all such efforts had failed. In practice some community of interests was obtained by the fact that a great many roads were in several organizations, and strove to produce harmonious action so that their interests elsewhere would not be affected adversely.

A certain amount of coöperation between the various pools was also obtained by an interlocking of pool officers.

Names such as Midgley, Carman, Daniels, Ristine, Faithorne, Tucker, and Bogue occur time after time as either commissioners or arbitrators of the various groups. This interlocking occurred in part because of the difficulty in finding capable men for these extremely trying positions, but it was also partly due to an effort to secure uniform management. These men ordinarily knew each other personally, and were able to produce some sort of coördination between the affairs of the various pools.

Primarily the pools were an attempt on the part of the railroads to stabilize rates. Early rates were as high as the traffic would bear. The charter of the Union Pacific specified "reasonable" rates, but the term was vague and could be interpreted only by an act of Congress or by judicial construction. Other lines were not limited even this much, and so they charged as much as the traffic would allow.

The building of additional lines soon meant that certain points were no longer controlled by a single road, and so at these places there was competition and the rates went down. Generally speaking, neither the railroads nor the shippers benefited by these conditions. The railroads lost by reason of the lower rates, while all shippers except those in the competitive area had to pay higher rates in order to make up for the drop elsewhere. Both parties were adversely affected by the violent fluctuation of rates.

Competition was further complicated by the practice which all roads soon adopted of giving extra rebates or lower prices to certain favored larger shippers. In this way they were able to secure large accretions of traffic, and even if the rate were so low as to be unremunerative it would be better than being forced to run trains without loads. This habit of making secret cuts became so universal that only the most insignificant shipper did not secure a rate lower than the one published. The size of the secret reduction depended on the power, ability, and influence of the shipper.

Because of these conditions the immediate reaction of both the railroads and the public to pooling was favorable. The railroads hoped to stabilize rates at a profitable figure, to stop secret cuts, and to divide traffic on an equitable basis. The public hoped that rate fluctuations would be eliminated and that competitive points would be made to bear their fair burden. As it turned out, neither side was entirely satisfied.

From the very first, it was evident that pools would never completely attain their objects. No road was willing to give up enough of its self-determination to permit its own injury, and without this final determinative power no pool could be thoroughly effective. As long as the central body did not have enough power to enforce obedience, no drastic action could be taken.

The continual change in western traffic conditions was also a disturbing feature. The building of new roads and the fluctuation of traffic because of changing economic conditions served to keep affairs in a constant state of flux. Nearly every road felt that it was not receiving the share of the traffic to which it was entitled, and consequently objected to the limit of its ability. Sufficient dissatisfaction necessitated a change. Sometimes this change evolved peacefully, but at other times it was preceded by a rate war.

Outside competition always remained a factor to be taken into consideration. As rates became more and more interdependent each pool was vitally affected by its connecting lines and by the groups parallel to it. Water competition was never met satisfactorily. These elements were directly responsible for the failure of the transcontinental association, and played their part with the other groups.

Even in the very significant matter of stopping competition the pools were by no means successful. Each road looked forward to a new division of the traffic and worked to secure a substantial margin over its old percentage in order to benefit by the new. It was true, that with minor exceptions, the published rates remained uniform. But secret cuts, instead of disappearing, became more universal. These rebates came to be given more and more to the large shipper, because it was his business that was the most significant in raising the total of the traffic carried. At times the pools themselves gave the large shipper special cuts in order to use his products to equalize traffic.

The small merchants and shippers of the West were further dissatisfied because of other railroad practices which they found distasteful. The railroads found it advantageous to localize their heavy traffic in order to reduce running expenses, conserve their equipment, and centralize their terminal facilities. This object was attained by giving certain favored towns and railroad centers lower rates than the rest of the country, and thus building them up as collecting and distributing centers. Naturally the small shippers of the neighboring towns objected.

Along with place discrimination went commodity discrimination. A single product could be handled more economically than a diversity of products, while at the same time this singleness of production made necessary the importation of a greater number and variety of other goods. The railroads were always embarrassed by the greater bulk of eastbound than westbound products, and the encouragement of a single product, such as wheat in the Northwest, made for a more complete utilization of car space.

Most railroad users soon saw the trend of the business, and tried to meet it as best they could. Small shippers did not object so much to the existence of discrimination as to their failure to benefit by it. While on the one hand they were willing to urge government control as a possible means of correcting the existing defects, on the other hand they tried to turn those conditions to their own advantage.

Groups of small cattle and grain dealers gathered together and tried to secure collectively what they had failed to obtain individually. Such associations frequently became large and wealthy, so that the railroads were forced to give in at least in part to their demands in order to secure their business. The conditions were never satisfactory at best, however, for every shipper or group of shippers felt that someone else was securing a better rate.

Town and city shippers moved to the same end through their chambers of commerce or through newly formed transportation committees. The railroads were either cajoled or threatened, depending upon the situation and the humor of the merchants. Every railroad in a given town might be threatened that unless it gave a lower rate all of the town's business would go to one of its competitors. A reduction by one line would be used as a bludgeon to secure the same concessions from the others.

Additional railroad or water competition might be aided with land and money on the condition that it would give lower rates than its competitors.

Notable among the city organizations was that of Kansas City, headed by Vanlangdingham, which did much to make Kansas City an important shipping point. Further west, J. S. Leeds was extremely active as head of a California shippers' organization. At one time this body subsidized water transportation in order to lower the California rate. Many of such committees were headed by former railroad men; Leeds had been formerly the general manager of the Missouri Pacific.

The weaker of the railroads proved the most vulnerable to such committees of shippers. These roads were in perpetual fear of being ruined by their larger neighbors, and were anxious to seize any possible advantage. Equal rates for equal distances would very frequently have driven them into bankruptcy, and the pools were forced to recognize this potential danger. Either they had to have a slightly lower rate to offset the poorer route, or else they had to be guaranteed a reasonable proportion of the proceeds of the pool. The latter solution proved the more acceptable under pool conditions, but did not entirely stop all trouble.

The real crux of the railroad situation during the eighties lay in the attitude of the consuming public, which was ultimately the most affected, and possessed of final power. The feeling of the public had been shown quite clearly during the granger movement of the seventies. This anti-railroad wave had receded somewhat in the subsequent years, but showed signs of revival during the eighties. Feeling continued to grow in spite of the fact that the decade was one of material prosperity, and railroad rates, along with the price of other commodities, showed a progressive decline. Discriminations of all types were resented by the consuming public. Exceptions in favor of persons, places, or commodities were only of advantage to a comparatively small number of persons, and the remainder of the population was unconcealedly hostile. Instead of such inequalities being reduced as time went on and more roads were built, they became increasingly great and complicated.

Non-competitive points were particularly bitter in their attitude toward the railroads. Whereas some advantage could be shown to points having several lines, none was evident elsewhere. Low rates in competitive areas meant that the operating income had to be expanded at the expense of regions in which a monopoly was enjoyed. Frequently the rate from a city to an inland town was as large or larger than to a city twice as far distant. The intermediate population did not feel the logic of the situation.

The most direct test of the efficacy of the railroads to the consuming public was whether or not they tended to lower prices. In general the public felt that the answer was "no," and that the reason for this situation lay in monopoly control. Each road controlled its own field and set its rates at will, while the pooling agreements tended to give the railroads of the country a strangle hold on economic conditions. It had to be admitted that rates had declined, but on the other hand it was argued that they had not gone down as fast as prices elsewhere, and thus had retarded instead of aided the country's growth.

State regulation was used as an ameliorative, but with little success. Sometimes the rates provided in the law were too high to have any effect at all. Frequently the regulatory commission lacked any real power, and was confined to the making of recommendations which were never acted upon. The position of railroad commissioner was new, and most of the men who were on the state boards were slow to act because they had no well-defined precedent to follow.

The attitude of the railroads did not make the enforcement of state regulation any easier or more effective. The roads tried to outwit the law and to make their rate structures as ridiculous as possible in order to discredit the state legislation. They even went so far in some cases as to threaten to stop construction unless the objectionable act were repealed. They maintained that such regulation was an unwarranted interference with private property, and made it impossible for them to do a profitable business.

In point of fact, the state laws probably had very little effect either one way or the other, except in comparatively few instances. A slight amount of trouble was created by the conflicting provisions of the various states. Not only was such legislation either inadequate, lacking in power, or poorly enforced, but by the very nature of things it must necessarily have been ineffective. State laws could control only state traffic, and the development of the railroad business was all in the direction of interstate hauls. Whether for better or for worse it was becoming evident that federal legislation was the only possible means of effective regulation.

The whole significance of the eighties in western railroad history was their importance as a period of transition from pioneer conditions to those of the present day. Problems of construction and engineering gave way to those of operation and manipulation. The widespread existence of pooling agreements showed that the network of rails was well on the way to completion, and that the new struggle was to be for the control of existing business rather than for the first entrance into new fields. State legislation gave way to federal regulation, and by the end of the decade conditions had become such that the present-day user of the railroad would have found himself pretty much at home. The pioneer had given way to the permanent settler.

CHAPTER XV

Labor is usually taken for granted in the discussion of early railroad building, not because it lacked in importance, but rather because it failed to become spectacular and attract attention to itself. The first important railroad strike occurred in 1877, and served to call the attention of the country to the fact that there was a labor problem, and that it might at times assume menacing proportions. The eighties and the early nineties saw the advance of labor to a position of importance, with a consequent interest in how it happened to be there and what it might do.

Early western railroad labor was exceedingly scarce. Practically every immigrant from the East had visions of his own home and farm in the newer sections of the country, and was not long content with anything short of economic independence. With the attractive terms offered by the government on the public domain, he was not long in fulfilling his dreams. At best he worked for only a few years on the railroads.

A certain amount of unskilled labor did, however, come from the East, particularly before the Civil War. Many boys, usually from the central and northern states, became dissatisfied at home and set out to make their fortunes elsewhere. New England furnished the largest quota. Here the soil was sterile, the families large, and transportation was poor, while at the same time the change in agricultural methods and products lessened opportunity. The ambitious sons of large families saw but little chance of success at home, and so began to consider seriously the idea of taking up some of the rich land of the Middle West, whose possibilities they frequently heard neighbors and friends extol.

The majority of the migrants were young men in their late teens or early twenties, who had not as yet become settled in the East. Sometimes they took along young brides, while in other cases they worked in the West until they secured additional capital, and then came home to get the girls of their choice. In many cases these young pioneers went in groups, with sometimes one or more going ahead to survey the conditions, and report on the most desirable place for settlement.

People from the same eastern community tended to gather together in similar communities in the West. This process was repeated continually as settlement continued to progress, so that there would frequently appear a whole line of western communities which would trace their ancestry to the same region of the East.

The eventual aim of all these migrants was to become independent. Those who had sufficient capital immediately secured land or started their own small businesses, depending upon their inclination. Those who knew surveying were particularly fortunate because the demand for surveyors continually exceeded the supply. Some taught school until they saved sufficient money to purchase land.

Those who were both poor and untrained furnished suitable material for all kinds of unskilled labor, and the newly opening railroads received their full quota. Unfortunately such persons constituted a fluctuating labor supply. The same unrest and ambition that had sent them West originally led them to change jobs frequently in order to receive more pay or better conditions. As soon as they had collected sufficient capital they took up land or started businesses of their own. Periods of depression sometimes brought some of them back into the ranks of unskilled labor.

A larger source of labor supply lay in the increasing immigration which began in the middle forties and extended throughout the fifties. The potato famine in Ireland and the political disturbances of Germany created a stimulus which resulted in sending great numbers of the inhabitants of these countries to America. Many of them remained in the East, but a considerable number saw the possibilities of the West, and migrated there at an early date.

The Germans tended to take up land and start farming in the newer states of the period—Wisconsin, Iowa, Missouri, and Illinois receiving large numbers. The Irish tended to remain in the East and settle in the large industrial centers, where they furnished the unskilled labor on the public works of the period. Some of both groups, however, took part in western railroad construction. The Irish were also a factor in driving out the native American unskilled worker in the East, and sending him West to recoup his fortunes.

The railroads of the United States had every reason for encouraging this immigration. If for no other reason, it was valuable for the cash fares that it would bring. The roads early banded together in order to facilitate the movement of the immigrants and to divide the proceeds of this type of business. Such traffic was ordinarily carried at reduced rates.

All roads, and especially those of the West, needed the cheap labor which the immigrant offered. Many of them had government land grants which might be sold at a profit, while at the same time the settlement of the immigrant would produce traffic which might be expected to yield a profit indefinitely. Even without government land, the railroads saw it to their advantage to settle these newcomers along the line of the road and thus create business which only too often was sadly lacking.

Many western railroads were so impressed with the desirability of immigration that they advertised extensively in Europe. Such immigrants as could afford it were sold land immediately, while others were promised work and were put into construction gangs when they arrived. Many times they worked for the road for a number of years as unskilled labor and then invested their savings in railroad land, settled along the line of the road, and afforded a profit forever. Surely such a process was most desirable from the standpoint of the railroad.

As in the case of the easterner, the European immigrant was never an entirely satisfactory source of labor. Many bought farms immediately; some moved from place to place; others went to work for other companies; while still others soon saved enough money to retire from railroading and buy their own land. In any event the railroads could never feel assured of a constant supply of labor at a price they were willing to pay. It must be remembered, however, that speculative roads, built mostly on imagination and hope, were in no position to pay a top-notch price for their supply of unskilled labor.

The Central Pacific was the one early road to solve its labor problem in a manner satisfactory to itself. The opening of communication with the Far East during the fifties brought with it an influx of Chinese coolies. Few in numbers at first, they gradually increased in volume as relatives and friends in China began to hear of the broader opportunities in America. Here was a supply of labor of which even the most hardheaded of railroad builders was forced to approve. Cheap, docile, hard working, the Chinese coolie gave the Central Pacific the most satisfactory labor supply that "big business" has as yet seen. Costs were reduced to a minimum, the turnover was very small, and labor troubles were non-existent.

The Central Pacific was practically the only road to benefit from Chinese labor to any great extent. Part of the immigration was brought over by the company itself. All of it necessarily landed on the Pacific coast, and the usual port of debarkation was San Francisco. The one big opening for unskilled labor at that time was railroad work, which was all controlled by the Central Pacific, so that it is not at all remarkable that that line received a large proportion of such workers.

Unfortunately for the railroads the coolies were not at all acceptable to other labor. Natives objected to the competition of foreign workmen of an alien race, which seemed entirely uninfluenced by the usual considerations which affected labor. Even the European immigrants were highly antagonistic, and when the Irish workmen of the Union Pacific came into contact with the Chinese of the Central Pacific there was considerable excitement.

In spite of the growing objections to the use of the Chinese, the Central Pacific continued to encourage this immigration as long as the road continued its rapid construction. Railroad men elsewhere were not unmindful of the advantages of such labor, and suggestions were made until well into the eighties that large numbers of Chinese should be brought to the East for similar work. No action was taken along this line, no doubt in part because of the fear of alienating other labor at a time when there was but little chance of filling all places with the Chinese.

The Burlingame treaty finally gave the United States a free hand to stop Chinese immigration, and Congress immediately took advantage of the opportunity. By that time, however, the greater part of the Chinese had dispersed to other occupations, and were no longer used extensively for railroad work. Their places were later partially filled by the Japanese, but this race did not like railroad work, and soon left for more congenial occupations.

Unskilled labor for western railroads was a difficult problem, but it was no more knotty than that of skilled labor. After all, any able-bodied man with proper guidance could grade track and lay rails, while it was comparatively few who could furnish the guidance or who could run engines or perform repair work. Even in the East it was very difficult to obtain skilled railroad labor, and frequently in the case of the very early roads it was imported from England.

Being a new country, the West had to rely upon the East for its supply of skilled labor. Surveyors, construction engineers, locomotive engineers, firemen, skilled mechanics, and managers of all kinds had to come from the East. Enthusiasm was practically the only thing that the first western railroads obtained locally. For the rest it meant eastern plans, eastern money, eastern brains, eastern material, and eastern labor.

Many skilled railroad men were of a roving nature and followed the general push of the frontier. An individual who started his working life on a Pennsylvania or New York road might well end it on the plains of Kansas or Nebraska. Periods of depression in the East saw many of these men start toward the newer lines of the Middle or Far West. It was from this itinerant group that the first western railroads received their supply of skilled labor.

Any adequate training for skilled positions was very slow in making its appearance. For many years the western roads depended on the East for their skilled mechanics. Any local products were more or less the result of accident. A man worked until he learned his job, and then if he was satisfactory he was promoted. The idea of teaching the man the job in any systematic way did not have any currency until the close of the century, and even then it was the exception rather than the rule.

In the same way as with skilled and unskilled labor, managerial positions depended largely on an eastern supply of men. The western roads filled most of their responsible positions with men who had "made good" on older and better established lines. As time went on, however, the West began to develop its own men who had worked up from the bottom, and by the last quarter of the century there could be found many responsible posts on the western roads which were filled by men who had received their experience west of the Mississippi.

The Civil War produced a considerable change in western labor conditions, both immediately and ultimately.

The immediate effect was to make labor exceedingly scarce. Able-bodied men from all over the country, including many of the newly arrived immigrants, went into the army. Many of these persons had formerly belonged to local militia companies, and were now mustered into the federal service. For the time being it meant that labor was almost impossible to obtain at any price.

The war made it highly desirable that the existing roads be made as effective as possible, and their importance in the outcome of the war can not be exaggerated. Especially in the North, with the closing of the Mississippi route, was it highly desirable that the railroad system of the country be made effective. Both North and South realized to some extent the importance of railroads, but both were slow in utilizing them to the fullest extent.

Both the North and the South found it essential that the armies make use of the existing railroad systems. The first development in both sections was for the armies themselves to take over and operate any necessary lines. This meant that a certain number of soldiers had to be deployed to do the necessary work. Usually a considerable number of experienced men could be found, but if such were not the case, then any available groups had to be used. Soldier labor was not a particularly desirable way of operating railroads. Even the use of volunteers who had knowledge of railroad work did not prove an ultimate solution. As the war progressed more and more railroads came under army control until at one time the northern armies were operating some 2600 miles. This situation meant that unified control by railroad men was an absolute necessity.

The development of Northern railroad control of con-

quered roads in the South during the war is a fascinating
study in organization. Before the end of the war all such
railroad activity was controlled by D. C. McCallum. A
complete railroad department had been constituted, with
sufficient men and materials to both construct and operate
all of the important conquered roads. The organization
was developed on a military basis, and greater speed was
acquired than anything hitherto known. Track-laying
and repairing was made a science, to be carried on with
machine-like precision and rapidity. In the South the
development of railroad control proceeded more slowly
and never attained an equal amount of effectiveness.

As soon as the war was over the government withdrew
from its railroad activities as rapidly as possible. Large
numbers of both skilled and unskilled workmen were
thrown out of work and had to look elsewhere for positions. Nothing was more natural than that a great number of them should turn to the traditional refuge of the
unemployed and dissatisfied—the West, where labor was
in great demand, both on the newly opening railroads
and elsewhere.

Both operating officials and labor went West in large
numbers, and there they left an unmistakable trail. The
most spectacular of their achievements was the building
of the Union Pacific. General Dodge, who had advanced
during the war from his former position of colonel, was
given charge of construction. A large number of his men
were former army men or employees of the army railroad service. He himself, besides his earlier training and
experience, had done a considerable amount of railroad
work while he was in the army. As a result the methods
and achievements of McCallum were transferred to the
building of the Union Pacific, and by the time that it

neared completion as much as seven miles of track was being laid in a day.

Former army men spread in the same way to other western roads. It frequently happened that men who had been identified with the army work were given charge of new western projects, and that at least a nucleus of their employees were former army men. Not all of these men had done railroad work during the war. Many of them had been in the army and had found difficulty in readjusting themselves to civilian life and so had followed the demand for labor westward.

This large increase in the available labor supply after the war was one of the important reasons that railroads were built so rapidly. Added to this was the surplus of capital which came into existence after it was no longer needed for war purposes. Then, too, the return of the army forced a great many people out of employment, particularly when industry was contracting rather than expanding, which meant that there was a large addition to the number of people going West, either to take up government land or to find employment.

Another post-war factor of importance was the increase of immigration. It had fallen off during the war period in spite of the passage of the only encouraging act in the history of United States immigration. War conditions did not serve to attract any large amount of alien labor, and so at the very time that additional workers were desired most ardently the tide from Europe reached a low ebb.

Immediately after the close of the war immigration again began to increase, reaching a high point of 800,000 by 1880. Again foreign labor supplemented that of the native worker, particularly in the unskilled occupations, and this new influx was used largely in the railroad construction of the seventies and after. It was during this period that the old German and Irish immigration gave way to that of other countries—Scandinavia, Russia, Italy, Greece, and minor European nationalities. By the nineties the character of the newcomers had changed noticeably from the northern Europe Nordic type, to the southeastern Europe Slavic and Mediterranean types.

In practice only a very small proportion of the immigrants were ever available for work on the western railroads. Their effect was more indirect, but just as important. The immigrant, particularly of a later date, usually settled in the East and worked in the mills and in the mines, where cheap, unskilled labor was needed. His lower standard of living served to reduce wages and drive the native workman and the older immigrant out of their former places. Many of these men moved west and started life over again under new conditions. The immigrant at least started a wave of movement which eventually reached the Far West.

The competition of alien labor was supplemented by increasing industrialization and by periods of hard times in the East. Farmers and farm labor were ruinously affected by the fertility of the virgin lands of the West, while many of the unemployed made haste to move further west to "grow up with the country." Many of these people were poor and had to work at least for a time at some manual labor before they could collect enough capital to buy their own farms or to start their own businesses.

The liberal homestead policy of the government tended to reduce the amount of time which it took for an individual to secure his own farm, but at the same time it still required a certain amount of capital to move, to prepare the ground, to buy seeds and implements, and to live until the first crop was sold. Many people were in too much of a hurry to start farming, and were later forced to work elsewhere in order to retain financial solvency.

The greatest western flood of population occurred during the latter seventies and throughout the eighties. Ministers, school teachers, farmers, and every other type of the population took part in this vast exodus to the West. Many of these, either because of inclination or lack of capital, worked on the railroads, at least for a time.

To these groups should be added also the unfortunate one of the unsuccessful western farmer. The scarcity of ready money in the West led many land owners to mortgage their property at excessive rates of interest, and frequently when the crops were poor and refused to yield an adequate return such persons were forced to dispose of their holdings and take up some other kind of work. The immense catastrophe of this kind was the drought of the latter eighties, which caught thousands of the farmers of western Kansas and Nebraska, who had gone too far west. Many of these men were forced to do something, such as railroad work, in order to make a living and to support their families.

Up to the last quarter of the nineteenth century, the railroads had little interest in their employees except as a certain necessary part of the machine. The only phases in which they were interested were whether the work was done satisfactorily and whether the rate of pay was sufficiently low. Any other factor was the business of the employee. This attitude was well stated by the president of the Chicago, Burlington and Quincy, who in 1892 wrote in regard to old age insurance—"American citizens should and will insist upon being paid full rates for their services; and they will provide their own pensions and superannuation fund out of what they themselves earn."

In spite of any abstract theory on the subject, the older individualistic concept of the relations between employer and employee showed signs of breaking down during the eighties. Such roads as the Chicago, Burlington and Quincy, the Atchison, Topeka and Santa Fe, the Atlantic and Pacific, the Northern Pacific, the Southern Pacific, the Texas and Pacific, the Union Pacific, and the Wabash began to make some provision for their employees outside of the actual necessities of the case. This movement generally took the direction of club rooms, recreation centers, library facilities, and eating houses. The railroads were beginning to realize that satisfied workers were the one good guarantee of satisfactory work.

Aid for hospital service was one of the important innovations which had its origin and growth during the eighties. Most of the roads founded such service on a periodic payment by the employees, but nearly all of them contributed something, such as land, buildings, or the money necessary for operating expenses. The basis for such plans was ordinarily a periodic payment by the employee of somewhere between twenty-five cents and a dollar a month, and the size of this payment frequently depended on the amount of his salary. Sometimes provision for a burial fund was also included.

The development of technical education was exceedingly slow. Up to 1900 little advance had been made, practically all roads depending on their employees learning the business through actual contact with the work.

Sometimes an apprenticeship system was used. Technical schools under railroad auspices were so infrequent as to be practically non-existent. Eventually this deficit was partially remedied by the development of the public school system.

The interest of Congress in the condition of labor dates from about the nineties, when automatic brakes operated from the engine, and automatic couplers were made compulsory (1893—went into effect in 1898). Ten years elapsed before any further action was taken, but then legislation became more frequent. Reports of accidents were enforced, the liability of the carrier in the case of accidents was increased, ash pans were regulated, boiler inspection was instituted, the carriage of explosives was safeguarded, and the maximum length of the working day was defined. The purpose of these acts, however, was often more the protection of the traveling public than the protection of the railroad employee.

CHAPTER XVI

LABOR ORGANIZATION

Labor organization with its accompaniment of collective bargaining and the use of the strike, was a product of highly developed industrial conditions. As long as labor remained comparatively small in numbers and widespread, it was disorganized. In consequence, it was not until the western railroad net was well developed that labor disturbances occupied any important place.

The first large scale labor upheaval, and one which served to call attention to the American "class struggle," was the railroad strike of 1877, which assumed sufficiently large proportions to threaten to tie up the entire transportational system of the United States. Its rapid spread, however, was due more to a similarity of conditions all over the country than to any feeling of solidarity among the employees, even of the same industry.

The depression of the seventies had led to a necessary curtailment of the expenses in all kinds of business. To the workers, conditions seemed to grow progressively worse, and when the Baltimore and Ohio advertised a ten percent reduction of pay in 1877 the firemen went out on strike. Through both persuasion and intimidation others followed their example, so that train movements came to an end. The employees of other roads, being in much the same position, followed suit, and the disturbances extended as far west as the Missouri River.

The workers had no organization, and so with the calling of state and federal troops the strike collapsed, although not before considerable damage had been done, particularly in Pittsburg. In itself this strike was not particularly important to the western roads, but it marked the opening of a new era, in which labor, more confident of itself, was to organize effectively and to fight its own battles.

The labor organizations which were later to become important had their origin in the sixties and seventies. During this period all of the more important groups of skilled employees began some sort of organization. Usually they had their beginning in periodic social and informative meetings, frequently with the idea of mutual insurance as one of their primary objectives. They soon divided themselves into two main groups—the discussional and informative societies, as opposed to those corresponding to our present day labor unions.

The first of these groups may be typified by the Master Car Builders Association, the Master Car Painters Association, the Railroad Claim Agents, the Railroad Purchasing Agents, the Railroad Traveling Auditors, the Railway Car Accountants, the Roadmasters Association of America, and other similar groups. These bodies never became labor unions, but remained only for discussional and fraternal purposes. They were interested primarily in the discussion of trade problems and in the adoption of uniform practices for their particular occupations.

The first of the important labor unions to come into existence was the Brotherhood of the Footboard, formed in 1863 to include engineers, firemen, and machinists; during the following year it became the International Brotherhood of Locomotive Engineers. In 1874 the position of Grand Master Engineer went to P. M. Arthur, who held it until his death in 1903. Throughout the first twenty years of its history the organization was officially opposed to strikes, although a few small ones occurred from time to time. Its outstanding feature was a benefit insurance system which originated in 1866 out of a voluntarily contributed fund for the benefit of widows, orphans, and totally disabled members. In 1867 a regular insurance system was adopted, which was made an integral part of the constitution two years later. In 1890 it became compulsory for all members under fifty.

The Order of Railway Conductors of America was organized in 1868 as a purely fraternal order, and with the exception of the Chicago, Burlington and Quincy strike of 1888, remained definitely opposed to all such disturbances. Its policy changed during the years of 1890-91, and this reversal killed the competition of its rival order, the Grand International Brotherhood of Railway Conductors of America, and left it supreme. Except for one year, the Conductors maintained an insurance system, but it did not become important until its provisions were recast in 1882. It became compulsory in 1891.

The Brotherhood of Locomotive Firemen was founded in 1873 as a mutual benefit association and did not take on the aspect of a labor union until 1885, in which year it become protective. Its insurance feature was established the year after the organization of the order, and was made compulsory four years later.

The fourth of the important groups was the Brotherhood of Railroad Trainmen, founded in 1883 as the Brotherhood of Railroad Brakemen. Its name was changed in 1890 so that it could include besides brakemen, train baggagemen, train flagmen, yard masters, yard foremen, and switchmen. It had an insurance feature throughout the entire length of its existence.

These four Brotherhoods were of somewhat similar origin and growth, and never became affiliated with the American Federation of Labor. Their later strength has been accounted for on numerous grounds—craft organization, the high training of the members, similarity of occupation and interest, good organization, central control, insurance features, moderation, business-like methods, reserve fund, and their strategic position. Whether any or all of these are the correct explanation it remains true that the Brotherhoods were destined to become the "aristocrats of the labor world."

Other groups of employees existed, and as time went on they tended to form unions. These lesser organizations came into existence for the most part during the middle eighties or later, and many of them were affiliated with the American Federation of Labor. Some of the important ones are the Order of Railroad Telegraphers (1886), Switchmen's Mutual Aid Association (1886), International Brotherhood of Maintenance-of-Way Employees (1887), Brotherhood of Railway Carmen, Brotherhood of Railway Trackmen, Switchmen's Union of North America, Brotherhood of Railway Bridgemen.

The early railroad unions emphasized the fraternal features, and particularly the insurance of members. The use of the strike as a collective weapon to secure concessions from the employers was of rather slow growth. Even in the general strike of 1877 the Brotherhoods took no part. There was a general fear on the part of the members that if the Brotherhoods took too vigorous action they would encourage the hostility of the railroad companies and would be forced to disband. As they became stronger they lost this fear, and tended to become more active in disputes affecting wages and conditions of labor.

Practically all of the strikes of the seventies were entirely local in their effect, and were universally unsuccessful. New men were immediately hired to take the place of the strikers, and if necessary troops were used to restore order. The railroads acted on the principle that they were bargaining with their employees individually, and in the event that any person did not like the bargain he could look for another job. The worker had neither a moral nor a legal equity in his job. As the *Railway Age* put it, it was "the working of the great law of supply and demand which it is useless for any man or set of men to attempt to resist by artificial means."

The one general strike of the seventies, that of 1877, was broken immediately. The western roads in general discharged any men connected with it, although in a few cases they advertised their generosity by allowing some of them to return. In a very few cases the roads concerned found it necessary to make certain concessions to the strikers. A strike of the Santa Fe engineers in 1878 because of a ten percent cut in pay was broken similarly; no violence occurred, but the militia was called out, the leaders arrested, and the places of all the strikers filled by new men. A similar incident occurred the same year in the Milwaukee shops of the Chicago, Milwaukee and St. Paul, and other incidents of a like nature might be mentioned.

The great need of the railroad employees, as of those in other industries, was a unified central organization which could assure permanence and stability, and back the local organizations in a time of stress. Various groups tried to take over this leadership, but the first to have any considerable success among western railroad labor was the Knights of Labor, established in 1869. This order both came into prominence and committed suicide in the middle eighties.

The small depression of 1884 had a similar effect to the one of the preceding decade. Men were discharged, wages were reduced, and discontent was general. At this time the Gould lines, centering in the Missouri Pacific, were a storm center. The component lines were over-built, over-capitalized, and under-repaired. Jay Gould was disliked bitterly in the communities through which his roads operated. At the same time the Knights of Labor were particularly strong in this same district, among the otherwise unorganized employees. All these factors combined boded ill for the future.

Wage reductions and discharges were begun on the Missouri Pacific in 1884. The Brotherhood of Locomotive Engineers was the first body to protest, and twice a compromise was arranged by a meeting of the officials of the company and of the union. This group of employees had a good organization, were highly skilled, and difficult to replace. Concessions were made that would have not been made elsewhere with a different group of men.

Conditions reached a climax early in 1885 when the shopmen of the Texas and Pacific, backed by the Brotherhoods, struck because of wage reductions. The strike quickly spread over the entire system, and even non-strikers refused to move the trains stopped by their fellow-employees. Traffic in the Southwest came to an abrupt stop, which meant ruin to the people of the district concerned. On the whole, the sympathies of the population were with the strikers because of their violent antagonism to Gould. The situation was serious enough to bring forth an offer of mediation on the part of the governors of Missouri and Kansas. A meeting was called which included representatives of both the company and the strikers, and an agreement was reached whereby the old wage scale was to be restored.

The victory of the strikers in 1885 came rather unexpectedly. Successful strikes were unique, and the employees began to feel a consciousness of power. The Knights of Labor, in particular, redoubled their efforts to unionize the railroad workers, and began to ask for the recognition of the union in collective bargaining. At the same time the position of the Missouri Pacific continued to become worse instead of improving as other roads were doing. More trouble seemed a foregone conclusion.

Early in 1886 trouble broke out anew. Neither side was satisfied with the effect of the agreement of 1885. The Gould roads continued to discharge men according to their own convenience, and to get work done outside of their own shops whenever they found it advantageous. The workingmen felt increasingly hostile to the arbitrary discharges, and felt that there was a conscious discrimination against the members of the Knights of Labor. The immediate pretext of the strike came with the discharge of one of the popular members of the Knights from the Texas and Pacific shops at Marshall, Texas. The men at that point immediately stopped work, and the trouble spread rapidly.

The Texas and Pacific was at this time in the hands of the receiver, who refused to make any concessions, or even to deal with the strikers. The principal demands of the Knights at this time were the right to organize and to be dealt with as representing all the workers, and a minimum wage of $1.50 per day for unskilled labor. Upon the failure of the receiver to take any action, the strike spread throughout the Southwest and all business was again stopped. Whereas in the preceding year the Brotherhoods had been found in favor of the strike, this time they were opposed, and had to be forced to leave work. The governors of Kansas and Missouri again offered to mediate the difficulties. Their offer was accepted by the company but refused by the strikers.

The strike soon came to center in St. Louis, and throughout the month of March traffic was crippled and acts of violence were not uncommon. Martin Irons, a local leader, soon came into prominence, and took control of the situation. By this time counsels of moderation were entirely unwanted, and Irons was only able to hold his supremacy because he was willing to advocate destructive action. Under his leadership the strikers planned to stay out until their demands were completely accepted.

In large part the success of the strike depended upon public sympathy, which the strikers felt they would receive because of the unpopularity of Gould. But as the strike progressed, public sympathy was alienated. The lack of transportation meant hardship, and people could see that the easiest solution was for the men to go back to work. The violence of the strikers was resented, while the willingness of the company to allow arbitration had a favorable effect. The tide turned definitely against the workers when the Gould lines refused to run any more trains as long as they were in danger of mutilation—which really meant until the end of the strike.

The strike in itself showed evidences of poor management and of the defects in the organization of the Knights of Labor. It had begun as a local issue and had spread in a haphazard fashion. At various times there were half a dozen semi-authoritative lists of demands made on the part of the strikers, including wages, hours, working conditions, the right of organization, and various other factors in varying proportions. To cap the climax came the leadership of Martin Irons and the widespread destruction of property. Irons, although a local officer, had taken complete control, and seemingly the central body of the Knights of Labor had no power to control the acts of its subordinates or to prevent unlawful acts.

The whole affair came to General Master Workman T. V. Powderly of the Knights of Labor quite as a surprise, but when he found out what it was all about he began negotiations with Gould. Progress was made, and finally he called the strike off when he understood that Gould was willing to arbitrate (April). In spite of this official action work failed to recommence. The local units of the organization felt their own independence and refused to have their action dictated by the central body.

At the same time that the strikers refused to return to work, Gould refused to arbitrate. He knew that the strike was practically broken and that public opinion was in his favor. Gradually the strikers were starved out, their places were filled by new men, and the operation of the trains was renewed. The workers were beaten so conclusively that for many years to come there were no labor troubles on the Gould lines.

More important than the immediate outcome of the strike was its effect on the Knights of Labor. The organization was discredited and began to decline rapidly in numbers and strength. Its place was taken by the American Federation of Labor, which was reorganized in 1886, and began to have its first large growth during this period. The Brotherhoods, however, were well established by this time, and did not affiliate themselves with the American Federation of Labor; they have continued to remain independent up to the present time, even though other groups of employees have from time to time been organized within the fold of the central body.

A notable proof of the unity of the Brotherhoods came with a strike of the locomotive engineers and firemen of the Chicago, Burlington and Quincy in February and March, 1888. The union men of other connecting lines refused to move the freight of the Burlington as long as the strike continued, and this action was sufficiently effective to provide an almost complete embargo. The differences which caused the suspension of work were finally compromised, but out of the disturbance grew a widespread strike of the yardmen and switchmen in Chicago. In this case considerable damage was done to property, and the strike was finally broken by the use of an army of city police and Pinkerton men. Ordinarily speaking, the Brotherhoods were very careful to avoid violence.

During the eighties the condition of labor was comparatively good, with wages advancing and the cost of living declining. As is usual in such a period, it was a favorable time for labor to organize and become strong, because it was at such a time that it was most in demand. The problem of organized labor was beginning to become acute, and the railroads were being forced to take cognizance of that fact. The use of conferences with employees and of arbitration and conciliation began to come into effect, with the result that many incipient disturbances were cut off at their source.

Economic conditions became poorer during the early nineties and by the latter part of 1892 retrenchment had begun to take place in the railroad field. Whereas in the few preceding years the result of depression had been almost entirely in the contracted building programs of the roads, now it was coupled with wage cuts and the discharge of all superfluous men. This condition, combined with the results of the panic of 1893, made labor generally unsettled, and a fertile field for discontent.

The youthful Eugene Debs was certain that the main possibility in the field of railroad labor organization was the development of one large central railroad union which would include all of the workers. He saw that while there were a number of strong organizations in the field there were a great number of men who were not affected at all, and that whatever solidarity existed came on a craft rather than an industrial basis. To remedy these defects Debs organized the American Railway Union, which was to include all railroad workers, and started to build up his organization in the Northwest.

The first test of the new body came in 1894, when it struck in protest against a pay reduction on the Great Northern. Traffic was practically stopped, and United States marshals and deputy marshals were pressed into service in order to assure the passage of the mails. Hill tried to divide the sympathies of the men by offering to restore the pay of the "old Brotherhoods," but the work of organization had been well done, and the effort failed. The issue was finally arbitrated by a committee of St. Paul and Minneapolis business men, and the decision in general favored the workers.

Encouraged by his success on the Great Northern, Debs transferred his efforts to the workers of the Pullman factories, and in the summer of 1894 that group went on strike for a restoration of wages. Sympathetic strikes occurred simultaneously on all roads entering Chicago which were manned by members of the American Railway Union. Traffic was stopped and the situation began to assume the aspect of a national crisis. In spite of the counsel of the leaders a certain amount of violence and destruction of property took place.

An attempt to keep order was made by the increasing of the Chicago police force, while shortly later a considerable body of state militia occupied the ground. The national government finally became worried, and a body of regulars was sent to secure the passage of the mails. With this assistance the Pullman company succeeded in breaking the strike. Debs was imprisoned and the American Railway Union went to pieces.

A noticeable change which occurred during the nineties was the development of a technique on the part of the railroads to counteract the organization of their employees. Union ringleaders were discharged and their names sent to other roads so that they would not again be employed. The roads gathered into organizations, as was the case in the Pullman strike, in order to be able to pool their resources, and to take common action. The employment of strikebreakers from the Pinkerton and other similar agencies developed rapidly. Usually these men were rowdies or criminals gathered from the slums of the cities, and given a free hand to do whatever they pleased in injuring the position of the strikers.

Also of note was the increasing participation in industrial disputes of the government in its capacity of repre-

senting the interest of the public. In both the Missouri
Pacific and the Great Northern strikes the interested governors had intervened to try to secure some sort of a
compromise. United States marshals and deputy
marshals were used widely to protect life and property.
State and national troops were used in case of severe
disorder.

The ordinary reason advanced for the use of troops by
the government was the protection of the passage of the
mails. The right of the men to strike was never ques-
tioned, and government officials were careful to maintain
an attitude of strict neutrality. On the other hand the
workers could see that when troops were brought in to
secure the passage of the mails, other cars and other
trains were also run, and that in consequence the effectiveness of the strike was greatly lessened, often leading
to its complete failure. In other cases where governmental authority was used labor discovered similar results,
and in consequence there developed a considerable
amount of bitterness on the subject.

Another cause of complaint by the workers was the
rapid development of the use of the injunction during
the nineties, and particularly in respect to its application to labor. For example, the court ordered in December, 1893, that a certain group of employees be restrained
from "combining and conspiring to quit, with or without
notice, the service of the road, with the object of crippling
or embarrassing its operation, and generally interfering
with the officers and agents of the receiver or their
employees in any manner, by actual threats or otherwise."

This particular injunction was later modified by a
superior court to allow the workers to leave their employment peacefully, but it still remained sufficiently

sweeping. In the injunction, railroad owners and receivers found a very serviceable weapon, and the employees saw a potent threat at the very heart of their right to organize, bargain collectively, and to strike if their demands would not be conceded in any other way.

The depression caused by the panic of 1893 saw a rapid rise in the number of unemployed, particularly in the towns and cities. Many of these people looked for the government to do something to relieve the situation, and most of them gave their allegiance to the Populist beliefs which were current at the time. Many of them moved from place to place in their search for positions, and in this wandering they were aided by the ease with which they could frequently avoid the payment of a fare. It was not uncommon that these workers in search of positions would band themselves together, and sometimes as many as from fifty to a hundred would travel together from point to point.

The most advertised scheme for giving work to the army of the unemployed was that of J. S. Coxey (Ohio), who proposed to use them to construct good roads at the expense of the state until economic conditions had improved to such an extent that they could secure work elsewhere. Together with Carl Browne (California) he conceived the idea of marching a large number of these men to Washington, there to make a personal demonstration in favor of his measure.

The march of "General" Coxey and his "army" to the national capital was one of the best advertised events of the day. The "army" made little impression on Washington, where its leaders were arrested for trespassing, and the "privates" were dispersed. The immediate effect of "Coxeyism" was unimportant; its significance lay in its position as a symptom of the same social and economic unrest which produced Populism.

The example of Coxey was followed farther west by half a dozen large groups and innumerable smaller ones. All of them tried to move east in the general direction of Washington, but their efforts met with varying amounts of success. The movement eastward was partly dominated by the example of Coxey, but it was also influenced by the hope of employment in the eastern industrial centers.

The general morale of these groups of men was very high and testified to the presumption that they were composed in large part of a high grade of skilled and unskilled labor, which was for the present unemployed and footloose. Naturally they acquired a fringe of less desirable elements—professional tramps, vagrants, criminals, and political and economic extremists. While the conduct of the groups was ordinarily beyond reproach, many towns and cities along the way feared their effect, and saw fit either to keep them out of town or to buy them off with supplies.

The one universal exception to the law-abiding history of the "Coxeyites" was their attitude toward the railroads. Populist anti-railroad feeling was very prevalent, and most of the armies felt not the least compunction in forcing a train to carry them or in seizing and operating a train—for were not the railroads the great monsters which were squeezing the life blood out of the country? Then, too, railroad transportation was the only way to cross the continent, and the unemployed had not the money to pay fares. It must also be remembered that riding free of charge was not unusual at the time, and carried with itself no feeling of moral turpitude.

The railroads were the subject of continual depredations. A train would be stopped by obstructing the track, and then the crew would be forced to carry the "army" into the next town. At other times the train would actually be taken over by the unemployed and run until stopped by a superior force. This ability to run trains was a significant evidence of the presence of skilled workers in the ranks of the "Coxeyites."

The attitude of the railroads varied according to circumstances. At times they carried the industrial armies in order to avoid trouble. At other times they resisted to the extent of pitched battles, even going to the extreme of entirely stopping train movements and of tearing up a portion of the track. In many cases United States marshals, aided by hastily sworn deputy marshals, were called upon to protect railroad property.

The general orderliness of the disturbers, combined with the anti-railroad feeling of the time, made punishment difficult. Most of the men who were rounded up by the police were freed in a very short time with only a warning. Now and then the leaders were jailed, and even in a few cases large numbers of the men were sentenced to a few days in the workhouse.

A movement of the unemployed such as existed in the industrial armies could not be permanent, and as economic conditions improved the armies gradually disbanded. By the fall of 1894 they had ceased to interest the public, and in a year or two they had disappeared entirely. The middle nineties saw a rapid industrial improvement, and when the war with Spain broke out the last excuse for an able-bodied man being out of work was gone. By the opening of the new century prosperity was again in full swing.

Congress took cognizance of the railroad labor situation for the first time in 1888, when it passed a law providing for voluntary arbitration of disputes and for the investigation of disturbances. The only time that the act was put into effect in its ten years of existence was when the President appointed a commission to investigate the Pullman strike.

The arbitration act of 1888 was repealed by the Erdman Act of 1898, which provided that upon the request of either party to a controversy the chairman of the Interstate Commerce Commission and the Commissioner of Labor were to try conciliation and mediation; in the event that this effort failed, the parties concerned would use arbitration, one member to be selected from each side, and one jointly. Provision was made that the findings of the arbitrators be accepted as final.

The provisions of the Erdman Act were used only once prior to the latter part of 1906. After that time, however, it had many successful applications, until modified by the Newlands Act of 1913. This law was on the same basis as its predecessor, but was expanded to remove objections. The outbreak of the war saw government operation and then the creation of the Railroad Labor Board. The developments during this period are a part of current economics.

CHAPTER XVII

EQUIPMENT

The material surroundings of railroad progress constitute a factor which is intensely important, and which cannot be localized. Improvements of track and equipment are elements of progress for the whole railroad industry, so that it becomes impossible to discuss them entirely in reference to the roads of one portion of the country. At the same time their significance is so great that a brief discussion of the elements most important to the western roads, and of those most influenced by them, becomes a necessity.

Railroad equipment had passed through its experimental stage and its early formative period before any railroads had been built west of the Mississippi. Locomotive engines of the horizontal type had been replaced by vertical, multi-tubular boilers, which served to produce a steadier supply of steam at a higher pressure, and with less heat. Wheels were being increased in number to distribute the weight and to produce greater tractive power.

Day coaches had been developed until they were being built for the most part on present day lines, although Pullman and dining cars were still unknown. Flat cars and box cars were in use, but specialized services such as refrigerator cars, oil cars, and mail cars were non-existent. Part of the reason for the late development of various types of car service was the lack of necessity. As long as all roads were short and the trains made frequent stops there was no immediate call for sleeping and dining cars. Until industries such as oil producing and meat packing developed on a large scale there was no reason for specialized freight service.

In the track, the early use of wood had disappeared before 1850, and iron had taken its place. The flanges to hold the wheels on the tracks had been transferred from the rails to the wheels. The first turn-table was used in the West in 1857. Automatic signals were put into use during the latter forties and the fifties. Practically all the essentials of effective service were at least in rudimentary form by the middle of the century.

The width of the early railroad tracks was governed by the assumption that such lines were to be used for public toll roads, open to anyone who would pay the rate. For this reason they were made of a width to accommodate the ordinary carriage. This idea can be traced down into the latter forties, even west of the Mississippi, and served in some degree to standardize the width of the track. An additional influence lay in the fact that many of the early locomotives were brought from England, and the American track had to be of the correct width as measured by the ordinary English standard.

The existing influences tended to standardize the width of the track in the North at the same figure as that of England—4' 8½". While this gauge was the common one, it was by no means universal. During the fifties there were at least half a dozen gauges, varying from 4' 8½" to 6' in common use in various parts of the United States. Significant was the 6' gauge of the Erie, the

4' 8½" of the New York Central, the 4' 9" of the Pennsylvania, and the 5' of most southern roads.

Western roads had a hard time deciding upon the track width which was most desirable. They founded their decisions on the cost of equipment and the comparative economy of operation, since there was very little idea that eastern and western lines would ever be linked together. The roads building west from Chicago naturally accepted the common northern gauge of 4' 8½", and the majority of other lines followed their example. Numerous exceptions might be cited; the Missouri railroads, for example, were made 5' 6" in width, and the California roads 6'.

The especial contribution of the West to the history of track width, was the development of the so-called "narrow gauge"—3' 6". Obviously, one advantage claimed for this width was the very evident economy in constructing the road bed and in purchasing equipment. More important, however, was the general acceptance of the idea that a narrow gauge road was better suited for mountainous country, because the tractive power would be greater for steep grades. Controversies on this subject were voluminous and bitter, and frequently remind one of the final mathematical proof which was offered to show that the early Baltimore and Ohio trains would not be able to make the grades of the track. The only fault of the proof was that practical operation showed entirely different results.

The advantages of a standard gauge for the entire country are fairly obvious, but failed to become important as long as the railroads remained short, disconnected lines. While the eastern lines were expanding and consolidating during the fifties, there was little effort toward uniformity because most of them were of the same gauge and there was but little interchange of traffic. Almost no business went north and south, so the southern roads were left to their own devices. In the West the Mississippi River seemed an insuperable barrier, so that it seemed to make little difference as to what the width of the track should be. A certain amount of uniformity was secured by the building of the Chicago roads and their connections.

The increasing amount of mileage and traffic during the sixties, as well as the influence of the Civil War, tended to produce uniformity. The development of through traffic made it exceedingly embarrassing to reship all goods wherever two roads connected. Cars of adjustable gauge were tried, but with no great success. Fast freight lines grew up, and threw the weight of their influence toward standardizing track widths, so that the duplication of equipment would not be so great.

In the West, the gauge of the Union Pacific had important effects. Its connecting lines in the east and in the west found it very advantageous to have the same track width. The original Union Pacific act designated the gauge as 5′, but in 1863 Congress was induced to change this figure to the standard width of 4′ 8½″, and the influence of the first transcontinental line was thrown in favor of the northern standard.

Another important factor toward the development of uniform gauge was the rapid improvement in bridge building. The first bridge over the Mississippi south of St. Paul was built by the Mississippi and Missouri River (Chicago and Rock Island), and was comparable in importance to the Niagara suspension bridge, finished about the same time. The first contracts were let in 1853, and the entire 1535 feet of bridge was opened for traffic three years later. It marked the beginning of a new era in western transportation, even though it was another decade before an additional bridge was opened.

A bridge over the Mississippi meant a new trend in western traffic, and was particularly objectionable to all persons interested in river business. At first the bridge was "accidentally" burned, then rebuilt, and then the status of the whole affair was brought before the courts. The contention that it obstructed river traffic and was a public nuisance was not sustained. The work was found vulnerable, however, on the side of authority for its construction. It was inter-state in nature and so was finally forced to secure the approval of Iowa, Illinois, and the United States. Protracted litigation seriously hampered the company and finally drove it into bankruptcy, but the bridge remained, being rebuilt during the sixties.

The bridging of the Mississippi was undoubtedly the most important single influence toward gauge standardization on the roads west of the river. In the sixties several new structures were put into place, and before the end of the decade it only remained a question of time until all connections with the East would be made by rail. Soon after the Civil War the railroads of Missouri changed their track to standard gauge, and other roads followed suit. The Texas roads were the longest to hold out, not changing their gauge to standard until through connections were finished in the seventies.

The most persistent variation was that of the narrow gauge roads, and particularly the Denver and Rio Grande. Throughout the seventies there was an acrimonious debate as to the comparative advantages of narrow and

standard gauge roads, but by the early eighties it was
generally admitted that the standard gauge was at least
necessary in practical railroading. The Denver and Rio
Grande at first laid a third rail in order to accommodate
connecting lines, but gradually it began to widen its
track, so that by 1890 its entire line, including the Denver
and Rio Grande Western, was standard. Other narrow
gauge roads were also widened, although some still remained.

By the middle eighties the use of standard gauge was
universal north of the Ohio and west of the Mississippi.
The South was slower in becoming standardized because
of the post-war depression and because very little traffic
moved north and south. It came into line in 1886 when
by common consent the whole southern network was
changed to 4′ 9″. This width agreed with that of the
Pennsylvania Railroad, and the extra half inch was of
very little significance.

Along with the standardization of gauge came the improvement of the track itself. Iron had replaced wood
at an early date, but its wearing qualities were not entirely satisfactory. Experiments with steel were carried
on during the early sixties, notably by the Pennsylvania,
but at that time the cost was almost prohibitive. During
the decade the perfection of the Bessemer process made
steel available for commercial purposes, but for the time
being its great cost made it available only for the more
heavily traveled portions of track.

The earliest user in the West was the Chicago, Rock
Island and Pacific, which experimented with some of
the new rails in 1865, at a price of $234.38 a ton. The
trials were successful, and so steel gradually replaced
iron on the main line. The entire main line was changed

by 1880, being the first all steel track from Chicago to the Missouri River.

Steel production in the United States was begun in 1867, but the price was prohibitive for such extensive use as on the railroads. Not until after the depression of the seventies were steel rails introduced in any large quantity, but after the process was started it was carried on with great rapidity. *Poor's Manual* estimates that by 1881 about one-third of the railways of the United States had steel rails. The transition was practically completed in the course of the decade.

The introduction of steel rails made possible increased traffic and heavier equipment. Vice versa, the heavier cars and engines, and the increasing traffic produced heavier rails and better road bed. Many roads, such as the Santa Fe, found it necessary to practically rebuild their main lines during the course of the eighties in order to make provision for the increased weight of traffic carried. Many of the important lines were double tracked because of the vast increase in the amount of business.

Increased traffic, longer hauls, and more interchange of business served to call attention to the situation in respect to time standards, as well as to that of gauge. Prior to 1870 there was no attempt to secure any commonly accepted standard of time. Each important center had its own "sun time," which was accepted by the surrounding country. The railroads usually accepted the time standard of their most important terminus, although sometimes they had independent times of their own. The result was a condition which was little less than chaotic. Time varied between road and road, between town and town, and between road and town, so that adequate connections were absolutely impossible.

The idea of standardizing time was one which should have had ready acceptance, but it was held back by the lack of a champion. Such an exponent appeared in W. F. Allen, who had the proper medium for the expounding of his views when he founded the *Official Traveler's Guide*. In 1872 a gathering of railroad managers tried to correlate the time and the train schedules of their respective roads. The benefit of this action to everyone concerned was so apparent that future similar meetings were at once determined upon.

Out of this first gathering grew the General Time Convention, which met regularly after 1874. Gradually the sentiment for a definite standard of time which applied to the entire United States and Canada became so universal that its existence could no longer be ignored. When the convention proposed such action in 1883 and referred it to the various roads for final action, it was accepted almost unanimously.

The time system adopted in 1883 is the one of today. Zones were created in such a fashion that there was an hour's difference between the meridians of 75, 90, 105, and 120. The time changed halfway between these meridians, and the whole zone went by the same standard. The General Time Convention, which had sponsored the change, was consolidated with the Southern Railway Time Convention in 1886, and in 1891 became the American Railway Association. Its activities were increased to include a discussion of signals, car rules, movements of trains, and safety appliances.

The use of standard time was accepted immediately by all sections of the country, in spite of the fact that it had no governmental authorization. Congress did not act until March 16, 1918, at which time it made the railroad standard legal in the act which established "daylight saving." The provision calling for the annual advancement and retardation of the time was repealed the following year, but the remainder of the act continued in force.

Increased traffic and the development of through business also implied a more specialized equipment on the part of the railroads. In the passenger field, for example, day coaches were moderately satisfactory as long as the main traffic was local. Longer trips by the average passenger, and faster time with less stops by the train, made necessary some provision for eating and sleeping during the course of the trip.

The first additional equipment was the sleeping car, which developed from the bunking car which was used to some extent to house the labor of various roads. The Chicago and Northwestern used sleeping cars as early as the latter fifties, but they did not become common until Mr. Pullman had perfected them on a commercial basis. The Chicago and Alton claims to have used the first Pullman car in 1859 from Bloomington to Chicago. At that time many people considered it a white elephant, but it soon proved its utility and value.

Dining cars were a later development and were not introduced on the western roads until the latter seventies. The railroads had always made provision for stops at meal time, and considerable revenue was produced by the station restaurants or by the granting of eating-house concessions. In consequence it took considerable length of time both to develop the necessary equipment and to prove to the railroads that it was desirable.

The development of the mail service may well be considered as a part of the discussion of passenger equipment. The Hannibal and St. Jo. claims the honor of the idea of the postal car. In 1858 it fitted out a car so that the mail could be sorted en route, in order to hasten its final delivery; the primary object was to expedite the progress of the overland mail. The first real postal car, built for the purpose, was put into operation by the Chicago and Northwestern in 1867 on its Council Bluffs line.

Freight equipment had its first great development under the auspices of the fast-freight lines which flourished throughout the sixties and seventies. During the eighties the railroads began taking over their own freight service, and the private lines were gradually driven out of business. The precedent of privately owned special equipment had been established, however, and much of it remained in the hands of independent companies or of large private shippers.

Special stock cars came into existence at the time of the great growth of the cattle business during the seventies and early eighties. This business became so important and the necessity for prompt shipment so great that many of the roads established the practice of running fast all-cattle trains on regular passenger train schedule. Of course provision had to be made for the feeding and watering of the stock en route; employees of the shipper were given this privilege, and gradually the number which could attend each carload was made uniform.

The development of the cattle business made it extremely desirable that large packing centers be established, both for the more economic handling of the meat and for the convenience of the railroads. Centralization meant inevitably that some way for shipping the finished product had to be devised. As late as the seventies it was impossible to ship meat products any considerable distance because of the danger of their spoiling.

Experiments with refrigeration for railroad use were carried on continuously throughout the sixties, but it was not until 1872 that the first successful shipment took place. Another fifteen years elapsed before refrigeration had proven a practical success and it was certain, for example, that southern and western garden truck and fruit could be consumed in New York City. The main difficulties encountered were the construction of sufficiently air tight cars, the provision for icing, the separation of the products so they would all be chilled, and the proper balancing of the car in the case of meat hung from the ceiling.

The development of the refrigerator car, combined with the invention of the tin can, made meat packing a national industry. The Chicago and Kansas City packers, who had already driven out all local competition, now expanded to cover a national field, and soon dominated the entire industry. Coöperation between the two centers, with the virtual fixing of prices, was not long in coming.

All these improvements in track and equipment meant larger and faster trains. In 1876, centennial year, a passenger train ran from New York to San Francisco (3200 miles), in 81 hours and 28 minutes, furnishing a practical demonstration of the vast advance of the preceding years. Train service had become comparatively good by the decade of the eighties. Further strides were made with the introduction of automatic electric signals.

Increased speed, particularly with heavy trains, increased the importance of brakes, and during the eighties railroad men were particularly interested in this kind of equipment. The early hand brakes and rudimentary air brakes had soon proved entirely unsatisfactory. The operation of a brake on each car necessitated a considerable number of employees, while at the same time the lack of unity in action produced a bumping of cars, and flat wheels on the cars that were braked too rapidly.

The first important improvement came in 1872, when George Westinghouse patented his automatic, high pressure, triple valve air brake. A reservoir of air was installed on each car, and the engineer could operate the whole appliance as a unit. This change obviated many of the former difficulties and for a time was satisfactory. With the increasing of the length and weight of the trains, however, it became evident that there were still some defects to be remedied. The trials held by the Master Car Builders Association at Burlington in 1886-87 showed that the braking process was entirely too slow and that the back part of the train ran into the front, due to the slower application of the brakes.

The introduction of electricity at about this time offered a possible improvement. In 1888 electrically operated brakes were used with satisfactory results. At about the same time Westinghouse improved his automatic air brake to such an extent that he was able to brake a train of fifty cars in two seconds. With these two developments the railroad train brake entered the modern era, and there was no longer any fear that equipment would ever become too heavy to be handled satisfactorily.

The development of brakes and automatic coupling devices proceeded so rapidly that in 1893 Congress ordered that all trains engaged in interstate traffic be equipped with automatic couplers and with brakes which operated from the engine for the whole train, such improvements to be made by January 1, 1898. This act was later made more strict, and supplemented by other safety legislation—notably concerning engine ash pans and boilers, and the carriage of explosives. Also the Interstate Commerce Commission was given authority and an appropriation in 1906, 1911, and 1913 for the investigation of automatic signals and similar devices.

Electricity proved both an asset and a liability to the railroads. It was immensely valuable in all kinds of lighting, braking, and signalling, but at the same time produced new competition in the street car and the interurban. Thomas Edison put his first electric railway in operation at Menlo Park, New Jersey, in 1880, and in 1887 the first successful street railway was opened at Scranton, Pennsylvania. New York City opened the first elevated railway before 1880, but it was quite a number of years before it was electrified. Immediately, of course, electricity did not offer any serious competition to the steam railroad.

The telegraph was developed at practically the same time as the railroad, and was a very valuable adjunct. By nature it was a monopoly, and the various telegraph lines tended to consolidate. The most important of such consolidations was in 1881, when the Western Union, controlled by Gould, absorbed the Atlantic and Pacific and the American Union by an exchange of stock. Two years later the Mutual Union was added, which gave an almost complete monopoly of the field.

In general the period of the eighties saw a transition from primitive to present day conditions of railroading. By 1890 the present day shipper, traveler, or railroad man would have felt at home in the midst of the existing conditions. Outside of refinements and enlargements, the most significant change of more recent times has been the electrification of certain terminals and of some strips of road. A few minor improvements, such as the gasoline hand car, the all steel train, and the better control of traffic, have also been added, but in the main the present day railroad system had been developed by the latter eighties.

CHAPTER XVIII

THE RAILROADS AND WESTERN SETTLEMENT

The building of western railroads and the advance of settlement went hand in hand. While the expansion of the American people had been rapid before railroads came into existence, it became still more rapid. The building of the transcontinental lines, in particular, ushered in a period of expansion which was greater than anything which ever preceded it.

Railroads first began to reach the Mississippi during the fifties, and before the end of the decade were built well across the first tier of trans-Mississippi states. By the outbreak of the Civil War they had reached the farming frontier, and had caught up with the important advance of settlement. Future building was to put them in advance of the main body of settlers, and was to place them in the position of pioneers in the opening of the Far West.

The railroads did their part in helping to fill up the first tier of states, which became fairly well settled by the end of the fifties. At the same time a thin trickle of settlers pushed still farther west—to Kansas and Nebraska and to the Pacific coast. The discovery of gold in California proved a very effective incentive, and was succeeded by the discovery of precious metals in Colorado, Utah, and Nevada during the latter fifties and early sixties. At the same time the Kansas-Nebraska troubles served to advertise those territories and to draw considerable numbers of people to the Middle West. The immigration of miners, traders, and settlers soon became a steady stream across the plains.

These new settlers were usually in advance of the government surveys, and while some of them were able to acquire their land legally by preëmption, a great number of them merely "squatted," hoping that the government would confirm them in their possessions at some later date. Such action proved exceedingly embarrassing to the federal authorities, who were averse to unauthorized settlement, and yet did not feel willing to eject any large number of people from the public domain.

The advancing tide of immigration served to push back the Indians, and the federal government was forced to take cognizance of the situation. The "permanent" frontier was once more proved inadequate, and new Indian treaties moved the tribes farther west. Naturally the Indians were dissatisfied with the situation in which they found themselves, and objected violently to their further removal. Trouble was continuous on the frontier.

Increasing overland traffic necessitated better transportation and the old route around the Horn soon proved inadequate. The Panama route was opened in the middle fifties by the completion of the railroad across the isthmus. Connections were made at each end by the Pacific Mail Steamship Company. Wagon traffic over the continent also increased in volume, being aided by the establishment of the overland mail in 1858 with its numerous stations. From this year until the completion of the Union Pacific in 1869 the overland traffic continued to increase with great rapidity.

The railroads had but little part in the transcontinental business of the fifties. The Hannibal and St. Jo. was the greatest beneficiary, hauling mail and freight to the end of its line, on the way to the coast. Up to 1860 this was the only road to reach the Missouri River, and owing to its excellent position secured a monopoly of the carrying of goods from the Mississippi to the Missouri on the way to the Far West.

The Civil War marked a very definite change in conditions in the West. For the time being immigration was lessened, giving the railroads a chance to secure an advantage in the race for the Far West. At the same time federal legislation prepared the ground for the expansion of the future. The Homestead Act of 1862 reduced the cost of land to almost nothing. The chartering of the Union Pacific, and later of other land grant roads, gave promise of the eventual completion of transcontinental railroad connections.

Railroad work was not entirely stopped during the course of the war, and immediately thereafter was pushed with vigor. The Union Pacific was completed in 1869, while other lines began jutting out into the territory which the Indians had been assured was to be theirs forever. By this time the railroads were beginning to be built entirely in advance of settlement, and many of the roads went through regions to which the settlers had not yet penetrated. In part, the government land grant policy was responsible for this rapid construction.

The influence of the railroads in encouraging settlement in the new West can hardly be overestimated. The Union Pacific, for example, had an influence along the entire line of its road, and from Montana to New Mexico. Before it reached Wyoming in 1867 there were almost no settlements, but within a year the region was considered well enough populated to permit it to be made a territory (July 25, 1868). Other factors entered into the situation, but did not entirely detract from the significance of the rapid increase in population.

The Indians naturally viewed with alarm the continued extension of the railroads and the rapid influx of miners and settlers, and retaliated in the only manner which they knew—war. In November, 1866, the Union Pacific was sufficiently advanced to begin carrying the overland mail to Fort Kearney, and during the same year there was an outbreak of the Sioux in the region of the fort. It was followed by disturbances by the Cheyenne and Arapaho tribes of Colorado and Kansas. Army campaigns of the following year were victorious, and peace was made in 1868. This action really constituted only a lull in the fighting, for no permanent pacification had been effected.

The nation-wide celebration which marked the completion of the Union Pacific was the signal for the attack on the remainder of the public domain. The Indians still remained, but Generals Sheridan and Sherman reduced them to submission by the early seventies. During this period the railroads were making secure the conquest of the second tier of states, while individual lines were beginning to push still farther west in the wake of the Union Pacific. Railroad construction and settlement progressed together, and each reacted upon the other.

The panic of 1873 slowed both the railroad construction and the advance of population, but when prosperity returned, both movements reached their height. The completion of the transcontinental roads during the early eighties brought with it the conquest of the last frontier and destroyed the "Indian country" forever. Incidentally it also destroyed the possibility of any future serious Indian trouble. The frontier, which had held with but few changes from 1850 to 1880, was completely annihilated.

The remarkable expansion which occurred during the eighties can best be shown in a comparison of the census population maps of 1880 and 1890. In the former, the old frontier can still be seen in fairly definite form. In the latter, strips of settlement have completely united the East and West, so that the frontier, which had existed since the earliest settlements in America, had disappeared.

The part of the railroads in the disappearance of the frontier was mainly one of acceleration. After the Civil War many of the roads were in advance of the population and served to hasten the settlement of newly opened areas. It was due to their opinion of the value of particular districts and of particular locations that some of the country developed before the rest, and that favored towns became important. They pointed out the direction of the future development of the West.

The most obvious interest of the railroads was the carrying of settlers, both for the fares involved and for the additional traffic which settlement would mean. Before the coming of the railroads the ordinary progress of the frontier was slow—trappers were followed by woodsmen and miners, and then by settlers, who at first came in small numbers. With the addition of the railroad this process was immensely hastened because of the lesser initial hardships. Communication assured the new settler supplies and news from the East, and also made it inevitable that there would soon be other settlers, bringing with them companionship and an increase in land values. This lessening of frontier hardships meant the inclusion of groups which had never before been willing to risk the terrors of the wilds.

The new country of Kansas, Nebraska, and the Dakotas was particularly suitable for rapid settlement and cultivation because of its very nature. Hills and trees were both scarce, so that it was not necessary to devote a year or more to clearing the land. Plowing and planting could start immediately. In consequence, new settlers poured in by the thousands, including everyone from land speculators to school teachers and salesmen. Land was practically free, and everyone saw the opportunity to become independent, even if only by land speculation. The railroads took these prospective citizens and literally sprayed them over the land.

The laborers which the railroads employed also had a habit of leaving their jobs and taking up land. Many of them were working for that purpose, and as soon as they had saved enough money they quit their places. Others came into contact with excellent land in the course of their work and were persuaded by its excellence to leave their employment and start to work for themselves.

The railroads were one of the big industries to encourage immigration. They supplemented state agencies for this purpose by agencies of their own, and advertised extensively the advantages of the West. Prospective immigrants would be encouraged to leave their native land and told how to secure their passports and ocean transportation. When they landed in the United States they would be met by other railroad agents, directed as to the proper trains to take, given special rates, and settled along the line of the most active agent's road,

In this way the German and Irish immigrants were handled during the fifties. Then came the Swedes, Norwegians, Danes, Poles, Russians, Italians, and Greeks. The period in which a particular group or a particular nationality came to America can be estimated with a fair degree of accuracy by observing the part of the West in which it settled. Normally the people of any nation or race tended to settle near together.

One of the important influences in causing the railroads to encourage immigration was their possession of large land grants. While some of the roads held portions of their grants for future speculative profits, the majority sought to sell as soon as possible. Such sales furnished much needed ready capital and at the same time built up the traffic along the line of the road. In practically every case where it was possible to sell the land at a reasonable figure, the traffic to be gained was more important than any possible later increase in the value of the land.

Railroad land was advertised extensively both in this country and abroad. Its price ordinarily ranged from $4 to $20 an acre, depending upon its location and fertility. Sales were slowed down by the competition of government homestead land, so that the railroads had to be able to show compensating advantages for their own possessions. Their biggest attraction was that their land always had good transportational facilities. Usually it was of good quality, because the road had seen to that matter when it had surveyed the route. In most cases a partial payment plan was used, so that the cost of the land could be spread over a number of years.

The first foreign railroad land agencies were carried on by the combined efforts of several roads; notable among these joint agencies was the National Land Company. When Jay Cooke took hold of the Northern Pacific, he was intensely interested in the possibilities of settlement, and began the practice of having his own agents, which he spread over the most of Europe. Glowing pamphlets described the possibilities of "Jay Cooke's banana belt"; agents abroad got the immigrants started; others in the United States routed them west with reduced rates, while still others conducted them personally to the land, even furnishing accommodations at times until they were settled.

Other roads soon followed the same general policy in order to encourage immigration and to have it settled along the line of the road concerned. Frequently the immigrants came in considerable groups, buying their land all in one region. One of their number was sometimes sent ahead in order to become familiar with the situation and to pick out the most desirable region. There was a great deal of competition between the agents of the various railroads in their efforts to interest such a person in their particular localities.

One of the most outstanding characteristics of all these settlers, both from the East and from Europe, was their unbounded optimism. Each individual expected to become wealthy, and each town was fully prepared to become the metropolis of the West. This attitude was well expressed by a correspondent of the *Commercial and Financial Chronicle*, who wrote (May, 1870),—"I expect to live to see a city not far from where Burlington, Iowa, is at present situated, far superior in population and permanent power to Chicago. The currents of trade get every year further south. Frozen lakes . . . must sooner or later kill the rapid growth."

The unrestrained enthusiasm of the average settler furnished an excellent field for the land speculator, and the railroads sold much of their land to such persons, either in the United States or abroad. These speculators tried to get control of good agricultural or timber land, mining properties, water power, and town sites. Frequently a railroad would form its own subsidiary land company, both for the sale of land and for the holding and development of valuable portions of the grant. Often the land or an interest in the land company would be given as a bonus on the purchase of stock or bonds.

Many of the railroads helped to advertise their lands by encouraging public speakers or by giving excursions. The Northern Pacific was the first road to make extensive use of public speakers. The excursion of 1875 on the Santa Fe was for the benefit of newspaper men. A similar excursion in November, 1880, headed by the Union Pacific, the Northern Pacific, and the Burlington, and including many of the land grant roads, gave a rate of a cent a mile in order that prospective settlers might see the land. Ordinarily the results of such expeditions were favorable, but now and then some unforeseen accident occurred or the sun refused to shine, and the trip became a failure.

The sale of large sections of land to land companies, either for future subdivision or for ranching purposes, did not occur until the latter seventies and the eighties. Possibly the earliest sale of this kind was in 1857, when the Dubuque and Pacific contracted in England for the sale of 6,000,000 acres. The amount actually disposed of was finally reduced to 500,000 acres, which was later subdivided and settled. As long as large portions of the public domain remained open for settlement and for the grazing of live stock, there was very little incentive to the purchasing of large tracts.

The development of the cattle business, combined with the end of the long drive caused by the encroaching line of settlement, led to the purchase of large sections of land both by American and foreign capitalists for ranching purposes. The railroads took advantage of this situation by disposing of large tracts of land which were unsuitable for agricultural use. The greatest gainers were the Union Pacific, the Northern Pacific, and the Atlantic and Pacific.

Foreign land holdings secured a considerable amount of attention during the eighties, and the Populist platform of 1892 took a strong stand against them. Most of such land had been bought from the railroads, which the Populists also opposed, by English and Scotch companies. The *Commercial and Financial Chronicle* estimated in 1886 that these holdings comprised 3,300,000 acres of land, accompanied by 672,000 head of cattle. Whether or not the figures are accurate, they indicate that these foreign holdings, usually in the poorer parts of the country, were never any great menace to the land poor of the United States. Single individuals, citizens of the United States, have owned two or three times as much as the entire foreign holdings combined.

The rapid settlement which occurred during the seventies and eighties soon began to exhaust the railroad land. The St. Paul and Pacific sold its last in 1880 (English firm), the Kansas Pacific in 1882 (American purchasers), the Chicago, Milwaukee and St. Paul in 1882 (Danish settlers), the Santa Fe in 1883 (Topeka firm; not including the Atlantic and Pacific grant), the Little Rock and Fort Smith in 1886 (New York firm). These were all of the more eastern group of grants. Some of the more westerly land, sometimes poorer in quality, was not sold by the end of the century, and some roads, such as the Northern Pacific, still retain some of it today.

The boom of the eighties settled the land faster than was altogether desirable. The price of farm products immediately responded by declining. This drop was somewhat offset by a corresponding reduction in railroad rates, but it still remained true that a large proportion of the profit from farm produce went to the railroads in the form of rates. It was a continual struggle for the man who was without capital to pay the cost of sending his grain to market.

Most western farmers were "land poor." Starting with plenty of land but little capital, they were never sure that they would be able to weather the coming year, and were entirely dependent on good climatic conditions. Besides the troubles which each individual had with his own finances, he also had part of the expense which the community had to meet in the building of schools, hospitals, churches, roads, and all things necessary for producing a real civilization in the wilderness.

Part of the difficulties of the western farmer were met by a surplus of capital in the East. Business was booming, and millions of dollars were available for investment. Nothing seemed more desirable than that a considerable portion of this money be invested in first mortgages on Kansas, Nebraska, and Dakota land. The number of companies doing this kind of business increased with immense rapidity, and most of them received capital from the East faster than they could find investments for it. Soon they were competing with each other for the privilege of making loans. Large investors bought freely of western municipal, county, and state bonds, while capital flowed freely into the railroads which were then being constructed.

The excess of enthusiasm raised the prices of western land to a figure which was entirely unwarranted when considered in view of the earning power. Land near Clifton, Kansas, which had earlier been considered worthless, sold in 1887 at $6,000 a quarter section, and there were similar situations elsewhere. Booms were common, and in their wake always came the land speculator and the fraudulent agent. Just how much fraud existed will probably never be determined, but there is no doubt that it was considerable.

The excessive amount of eastern capital which was available led the farmers to mortgage their land in large quantities in order to pay their debts or to make improvements. Ready money at low rates proved a very attractive alternative to scrimping throughout the year, and every true westerner was convinced that prosperity was only a matter of time. The size of a man's debts did not matter, because everyone expected that with the fertility of the land a payment could be effected a few years hence.

The bubble of buoyancy was pricked when the excessive rainfall of the eighties turned into a drought in the decade of 1887-1897. Crops were hopeless, and in some of the overbuilt portions of western Kansas and Nebraska no crops were harvested for half a dozen years. A failure of crops meant hard times and a contraction of credit. Interest rates went up. The farmers had already mortgaged their land and nothing was left but to mortgage their stock and buildings at the higher rate, thus increasing their burden of debt to hopeless proportions.

The *American Wool Reporter* investigated the farm mortgage business in Kansas in 1888 and found seventy-two companies operating in fifty-two counties, and that during the prior six months there had been a total of 607 foreclosures. 11,122 foreclosures occurred in Kansas during the years 1889-93. This condition was particularly prevalent in the second tier of trans-Mississippi states, although it also existed to some extent elsewhere. The farmer was finding it difficult to keep body and soul together.

The hard times in the West absolutely stopped any further expansion of the population for the time being. The western tier of counties in Kansas and Nebraska actually decreased in the number of their inhabitants. Values of land, buildings, and stock descended. Some of the settlers managed to weather the storm and to eke out a precarious existence. Others either returned east, went farther west, or entered other lines of work.

The depression was particularly bad in its effect on the railroads. All of them were overbuilt and dependent upon continued prosperity, while many of them were depending upon the future expansion of the West to make any profit at all. Some of the weaker ones succumbed to the strain immediately, while all of them at least contracted their building programs and started to economize. Construction was practically stopped during 1887-88, except for the completion of partially built through lines. Many roads did what they could to alleviate conditions by distributing food and seeds, in the hope that the depression would be brief.

Decreased crops meant decreased traffic, and so instead of rates continuing to decline, they started to rise. The result was perfectly understandable from the viewpoint of the railroads, which were trying to keep up their operating incomes, but it was a great hardship to the farmer who was suffering from the drought and could hardly afford to ship his grain at the old price.

The farmers who found themselves in the grip of bad conditions were confident that it was through no fault of their own, and so they began looking for a place to put the blame. The Populist movement, which was the outgrowth, was aimed primarily at the eastern capitalist, who it was felt controlled and manipulated the credit of the country to his own mercenary interest. Along with the eastern capitalists were placed the railroads, controlled for the most part in the East, as one of the chief factors in the existing situation. The results of this feeling of resentment will be discussed in the next chapter.

By the latter eighties the West had been settled and was well on the way to becoming a normal, prosaic part of the United States, differing very little from other sections of the country. In great part the railroads were responsible for the rapidity with which this change had taken place. The old romantic West had disappeared in favor of the settled, orderly, law-abiding country of the present. While this result had been the dream of statesmen for a hundred years, it did not take place without arousing the regret of men who had idealized the old Homeric West. As Emerson Hough wrote in the *Century Magazine*,—

"The West of steam-transportation has not so much impressed itself, and in reason could not be expected so to impress itself, upon its population as did that West when the wheels moved slowly and the natural difficulties to be overcome were so vastly greater for the individual. The old West begot character, grew mighty individuals, because such were its soil and sky and air, its mountains, its streams, its long and devious trails, its constant stimulus and challenge. That which was to be has been. The days of the adventurers have gone. There are no longer any Voices to summon heroes out in voyage of mystic conquest. It now costs not so much heroism, but so much money, to get out into the West, and it costs so much to live there. As a region the West offers few special opportunities. It is no longer a poor man's country, nor is any part of America a country good for a poor man. It is all much alike. Our young men of the West are as apt to go East to seek their fortunes as to try them near at home. There is no land for the free. America is not American."

CHAPTER XIX

The "granger movement" left a legacy of resentment against the railroads which continued and even expanded during the prosperous period of the eighties. It did not again become openly violent, however, until the depression of the latter eighties and early nineties. The Popuist movement merely served to give expression to a feeling which had lain dormant for a decade and a half.

The changed attitude was particularly apparent in the financial assistance which was given to the various roads. Private subscriptions were never very numerous in the West, but now they came to an almost complete end. Local aid had practically ceased to exist during the seventies, and was not revived. State financial assistance was also no longer given. The railroads were obviously and immediately under the control of eastern capitalists, and there was no indication that conditions would ever change. The farmers felt that any sympathy which they received was more apparent than real.

The same objections which the farmers advanced to the railroads in the seventies were even more applicable in the eighties. Railroads were large foreign corporations, controlled either by eastern or alien capital. Rates were made according to what the traffic would bear and not to the needs of the users. Personal, place, and commodity discriminations were in operation on an increased scale.

Rate reductions were ordinarily the result of war, and had little relation to the wants of the farmers. Even this source of reduced rates was becoming less common because of the increasing use of pools and rate agreements.

The underlying cause of the trouble between the railroads and the farmers was a lack of sympathy and understanding. The farmers talked about watered stock, excessive rates, and monopoly control, while the railroads feared governmental action and hard times. Neither made any study of the difficulties and consequent viewpoint of the other, and so they continued to work at cross purposes.

The changing financial practice of the railroads was a prolific cause of misunderstanding. In earlier times the sale of stock had been the most important way of securing funds. Now the use of bonds was becoming more and more important. Large numbers of investors had no chance to ever see the property in which they were interested, and felt that bonds were a safer investment than stock. Most of this business went through the large banks and trust companies of the East, and these concerns began to take a more active interest in railroad affairs. Members of interested banking houses were put on the board of directors, and were consulted with respect to management, rates, pools, and similar matters.

The increasing interest of eastern bankers in western railroads served to make the farmers absolutely sure that the bankers of New York were directly responsible for western economic ills. They saw an indirect control, not called for by stock holdings, by a group of people who had absolutely no interest in the West except for the amount of money they could make. It was hard to try to think of them as disinterested benefactors, which they certainly were not.

Western grievances as usual led to legislative action. Iowa established a railroad commission in 1878, California in 1880, Texas repealed her land grant act in 1882, Kansas passed a regulatory act in 1883, Minnesota added a warehouse commission in 1885, Arkansas repudiated her railroad debt in 1885, Nebraska and Dakota Territory created railroad commissions in 1885, Colorado had an extensive railroad investigation in 1885 and created a regulatory commission, and Oregon passed her first restrictive legislation during the same year. This large amount of legislation during 1885 was due in large part to the panic of the preceding year.

The Dakota Grain and Warehouse Commission was created in 1887, and during the same year was established the Oregon commission, which was given increased power in 1891. The Texas commission was established in 1891 under the charge of J. L. Reagan, who had been exceedingly active in Congress during the preceding twenty years in favor of restrictive railroad legislation. The powers of the Iowa commission were increased in 1888, Missouri secured a new law in 1887, while the Minnesota law was amended in 1891. All the new states of the period—North Dakota, South Dakota, Washington, Wyoming, Montana, Idaho, and Utah, had restrictive provisions in their constitutions.

Most of the acts creating railroad commissions, as those of the preceding decade, followed the precedent of Massachusetts, Illinois, and Wisconsin. The Massachusetts commission, headed by C. F. Adams, Jr., had a particularly significant influence. The writings of Adams were quoted all over the West as authoritative.

The development of state regulation produced a great variety of requirements and procedure. While there was some uniformity due to the copying of precedent, there were still enough variations to make the situation complicated. Both the railroads and the state commissions desired some sort of uniformity. To meet this demand, the commissioners of the various states began the practice of holding annual conventions in order to exchange ideas and to secure at least similar methods of bookkeeping.

The first convention of railroad commissioners was held in Springfield, Illinois, on July 20, 1875, and the second at Columbus, Ohio, in 1878. From that time on the meetings were held almost every year. After 1887 they were all held at Washington on the call of the Interstate Commerce Commission. Their mere existence aided materially in securing a measure of uniformity through the interchange of ideas and experiences.

At the same time that the various states were developing the control of their railroads, the federal government was coming to the point of action. Congress first turned its attention to the land grants with which it had aided various roads. Many of these gifts had never been claimed, and the rapid expansion of the seventies and eighties called attention to these large districts which were not open to settlement. At the same time the anti-monopoly and anti-railroad feeling did not lead people to think more leniently of a situation in which certain roads, which might never be built, could hold land in spite of the desires of actual settlers.

The original terms of the acts had provided that if the roads were not completed within a specified term of years the land would automatically return to the public domain. The Supreme Court nullified this provision when it decided in Schulenburg v Harriman (1874) that the grants were made *in praesenti*; the title passed immediately upon the making of the grant, even though subsequent actions were necessary in order to give precision to the title and to attach it to particular tracts. By consequence of this decision it was necessary for Congress to pass additional legislation if it wished to restore unearned grants or portions of grants to the public domain.

The movement for the repeal of the land grants started even before the last one was made in the early seventies. It was felt that sufficient land had been granted to create a satisfactory transportational system, that such a system was in process of building, and that all remaining land should be reserved for its real use—settlement. At a time when land was becoming scarce it was more important that all unearned grants be returned to the public domain than that the railroads should receive further encouragement.

The early movement for land grant forfeiture produced its first results with the repeal of a Louisiana grant on July 14, 1870. The sentiment in favor of such repeals continued to gain in strength throughout the seventies, but although there were a number of forfeitures during the latter part of the decade, the real problem still remained untouched. Sentiment did not become united until a majority of the transcontinental roads under construction were completed and land became a good deal more scarce.

By 1884 all the national parties favored forfeiture. The victory of the Democrats was the signal for the passage of a large number of forfeiture bills during the years 1884-86. Notable among them were the acts concerning the Texas and Pacific and the Atlantic and Pacific. The Democrats were particularly interested in land reform, and in their platform for 1888 it was their proud boast that they had "restored to the people nearly 100,000,000 acres of valuable land, to be sacredly held as homesteads for our citizens." Not all of this was former railroad land; a considerable share had been taken illegally from the public domain and was restored when Carl Schurz took control of the Land Office.

The Republicans, on the other hand, denied "that the Democratic party had ever restored one acre to the people, but declare that by the joint action of the Republicans and Democrats about 50,000,000 acres of unearned lands originally granted for the construction of railroads have been restored to the public domain, in pursuance of the conditions inserted by the Republican party in the original grants." The activities of Schurz were minimized.

After 1888 the attention of Congress was turned toward a general forfeiture act to cover all unearned land grants in the country. After many vicissitudes, such a bill finally became law on September 29, 1890. By this time, however, the majority of the large western grants had already been revoked, so that the effect of the act was confined in most part to the South.

The most important action of Congress during the eighties in relation to the railroads was in respect to regulation. The "granger" agitation of the preceding decade had reached into Congress to the extent of provoking a considerable amount of discussion and of calling forth the Windom report, which furnished an excellent summary of the existing situation. The main object of the men in favor of national regulation of railways at this time was to encourage competition. A government railroad or waterways or both were to provide additional competition, which was to result in lower rates. Possible federal control of rates was looked upon as being at best only a palliative. A regulatory measure governing live stock was finally passed in the early seventies, but was quite generally evaded.

The climax of the early regulative movement in Congress came with the passage of the McCrary bill by the House in 1874. Unreasonable charges or discriminations were forbidden. A board of nine, to be appointed by the President, had the power to prepare a schedule of maximum rates, and could secure any necessary books and papers. Roads which violated the provisions of the act were to be sued by the board, and were to be punished by fines ranging from $500 to $5000. This bill failed of passage in the Senate. The first of the Reagan bills was introduced in 1877, and from this time Congress was never without one of the bills of the Texas member.

Possibly the principal reasons why Congress did not act earlier than it did were the questions of constitutionality and the attitude of the courts. The belief that the railroads could be regulated by act of Congress did not secure general acceptance until the eighties. The courts, in a number of celebrated cases during the seventies, held that the state commissions were constitutional and could control all rates within the state, including portions of through rates. The implication was that the state commissions were the desirable bodies to exercise such regulation. The increase in the number of state commissions led many of the members of Congress to feel that federal action was at least unnecessary, even if it were constitutional.

As in the case of the land grant forfeiture, the crisis

came after the panic and elections of 1884. By this time it was certain that Congressional action was only a matter of time. In the session of 1884-85 the House passed the Reagan bill and the Senate passed the Cullom bill, both by substantial majorities. An apparent deadlock was reached when no compromise could be effected which was satisfactory to both Houses.

At this juncture the Senate took a further step by appointing a select committee of five, which in 1886 brought in the famous Cullom report, probably the most influential document of its kind. At about the same time the Supreme Court, in the case of the Wabash, St. Louis and Pacific Railway Company v. The State of Illinois, decided that the state commissions had no power over interstate traffic. Since this business was of prime importance, and could be regulated only by the federal government, the necessity of Congressional action became imperative.

The Cullom bill again passed the Senate in 1886, and again the House substituted the Reagan bill. The main differences, as summarized by L. H. Haney in his *A Congressional History of Railways in the United States, 1850-1887*, p. 292, were—"(1) the Senate bill did not forbid pooling; the House bill did; (2) the Senate long-and-short-haul clause was weak and might be set aside; that of the House bill was rigid; (3) the House bill provided no executive machinery in the shape of a commission, but left enforcement to the courts."

The House substitute for the Senate bill was immediately rejected and a conference committee was appointed. Finally a conference bill was evolved, which, while it was not entirely satisfactory to either House, secured enough votes for passage. It finally became a law by the signature of the President on February 4, 1887, and went into effect on April 5, 1887.

The act as it was finally adopted prohibited pooling, and this provision was seen by the Senate conferees as their great concession. All special rates and rebates, as well as discrimination in favor of persons, localities, and particular products, were forbidden. No greater charge could be made for a shorter than a long haul, provided that the first was included in the second. All rates had to be made public and could not be changed on less than a ten days' notice. A commission of five, appointed by the President, had charge of the administration of the act. Not more than three of this body could be of the same political party. The findings of the commission in any case were to constitute prima facie evidence in a court. Penalties for disobedience had a maximum amount of $5000 for each offense.

The Interstate Commerce Act was at first well received by the railroads, and the rulings of the commission were obeyed. It was true that a great many discriminations and secret rebates continued, but at least outwardly the roads strove to live up to the letter of the law. The fact was that both in the government and in the management of the various roads there was little understanding as to what the phraseology of the new act meant. Until it had been made clear, there was a cessation of activity.

Curiously enough, the first serious attack on the provisions of the act came in connection with the securing of evidence and in the judicial procedure. By successive interpretations, the courts gradually reduced the power of the commission to almost nothing. In spite of additional legislation by Congress the commission found itself seriously hampered in securing evidence and in securing convictions, and the number of cases which were appealed to it began to lessen.

The general attitude of the courts served to make the Interstate Commerce Commission a distinctly subordinate body. In spite of the provisions of the act which made the findings of the commission prima facie evidence, the courts soon proceeded to review all the evidence. New facts were presented by the roads, and accepted by the courts as invalidating the whole procedure before the commission and necessitating a complete review of the facts. This procedure transformed the Interstate Commerce Commission into a distinctly subsidiary organization.

The long and short haul clause was soon ruined by the generous interpretation of the courts. The courts tended to contract the meaning of the clause prohibiting a greater charge for a less haul until it meant almost nothing. The commission was also hampered by the excessive length of time which any case took. It had no special preference if it were appealed to the courts, and so by the time it was tried in four or five years, the conditions were no longer the same.

As the courts began to strip the commission of its supposed powers, the railroads became more restive and tried to hasten the process. The real heart of the whole situation lay in the power of the Interstate Commerce Commission to prescribe rates. Although no such power had been specifically granted, the commission felt that its power to decide what rates were unreasonable, carried with it the power to say what rates were reasonable, and to insist upon their promulgation. The courts did not agree with this assumption, and the commission soon lost its last vestige of power. True, it could force a road to change a rate, provided it were proved unreasonable, but this procedure had to be repeated indefinitely if the commission wished to arrived at any particular figure. The gradual emasculation of the Interstate Commerce Act led finally to new legislation. Even the railroads were in favor of certain changes in the law, without its complete abolition. The first changes were in procedure and in penalties. After some minor legislative action during the nineties, the Elkins amendments of 1903 revised the procedure for the proof of illegal rates, and also the placing of penalties for infractions of the law. Practically no opposition developed to this change, since it was equally acceptable to everyone.

The really vital changes in the original law occurred with the passage of the Hepburn Act in 1906, which united public sentiment secured over the very active resistance of an extensive and well paid railroad campaign. The field of federal regulation was expanded to include oil pipe lines, all special railroad equipment, and switching. storing, and handling. The most important advance in the powers of the commission was the ability to fix maximum rates and to apportion joint rates. The burden of proof in the case of disputes was placed on the carrier. The courts still had a full power of review, and the railroad rate still remained in effect until a dispute was settled. Settlements were expedited by allowing for immediate appeal to the Supreme Court, and precedence over other matters. The railroads were not allowed to ship products produced or controlled by themselves. Publicity of accounts was further aided.

The effects of the new law were on the whole quite satisfactory, and the power of the Interstate Commerce Commission increased rapidly. A long step was taken with the Supreme Court decision in 1910 that the courts had only the power to decide constitutional questions and whether the commission was acting within its delegated powers. This meant that the courts would no longer review the economic facts at issue, except as they bore upon the legal questions involved.

Disregarding minor developments, the Interstate Commerce Commission later extended its power over telegraph, telephone, and cable lines. Rates could be suspended until they were tested as to their reasonableness, and the commission could establish minimum as well as maximum rates. Provision was made for the valuation of the railroads in order to furnish one basis of rate making, and the commission was given somewhat more power over water transportation and over safety devices. The outbreak of the World War saw government operation, followed by the return of the railroads to their private owners under the terms of the Transportation Act of 1920. These developments are merely noted briefly in order to show the general trend of later railroad control.

Among other things, the Interstate Commerce Commission had a considerable effect on freight classification. Prior to the latter seventies there was no agreement as to the classification of freight except as two or three roads would reach an understanding. A uniform classification was adopted for the Northwest in 1877, and later expanded and used by the Southwestern Railway Rate Association. In 1882 there was an attempt to make practice uniform all over the country, but the meeting broke down. The western roads continued, however, and finally succeeded in agreeing upon the Revised Western Classification, which was accepted by all of the trans-Mississippi lines.

Immediately upon the formation of the Interstate Commerce Commission there was another attempt to secure uniformity, which failed because of the objections of the transcontinental roads. A House resolution requested the commission to secure action, and so it continued its efforts. A plan was finally drawn up which did not include the transcontinental roads, but after it was completed two other lines proved obdurate and again no agreement was possible. In the meantime a trunk line and a southern classification had been agreed upon, and developments gradually limited existing classifications to these two and to the western rate sheets. In spite of continued attempts, no national agreement could be reached. In December, 1919, these three classifications were combined under one cover as Consolidated Freight Classification Number 1.

One of the most significant and far-reaching of the effects of the Interstate Commerce Act came as a result of the prohibition of pooling. This form of railroad coöperation was widespread, and was one of the developments which looked most hopeful from the point of view of the railroads. The prohibition of rate agreements by the Interstate Commerce Act eventually meant that the railroads had to seek a new form of coöperation, thus giving an entirely new trend to railroad history.

The first reaction of the railroads was to try to find some kind of an effective legal traffic agreement which would take the place of the old pools. The gradual demoralization of rates in the West made some sort of agreement absolutely imperative. At the same time, the growing interdependence of all western rates, and the common danger of federal interference, led the roads to act together.

The first concerted action came in the Western Freight Association—a rate agreement covering the eastern half of the territory west of the Mississippi. The old northwestern, central, and southwestern groups retained their local autonomy, but acted jointly in matters of common interest. The executive committees, which had control under the original agreement, soon gave way to the commissioners, who were more able to act quickly and effectively.

Early in 1889 the agreement was expanded under the name of the Interstate Commerce Railway Association. The old organization still continued in existence, but a new body, the Trans-Missouri Freight Association, was added. The transcontinental roads still remained outside. Provision was made for a division of traffic in disputed cases, and there is evidence that such division took place. It was hoped that this action would not be considered illegal by the courts. At best the arrangement was rather vague, and when the Burlington forced matters to an issue in 1889, the association admitted its lack of power, and was forced to disband.

The widest territorial extent of pooling came with the formulation of the Western Traffic Association in the winter of 1890-91. A Lake division, Gulf division, Trans-Missouri division, and transcontinental division took in all of the West. Commissioners were elected for each division, but final power was vested in a central advisory board, composed of the president and a member of the board of directors of each road. Again it was a traffic division upon which the whole organization rested fundamentally, and again the association went to pieces because of its lack of control over its members. The various divisions maintained a somewhat precarious separate existence.

The last important attempt at general action came in 1894, but again the resulting association collapsed very quickly. Two years later a similar agreement failed of ratification. Even the coöperation of the smaller local groups failed to afford any satisfaction. Troubles were innumerable and disastrous. At the same time that the Interstate Commerce Commission was being stripped of its power to make rates by the Supreme Court, the railroads found their normal difficulties in maintaining rates to be further complicated by the anti-pooling provision of the act of 1887. Conditions were chaotic.

A further complication came with the passage of the Sherman Anti-Trust Act in 1890. The question was immediately raised as to whether or not the railroads were subject to its provisions, and if they were, what sort of an agreement would constitute a "combination in restraint of trade." The testing of these two acts in their relation to the railroads came in the Trans-Missouri Freight Association and Joint Traffic Association cases, both decided in 1897. Similar principles were upheld; all rate agreements, pools, or traffic diversions had the effect of destroying competition and fixing prices, and were consequently held to be illegal.

The old organizations broke down immediately upon these decisions, being succeeded by bureaus for the exchange and publication of information. Actually there was but little difference in rate conditions, because the old agreements had not worked. The only remaining method for securing unity was by the prosecution of all roads making secret cuts, but this practice was so universal that no road felt sufficiently blameless to start proceedings. The Interstate Commerce Commission tried to attain some uniformity by monthly meetings with the railroad executives, but the importance of such gatherings tended to lessen as time went on.

The one result of the breakdown of the pools was a propulsion toward government action, which finally led to the building up of complete control over rates by the Interstate Commerce Commission. On the other hand, the railroads tried to work out their own salvation by developing the idea of a community of interests by interlocking directorates, and also by the combining of several large systems under a single management. This tendency was a perfectly logical historical growth, and gives the tone to the succeeding period.

CHAPTER XX

The depression both preceding and after the panic of
1893 was one of the worst in the history of the United
States. It was particularly notable for the intense prosperity which preceded it. The peak of western railroad
construction was reached in 1887, and within two years
practically all construction had ceased. Rigid economies
did little more than to postpone the inevitable.

The beginning of railroad distress was sharply marked
by the collapse of the Gould lines in the middle eighties.
Even as strong a line as the Santa Fe found it necessary
to reorganize in 1889 to tide over the depression. As
was the case twenty years before, all the credit institutions were overloaded with non-negotiable paper. Gold
was leaving the country rapidly and the Treasury Department was having difficulty in maintaining an adequate
gold reserve.

The crisis came in the panic of 1893, and banks, manufacturing concerns, and railroads went to the wall quite
unanimously. The total number and capitalization of
western roads going into the hands of receivers was ap-
palling, and had no precedent. Among the larger lines
were the Santa Fe, the Northern Pacific, the St. Louis and
San Francisco, and the Union Pacific. The granger roads
were the one important group to maintain solvency, but
only because of rigid economies and because of their
strong financial backing.

The inordinate number of foreclosures and reorganizations during this period served to call attention to railroad finances. All of the evils of poor building, excessive expansion, and over-capitalization which had been evident at the time of the panic of 1873 were now illustrated on a still larger scale. They were augmented by the manipulation of funds which was found necessary to tide over hard times. It was at this time that people were beginning to become interested in these financial practices.

The process of reorganization, either with or without a receiver or a foreclosure sale or both, ordinarily meant an increase in capitalization. It was always possible to assess the stockholders in order to retire some of the bonds and pay off some of the floating debt, and thus make the road solvent, but this procedure was ordinarily not followed because the stockholders objected to spending money on which there would be no return. Any other conceivable plan would be preferable.

The usual process of reorganization was to decrease the fixed charges by converting bonds into stock. Dividends were paid on stock only when the road was making a profit, while the interest on bonds had to be met regardless of other conditions. Consequently in a period of depression the road would have greater chances of retaining solvency. Such a plan was always acceptable to the stockholders, who lost nothing, and saw a possibility of reviving the road so that it could pay future dividends.

The position of the bondholders was radically different. They would of course be unwilling to contract their holdings, and would be equally opposed to exchanging their well-secured bonds for questionable stock. On the other hand, if the road were sold at foreclosure, it would mean that in all probability they would be forced to exchange their bonds for stock. Therefore, it was ordinarily necessary to advance some sort of a compromise solution which would at least be moderately satisfactory. Sometimes the bonds were called in and a smaller issue made, with the difference in value being made up by stock; in such cases a stock bonus was ordinarily given in order to satisfy the bondholders. Sometimes the bondholders were given income bonds or preferred stock to a somewhat greater value than their original holdings, and additional capital was raised by a new bond issue. Such plans had infinite variations, but the underlying idea was to rearrange the securities in order to decrease fixed charges, and at the same time to satisfy security holders by increasing the face value of the paper which they held.

The usual result of reorganization was to increase the capitalization and reduce fixed charges. Such a process was hardly designed to produce a financially strong road. If it could not meet its obligations before the reorganization, it could certainly not hope to pay adequate dividends at a subsequent time. The whole process was cumulative. Increased capitalization meant more difficulties in the next financial depression, which again meant more capitalization, and so on indefinitely. The only break in the chain was when increased values and traffic kept pace with the increased capitalization.

The attitude of the public was that rates should be fair and reasonable for the service involved, regardless of the capitalization. If dividends could not be paid it was an indication that the capitalization was too great or that the road was poorly managed. It was conceivable that a newly opened road might fail to pay dividends for several years, but after that time the failure to make expenses indicated poor management. In any event, the railroads were primarily for the purpose of serving the people and not vice versa.

The railroads agreed with the proposition that rates should be reasonable, but they contended that no rate was reasonable unless it returned an income on the capital invested. While they were willing to admit that in some cases the capitalization was greater than the original cost of the road plus its improvements, they contended that the railroad property had increased in value to at least the amount of the capital involved. They held that it would be manifestly unfair to deprive the roads of the legitimate increase in value of their properties.

The Interstate Commerce Commission accepted the railroad argument in part, and conceded that a fair estimate of the existing value of railroad property was one of the considerations in rate-making. Up to the present time such valuation is still problematic. Congress gave the commission power to evaluate the railroads in 1913, and the process is not yet complete. Even with these statistics available, there is still very little agreement upon the basis which such figures should have.

The effects of the panic of 1893 remained in evidence practically until the close of the century. When they finally disappeared, a new era in railroad history was revealed. The western railroad net had been completed and the majority of the mileage was in the hands of the larger roads, with evidences of eastern control multiplying. The grouping of the roads into large systems had been practically completed, and future developments were in the direction of the manipulation of the larger groups.

The progress of the western roads toward consolidation had first been noticeable immediately after the Civil War. Earlier developments had been in the direction of securing a through line between two important points, such as from Chicago or St. Louis to the Missouri River. About 1870 the roads began to look elsewhere, and to build or acquire lines which gave them connections to other points. During the eighties numerous roads had succeeded in attaining good connections north, south, east, and west, as well as a network of branches to secure control of the territory traversed.

Expansion was carried on by construction or purchase, or by a combination of the two. Large lines might either charter their own extensions or purchase previous incorporations and carry them to completion. It was also possible to buy lines which were already completed and to attach them to the main lines. Such roads might be bought outright, controlled by the purchase of a majority of stock, or held on a long term lease. Frequently the method used was an exchange of stock.

Once the control of a new line was secured, there came the question of how it should be managed. Sometimes it was run independently of the mother company. At other times it was controlled and run as a subsidiary corporation, losing its identity almost entirely. It might even be consolidated into the parent line and lose its separate existence completely. This last course of action was particularly desirable from the viewpoint of economy of operation, but it was frequently made impossible by the incorporation clauses of the various states. At times it was also undesired by the railroads. The Gould lines felt that such a process would destroy certain speculative possibilities, while the Southern Pacific was not anxious to encourage the cry of monopoly by being in too close connection with the Central Pacific.

Railroad men generally favored the tendency toward consolidation. Large systems made possible the increased economy of large scale production, lessened the possibility of rate wars, and presented an opportunity for a more varied and complete service to the public. The competition between small lines was undesirable from every viewpoint. They injured both themselves and the public. Larger systems were able to equalize inequalities and to produce a high grade of service.

The attitude of the public was not so favorable. The average citizen feared monopoly control. The larger the system the more secure was its hold upon the territory which it occupied. With a secure grip on the situation, it could advance rates to the highest point that the traffic would bear, and reduce service to the lowest point that the railroad users would stand.

The truth of the situation probably lies somewhere between the two points of view. No such happy medium was reached, however, and each side of the argument tended to become more extreme. The railroads bent all their efforts to the creation of more extensive and complete systems and the formation of agreements among themselves, while the public looked for railroad commissions to lower rates and to enforce competition.

The depression of the nineties stopped the progress toward railroad consolidation for the time being and left the 5000 miles system in the heyday of its importance. Future growth by construction seemed impossible, while most of the important branch lines had already been acquired. At the same time the passage of the Interstate Commerce Act and the Sherman Anti-Trust Act had stopped the movement toward voluntary coöperation in pools and rate agreements.

When prosperity began to return during the latter nineties a new tendency began to be in evidence. Under the control of eastern bankers for the most part, the existing systems were treated as they had formerly treated branch lines. The securities of particular systems became centralized in certain banking groups which found their entire interest in adequate profits and not in the building up of one line at the expense of another. Only by large consolidations could a unity of action be effected and profits made secure.

The outstanding figure of the new tendency was E. H. Harriman. Harriman's first venture in western railroads was an interest in the Illinois Central, which he purchased in 1883. At that time he was a humble member of a group which included Kuhn, Loeb and Company, Vanderbilt, Gould, Stuyvesant Fish, and other similar names.

Harriman's rise to power was rapid, and in 1897 he purchased control of the Union Pacific, which General Dodge described as then being "two dirt ballasted streaks of rust. The stations along the mountain grades were tumbledown shacks, most of the equipment fit only for the scrap pile. From top to bottom the Union Pacific suffered from bankruptcy, brought on by political and financial intrigue."

At this time Harriman was acting in the interest of a syndicate of bankers, of which he was the railroad man. In the succeeding years he purchased sufficient stock to give himself absolute control, so that by 1900 he was dominant. His first effort was to reacquire the numerous branch lines which had been lost during the period of the receivership. By 1900 this process had been virtually completed; all the old properties of the Union Pacific had been restored, and in most cases the control was more absolute than had been the case at an earlier time.

The policy of Harriman in respect to the operation of his properties was distinctly sound. By means of reorganization the fixed charges had been reduced, and provision made for meeting the full debt to the government. Rigid economies in administration were made. Profits were used in great part for the repair and replacement of outworn equipment. Within a comparatively few years the Union Pacific compared very favorably in its physical properties with the best of western railroads.

The future developments of the Union Pacific were in the direction of solidifying and expanding its interests. The first important move in this direction was an attempt to purchase a considerable interest in the Chicago, Burlington and Quincy, which would give an independent line to Chicago, besides other important connections and innumerable feeders. The price proved too high, however, and the negotiations failed.

More fortunate for the Union Pacific was its experience in the Far West, where it had been trying for many years to secure an effective connection with the coast which would be independent of the Southern Pacific. In 1901 C. P. Huntington died, and his holdings in the Southern Pacific and Central Pacific were placed on the market. At first Harriman tried to secure only the Central Pacific, but finally he was forced to buy control of the whole system. For the first time in its history, the Union Pacific had satisfactory connections with the Pacific coast.

Harriman's connection with the Burlington did not end with his unsuccessful attempt to secure an interest

in it. Shortly later the situation was entirely changed
when Hill offered to purchase the entire stock of the
Burlington in the interest of his other lines, the Great
Northern and the Northern Pacific. He did not hesitate
at the price, and was soon in possession of complete
control of the Burlington.

While the Burlington was very desirable to the Union
Pacific as a subsidiary company, it was even more important and threatening in the hands of the more northern roads. Its line into Montana made it possible for
Hill to divert its very considerable Mississippi valley
business from the Union Pacific. At the same time its
line to St. Paul gave both the Great Northern and the
Northern Pacific a Chicago connection. With the Hill
interests in control, the Burlington could inflict a
considerable amount of damage on the Union Pacific.

Harriman was never willing to accept defeat, and decided to fight. It was impossible to buy into the Burlington, so he decided to concentrate his attention on the
Northern Pacific, whose control would give him a half
interest in the Iowa road. By the middle of 1901 he had
succeeded in securing a majority of the Northern Pacific
stock, in the course of which procedure he had driven
it to such a figure that it precipitated a stock exchange
panic. When the smoke of battle had cleared away it was
found that although he controlled a majority of the stock
he had only a minority of common stock, and that the
road's act of incorporation permitted the common stockholders to retire the preferred stock at any time. In
consequence, Hill still retained control of the situation.

The only trouble with Hill's position was that the
Harriman holdings were too large to be comfortable. The
administration could always be embarrassed, and it was

altogether possible that the control might some day change hands. Neither side wanted more trouble than necessary, and so a compromise was arranged. The only apparent term of the compromise was that two Union Pacific men were given places on the Northern Pacific board of directors.

It was now Hill's turn to take the initiative, and he decided to consolidate his northern holdings in order to free his hands for work elsewhere. Physical consolidation was certainly illegal by the terms of the Sherman Act, and so a holding company, the Northern Securities Company, was chartered to hold the stock of both the Great Northern and the Northern Pacific. Such an operation carried with it the control of the Burlington, and insured the harmonious operation of the three roads. The Harriman holdings were turned in to the new company, and three of the directors were Union Pacific men.

The government immediately started suit against the Northern Securities Company for violating the Sherman Act. The government won its suit, and the company was enjoined from operating either the Great Northern or the Northern Pacific and from collecting dividends on their stock. This result made Hill change his plans, and in order to retain a unified control he had the company dissolved by prorating the holdings. Each shareholder in the Northern Securities Company received equal parts of Northern Pacific and Great Northern stock, regardless of what his original holdings had been. In this way it was possible to disband the larger company and still have the control remain the same.

Immediately upon the adoption of this plan for dissolution, Harriman saw his chance to attain his old objective of the control of the Northern Pacific. He petitioned the court to set aside this method of stock distribution, on the plea that it would leave the control the same as before and thus be illegal, and also because the illegality of the Northern Securities Company should invalidate all of its actions, making each individual receive what he had put in. If this contention had been accepted it would have given Harriman control of the Northern Pacific, because at this time he was in possession of a clear majority of its stock.

The court ruled against the Harriman suit on the grounds that the Northern Securities Company was not illegal per se, but had only been restrained from performing certain acts; furthermore, the change in conditions made it utterly impossible by any human means to restore conditions as they had been. Upon this decision, Harriman was forced to acknowledge the impossibility of securing his aims, at least for the time being. Most of the Northern Pacific stock which he had purchased was sold on the open market, although enough was retained to secure some sort of coöperation between the two roads.

In addition to this holding of Northern Pacific stock, Harriman adopted the practice of buying into other important roads in order to be assured of satisfactory connections and traffic arrangements. The Baltimore and Ohio, the New York Central, the Santa Fe, the Chicago and Northwestern, the Chicago, Milwaukee and St. Paul were some of the more important roads in which he had significant holdings. In the case of the Illinois Central, 30% of the stock was held, which in ordinary times carried with it the control of the road. In fact, Stuyvesant Fish was forced from the presidency in 1906.

During the first decade of the twentieth century the

Union Pacific also secured one new transcontinental connection in the San Pedro, Los Angeles and Salt Lake City. This line was backed by Senator Clark, and was projected to run directly from Los Angeles to Salt Lake City. Its completion under independent management would mean, that in connection with the Denver and Rio Grande it would compete for most of the transcontinental business of the Union Pacific. The Union Pacific also controlled a road chartered along this route, and so after a struggle in both the courts and on the field, brought the new project to terms. The resulting agreement divided the control, giving half to each company, but actually it was the Union Pacific which was dominant. The road was completed in 1905.

The Harriman interests reached their height about 1907. About this time they included the Union Pacific, the Oregon Railway and Navigation Company, the Oregon Short Line, the Southern Pacific, the Central Pacific, the San Pedro, Los Angeles and Salt Lake City, and the Illinois Central, besides numerous smaller lines. An interest was also held in a great many lines such as the Santa Fe, the New York Central, the Baltimore and Ohio, and the Chicago and Alton. To be complete the list should also include steamship lines, street railways, coal, oil, land, and certain other miscellaneous holdings. The control of the southern transcontinental field was practically monopolized. The only independent road, the Santa Fe, was operated in harmony.

Conditions in the Northwest were similar, but here it was Hill who was in control. The ownership of the Great Northern, the Northern Pacific, and the Chicago, Burlington and Quincy carried with it a fairly complete monopoly of business in the Northwest, as well as a

considerable amount of the traffic of the northern
Mississippi valley.

The ambition of these two men seemed limitless. The
only thing that stood in the way of one or both obtaining
a complete control of the railroads of the West, or even
of the entire United States, was the existing federal anti-
trust legislation. At one time Harriman was examined
on this phase of the question. He was asked,—"And your
power, which you have, would gradually increase as you
took one road after another, so that you might spread not
only over the Pacific coast, but spread out over the
Atlantic coast?" Without hesitation, Harriman answered
with the single pregnant word, "Yes."

The end of the progress of the Union Pacific dates
from about the time of the death of Harriman in 1909.
Shortly later the Supreme Court decided that the combination of the Southern Pacific and the Union Pacific
was illegal, and ordered them separated. An attempt to
retain control of the Central Pacific failed because of the
opposition of the California railroad commission. Finally
a part of the stock was traded for Baltimore and Ohio
stock held by the Pennsylvania, and the remainder was
sold to Union Pacific stockholders.

Besides the two large groups of Hill and Harriman
there was a third dominated by Gould, Sage, and Rocke-
feller. This group included the Missouri Pacific, the Iron
Mountain, the International and Great Northern, the
Wabash, the St. Louis and Southwestern, the Texas and
Pacific, the Missouri, Kansas and Texas, and the Denver
and Rio Grande. It was dominant in the Southwest, but
also extended into the Far West and into the East.

George Gould conceived the idea of continuing and
extending his father's ideas to encompass a road from

coast to coast. As it was, the Gould properties extended from Buffalo by way of the Wabash to St. Louis, from there to Pueblo by way of the Missouri Pacific, and from Pueblo to Salt Lake City over the Denver and Rio Grande. The Western Pacific was chartered to build from Salt Lake City to San Francisco, and was completed in 1911. The entire plan failed, however, because of financial difficulties, caused in the most part by the lavish expenditures which were made in order to secure an entrance to Pittsburg.

The last of the present transcontinental roads to be completed was the Chicago, Milwaukee and St. Paul, finished in 1909. The line was an extension of that to Aberdeen, South Dakota, and was built slightly north of west until it came to its terminus at Seattle. This line inaugurated the novel plan of using electricity for the portion of the road which went over the mountains.

Aside from the development of large ownership groups and the completion of several new transcontinental lines, the most notable development of the early twentieth century was the growth of the community of interest idea. It has already been shown how the Union Pacific acquired interests in other roads in order to be assured of a favorable management. Other roads followed the same practice until there was almost a universal interlocking of ownership. Coöperation which could not be attained at an earlier time by the use of pools and traffic agreements was finally secured by stock purchases.

During the first decade of the twentieth century the history of western railroads becomes current economics. The railroad net is complete, the land has been settled, and all types of voluntary coöperation have been tried. The West no longer presents any distinctive features.

Trans-Mississippi railroad operation is just the same as that of the roads on the other side of the river. Regional problems have given way to national problems.

From the time that the first western railroad was considered, the West had distinct problems to differentiate it from the more settled part of the country. The physical obstacles to be overcome, the capital to be raised, and the labor and population which had to be brought into the new country, were all distinctively western problems. During the sixties the physical difficulties were well on the way to being conquered; the seventies began to give a definite trend to the development of the West; the eighties saw the main outlines of the railroad net completed and the population fairly well developed; the nineties witnessed the development of labor to conditions approximating those of today; the first decade of the twentieth century contained the final completion of the western railroads and the emergence of present day conditions in all fields. Western railroad history had merged into that of the nation.

BIBLIOGRAPHY

The following bibliography makes no pretense of being exhaustive. Neither does it pretend to contain the sources of the information presented in the preceding pages. Its only purpose is to collect the more important and significant material on western railroads in a form which may be available for more extended reading on any particular phase of the subject. Whenever possible the material has been limited to books. Magazine articles are quoted when they are particularly significant or when there is a paucity of other material. The same may be said of other documents such as court reports, railroad reports, commission reports, newspapers, and railroad periodicals. Complete bibliographical details are not always given when the material has been quoted earlier in the bibliography.

BIBLIOGRAPHICAL AIDS

The two most usable bibliographies of railroad literature are those in the two works of F. A. Cleveland and F. W. Powell—*Railroad Promotion and Capitalization in the United States* (N. Y., 1919), and *Railroad Finance* (N. Y., 1912). B. H. Meyer (ed.), *History of Transportation in the United States before 1860* (Washington, 1917) presents an extended, although not entirely complete list of publications on the period covered. Several lists of the books on the subject in various libraries have been collected, notably those for the Hopkins Railway Library and for the Library of Congress, and the catalogue prepared by the Bureau of Railway Economics.

GENERAL WORKS

Adequate railroad histories are practically non-existent. B. H. Meyer (ed.), *History of Transportation in the United*

States before 1860 (Washington, 1917) hardly touches the situation in the West. H. V. Poor, *History of Railroads and Canals in the United States* (N. Y., 1860) and H. M. Flint, *Railways in the United States* (Philadelphia, 1868) were both written before western railroads became important. J. L. Ringwalt, for many years editor of the *Railway World*, has a volume on *Development of Transportation Systems in the United States* (Philadelphia, 1888) which contains a large number of miscellaneous facts. For a brief summary of the history of any particular road *Poor's Manual of the Railroads of the United States*, issued yearly, is invaluable. G. R. Chatburn, *Highways and Highway Transportation* (N. Y., 1923) summarizes the development of the railroad. L. H. Haney, *A Congressional History of Railways in the United States to 1850* (Madison, 1908) and *A Congressional History of Railways in the United States 1850-1887* (Madison, 1910) present one phase of the subject.

General economic histories present some phases of the development of the railroads. A few of the better of such works are E. L. Bogart, *The Economic History of the United States* (N. Y., 1907); K. Coman, *The Industrial History of the United States* (N. Y., 1905); E. S. Cowdrich, *Industrial History of the United States* (N. Y., 1922); I. Lippincott, *Economic Development of the United States* (N. Y., 1921). To these should be added sectional accounts such as C. H. Brough, "Industrial History of Arkansas," in *Publications of the Arkansas Historical Association* (Little Rock, 1906), pp. 191-230, and J. L. Coulter, "Industrial History of the Valley of the Red River of the North," in *Collections of the State Historical Society of North Dakota* (Bismarck, 1910), 3:529-672.

Various works on certain aspects of railroad economics contain a considerable amount of history interspersed in their pages. A few of them will serve to show the general trend. F. A. Cleveland and F. W. Powell, *Railway Promotion and Capitalization in the United States* (N. Y., 1909); A. T. Hadley, *Railroad Transportation* (N. Y., 1886); W. Z. Ripley, *Railroads* (N. Y., 1912); H. S. Haines, *Problems in Railway Regulation* (N. Y., 1911); E. Jones, *Principles of Railway Transportation* (N. Y., 1924).

BIBLIOGRAPHY 323

A certain amount of information concerning railroad history in the West is given in the general histories covering the period since 1850. E. B. Andrews, *History of the Last Quarter-Century in the United States* (2 vols., N. Y., 1896); C. A. Beard, *Contemporary American History* (N. Y., 1918); C. R. Lingley, *Since the Civil War* (N. Y., 1920); F. L. Paxson, *The New Nation* (N. Y., 1915), *Recent History of the United States* (N. Y., 1921), and *History of the American Frontier* (Boston, 1924); J. F. Rhodes, *History of the United States from the Compromise of 1850* (N. Y., 1893-1922); L. B. Shippee, *Recent American History* (N. Y., 1924).

Western state or local histories usually present to some degree the railroad situation. Most of them are very poor and should be taken with extreme caution. A few of the better works might be mentioned. The numerous volumes of H. H. Bancroft on the states of the Far West afford a considerable amount of material; R. E. Cleland, *A History of California: the American Period* (N. Y., 1922); C. Cole, *A History of the People of Iowa* (Cedar Rapids, 1921); W. W. Folwell, *A History of Minnesota* (4 vols., St. Paul, 1921); D. H. Hardy and I. S. Roberts, *Historical Review of South-East Texas* (Knoxville, 1912); G. W. Kingsbury and G. M. Smith, *History of Dakota Territory* (3 vols., Chicago, 1915); J. A. Schafer, *History of the Pacific Northwest* (N. Y., 1918); J. T. Scharf, *History of St. Louis City and County* (2 vols., Philadelphia, 1883); J. C. Smiley, *History of Denver* (Denver, 1903); J. B. Thoburn, *A Standard History of Oklahoma* (5 vols., Chicago, 1916); O. F. Whitney, *History of Utah* (4 vols., Salt Lake City, 1893).

I. THE BEGINNING OF RAILROADS

The material on early railroads in both England and the United States is at best fragmentary. C. F. Carter, *When Railroads Were New* (N. Y., 1909) presents considerable material in a popular form. W. B. Brown, *The History of the First Locomotives in America* (N. Y., 1874), and J. E. Bloomfield, "First Application of Steam to Railways," in *Hunt's Merchant's Magazine and Review* (1846), 14:249-60 contain interesting suggestions. L. H. Haney, *A Congressional His-*

tory of Railways in the United States to 1850 (Madison, 1908) presents some of the early experimentation, and also an account of the early government surveys. F. A. Cleveland and F. W. Powell, *Railway Promotion and Capitalization in the United States* (N. Y., 1909) has a good account of the early transcontinental work in Chapters IX and XIV. The various histories of the Union Pacific, cited later, also contain such material. The Davis surveys of 1853-55 are discussed in G. L. Albright, *Official Exploration for Pacific Railroads* (Berkeley, 1921). F. H. Hodder, "The Genesis of the Kansas-Nebraska Act," in *Proceedings of the State Historical Society of Wisconsin* (1912) presents one excellent example of the sectional influence of the western railroads. F. A. Root and W. E. Connelley, *The Overland Stage to California* (Topeka, 1901) is an interesting record of the overland business. C. M. Fuess, *The Life of Caleb Cushing* (2 vols. N. Y., 1923) gives an account of the Cushing treaty which opened our trade with the Far East.

II. The First Construction

The Chicago convention of 1847 may be followed in its proceedings as reprinted in the *Fergus Historical Studies No. 18* (Chicago, 1882). The entire period of 1845-50 and the conventions of St. Louis and Memphis may be followed in three articles from the pen of R. S. Cotterill—"Early Agitation for a Pacific Railroad 1845-1850," in the *Mississippi Valley Historical Review* (1918), 4:396-414; "The Memphis Railroad Convention," in the *Tennessee Historical Magazine* (1918), 4:83-94; "The National Railroad Convention in St. Louis, 1849," in the *Missouri Historical Review* (1918), 12:203-15. The interest of T. H. Benton in western railroads is presented somewhat in his *Thirty Years' View* (N. Y., 1850), which should be read in connection with P. O. Ray, *The Repeal of the Missouri Compromise* (Cleveland, 1909). R. E. Riegel, "Trans-Mississippi Railroads During the Fifties," in the *Mississippi Valley Historical Review* (1923), 10:153-172 presents a general survey of the entire progress during the decade. There have been published numerous short accounts of individual roads—P. Briscoe, "The First Texas Railroad," in *Quarterly of the Texas State Historical Association* (1904), 7:279-285; A. Hebard, "The Original Survey of the C. B. and Q. Railroad Line," in *Annals of Iowa*, 6:216-220; Anon., "The Pioneer Railroad of Iowa," in *Iowa Historical Record* (1899), 13:123-134; R. I. Preston, "The Lyons and Iowa Central Railroad," in *Annals of Iowa* (1910), 9:284-301; R. E. Riegel, "The Missouri Pacific Railroad to 1879," in *Missouri Historical Review* (1923), 18:3-26. More extended treatment of the early Missouri railroads can be found in W. J. Thornton, "Early History of Railroads in Missouri," in *Missouri State Historical Society Proceedings* (1903), pp. 28-43; E. M. Violette, *Some Chapters in the Story of Missouri* (Kirksville, 1914); and J. W. Million, *State Aid to Railways in Missouri* (Chicago, 1896).

III. FEDERAL AID

By far the best two books covering the subject of federal aid are L. H. Haney, *A Congressional History of Railways in the United States 1850-1887* (Madison, 1910) and J. B. Sanborn, *Congressional Grants of Land in Aid of Railways* (Madison, 1899). Part of the same material is given in F. A. Cleveland and F. W. Powell, *Railway Promotion and Capitalization in the United States* (N. Y., 1909), Chapter XV, and in E. H. Talbott, *Railway Land Grants in the United States* (Chicago, 1880) and M. M. Orfield, *Federal Land Grants to the States with Special Reference to Minnesota* (Minneapolis, 1915). T. Donaldson, *The Public Domain* (Washington, 1884) is always indispensable in gaining exact figures on the public domain. G. W. Julian, "Railway Influence in the Land Office," in the *North American Review* (1883), 136:237-57, and E. C. Nelson, "Presidential Influence on the Policy of Internal Improvements," in *Iowa Journal of History and Politics* (1906), 4:1-69 present interesting sidelights. The attitudes in favor and in opposition to the land grant policy may be typified by B. B. Taylor, "The Policy that Built up the West," in *Overland Monthly* (1875), 14:201-7 and J. W. Johnson, "Railway Land Grants," in *North American Review* (1885), 140:280-9.

IV. ᴅᴛᴀᴛᴇ ᴀɴᴅ Lᴏᴄᴀʟ Aɪᴅ

The literature on the subject of state and local aid is practically non-existent. The best general discussion occurs in Chapters XII and XIII of F. A. Cleveland and F. W. Powell, *Railway Promotion and Capitalization in the United States* (N. Y., 1909). Municipal aid is discussed in W. M. Flanagan, "Municipal Aid to Railroads," in the *Virginia Law Journal* (1891), 15:465-6. The Missouri experiment in state aid is well presented in J. W. Million, *State Aid to Railways in Missouri* (Chicago, 1896). The Minnesota venture is described in W. W. Folwell, "The Five Million Loan," in *Collections of the Minnesota Historical Society* (1915), 15:189-214, and in R. S. Saby, "Railroad Legislation in Minnesota, 1849-1873," in *Collections of the Minnesota Historical Society* (1915), 15:1-188. Nebraska local aid is presented in C. E. Tingley, "Bond Subsidies to Railroads in Nebraska," in the *Quarterly Journal of Economics* (1892), 6:346-52.

V. Tʜᴇ Wᴀʀ Pᴇʀɪᴏᴅ

The war situation of the railroads is very well discussed in five monographs—C. R. Fish, "The Northern Railroads, April, 1861," in *American Historical Review* (1917), 12:778-93, and *Restoration of the Southern Railroads* (Madison, 1919); C. W. Ramsdell, "The Confederate Government and the Railroads," in *American Historical Review* (1917), 12:794-810; H. K. Murphy, "The Northern Railroads and the Civil War," in *Mississippi Valley Historical Review* (1918), 5:324-38; and R. E. Riegel, "Federal Operation of Southern Railroads During the Civil War," in *Mississippi Valley Historical Review* (1922), 9:126-38. References on the Union Pacific and the Central Pacific will be found under Chapter VI. The standard work on the Credit Mobilier is J. B. Crawford, *The Credit Mobilier* (Boston, 1880), which should be taken with considerable reservations because of its unqualified support of the organization. A good antidote may be found in the Congressional investigations as reported in *House Reports* 77, 78, 81, 82, and 95, 42nd Congress, 3rd Session. Possibly the best brief summaries of the operations of the Credit Mobilier may be found in W. A. Dunning, *Reconstruction, Political and Eco-*

nomic (N. Y., 1907), pp. 230-4 and in J. F. Rhodes, *History of the United States from the Compromise of 1850* (N. Y., 1906), 7:1-20. *Oakes Ames, a Memoir* (Cambridge, 1883) and O. J. Hollister, *Life of Schuyler Colfax* (N. Y., 1886) give defenses of two of the men involved, and other similar material might be added. Other points of view may be found in the references for the succeeding chapter.

Early construction in Minnesota is discussed in J. H. Bakes, "History of Transportation in Minnesota," in *Collections of the Minnesota Historical Society* (1901), 9:1-34; J. W. Bishop, "History of the St. Paul and Sioux City Railroad 1864-1881," in *Collections of the Minnesota Historical Society* (1905), 10:399-415; W. Crooks, "The First Railroad in Minnesota," in *Collections of the Minnesota Historical Society* (1905), 10:445-8; J. H. Randall, "The Beginnings of Railroad Building in Minnesota," in *Collections of the Minnesota Historical Society* (1915), 15:215-20.

VI. The Completion of the First Transcontinental Road

Haney, *Congressional History* and Sanborn, *Congressional Grants* are both invaluable. The only definitive history of the Southern Pacific is S. Daggett, *Chapters on the History of the Southern Pacific* (N. Y., 1922). J. P. Davis, *The Union Pacific Railway* (Chicago, 1894) and H. K. White, *History of the Union Pacific Railway* (Chicago, 1895) are both satisfactory. N. Trottman, *History of the Union Pacific* (N. Y., 1923), the latest work, is particularly admirable in its treatment of the finances. C. F. Carter, *When Railroads Were New* (N. Y., 1909) and F. A. Talbot, *The Railway Conquest of the World* (Philadelphia, 1911) both present interesting pictures of the construction of the Union Pacific. J. D. Cruise, "Early Days of the Union Pacific," in *Collections of the Kansas State Historical Society* (1910), 11:529-50, S. Dillon, "Historic Moments: Driving the Last Spike of the Union Pacific," in *Scribner's Magazine* (1892), 12:253-9, G. M. Dodge, "How We Built the Union Pacific Railway," in *Senate Document* 447, 61st Congress, 2nd Session, and G. F. Train, *My Life in Many States and in Foreign Lands* (N. Y., 1902) all give personal recollections of some phase of the construction of the Union Pacific.

VII. PROSPERITY

W. H. Stennett, *Yesterday and Today* (Chicago, 1910) is the official history of the Chicago and Northwestern and has been published in numerous editions. I. W. Cary, *The Organization and History of the Chicago, Milwaukee and St. Paul* (Milwaukee, 1893) constitutes the only existing history of that line. R. E. Riegel, "The Missouri Pacific Railroad to 1879," in *Missouri Historical Review* (1923), 18:3-26 reviews the development of the Missouri Pacific system. The remainder of the roads treated in the chapter still remain to be given individual treatment.

VIII. TRANSCONTINENTAL ASPIRATIONS AND THE PANIC OF 1873

The story of the Kansas Pacific-Denver Pacific line can best be followed in the histories of the Union Pacific cited under Chapter VI; A. Roenigk, "Railroad Grading Among Indians," in *Transactions of the Kansas State Historical Society* (1904), 8:384-9 treats of the situation on the Kansas Pacific. G. D. Bradley, *The Story of the Santa Fe* (Boston, 1887), is an adequate account, even though favoring the road. Interesting accounts of the "Rio Grande war" appear in Smiley, *Denver,* cited under general works, and in F. Hall, *History of the State of Colorado* (4 vols., Chicago, 1889). The Missouri Pacific is treated in Riegel, "Missouri Pacific," cited under Chapter VII. The history of the Northern Pacific is presented with entire satisfaction in E. V. Smalley, *History of the Northern Pacific Railroad* (N. Y., 1883) and E. P. Oberholtzer, *Jay Cooke Financier of the Civil War* (2 vols., Philadelphia, 1907).

IX. DEPRESSION AND OPPOSITION

The best discussion of railroad finances occurs in Cleveland and Powell, *Railway Promotion;* the same volume, Chapter XIV, gives the only satisfactory account of the reaction against state and local aid. Various aspects of railway finance may be considered in such works as C. W. Hassler, *Railway Rings and their Relation to the Railroad Question of the Country* (N. Y., 1876); E. L. Andrews, "The Watering of Railroad Securities," in *American Law Review* (1887), 21:696-714; and in the various Congressional reports on railroad regulation. The restrictive movement in Congress is well presented in Haney, *Congressional History*. The movement in the states is excellently presented in S. J. Buck, *The Granger Movement* (Cambridge, 1913); *The Agrarian Crusade* (New Haven, 1920), by the same author, is a more popular account which covers a good deal of the same material. The work of the Iowa commission is described in detail in F. H. Dixon, *State Railroad Control* (N. Y., 1896), and in P. A. Dey, "Railroad Legislation in Iowa," in *Iowa Historical Record* (1893), 9:540-66. The early events in Minnesota are recounted in Saby, "Railroad Legislation in Minnesota."

X. RECOVERY

The development of mining is discussed in W. J. Trimble, *The Mining Advance into the Inland Empire* (Madison, 1914). The best surveys of the development of the cattle industry occur in F. L. Paxson, "The Cow Country," in *American Historical Review* (1917), 22:65-83, and in *The Last American Frontier* (N. Y., 1910), by the same author. The packing side of the industry is presented in R. A. Clemens, *The American Livestock and Meat Industry* (N. Y., 1923), and H. C. Hill, "The Development of Chicago as a Center of the Meat Packing Industry," in *Mississippi Valley Historical Review* (1923), 10:253-73. J. B. Kendrick, "The Texas Trail," in *Wyoming Historical Society Miscellany* (1919), pp. 41-49, and J. G. McCoy, *Historical Sketch of the Cattle Trade of the West and Southwest* (Kansas City, 1874) both present pictures of the "long drive," which are drawn from personal experience. J. Nimmo, Jr., *Report in Regard to the Range and Ranch Cattle Business* (Washington, 1885) reports on the encroaching line of settlement and suggests a national cattle trail as the proper solution.

XI. The Gould System

The Union Pacific operations of Gould can be followed in
the references previously given on that road. The life of
Gould and a final history of his railroad system still remain
to be written; G. Myers, *History of the Great American Fortunes* (3 vols., Chicago, 1910) presents an unfavorable estimate of Gould's work; R. E. Riegel, "The Missouri Pacific
Railroad to 1879," in *Missouri Historical Review* (1923),
18:3-26, and "The Missouri Pacific, 1879-1900," in *Missouri
Historical Review* (1924), 18:173-96 give a suggestive summary of the development of the Gould properties. W. Q.
Gresham, "The Wabash Railway Receivership," in *American
Law Review* (1887), 21:104-26 gives one phase of the Gould
manipulations.

H. Fink, *Regulation of Railway Rates on Interstate Freight
Traffic* (N. Y., 1905) gives a survey of the history of most of
the important pools, by a pool manager. Two of the more
important western ones are discussed in R. E. Riegel, "The
Southwestern Pool," in *Missouri Historical Review* (1924)
19:12-24, and "The Omaha Pool," in *Iowa Journal of History
and Politics* (1924), 22:569-82. Two articles by J. W. Midgley, one of the pool managers, "A New Departure in Railroad
Management," in *Forum* (1899), 27:491-501, and "Railroad
Rate Wars: Their Cause and Cure," in *Forum* (1896),
20:519-30 treat of pooling. M. A. Knapp, "Some Observations on Railroad Pooling," in *Annals of the American Academy* (1896), 8:127-47 gives the viewpoint of a member of
the Interstate Commerce Commission. The entire subject
of railroad coöperation is discussed in C. S. Langstroth and
W. Stilz, *Railway Co-operation* (Boston, 1899).

XII. The Completion of the Southern
Transcontinental Roads

The principal references for the material in this chapter
have already been given under Chapters VI and VIII. F. E.
Prendergast, "Transcontinental Railways," in *Harper's*
(1883), 67:936-44 presents a contemporaneous account. C. S.
Gleed, "The Atchison, Topeka and Santa Fe," in *Cosmopoli-*

tan (1893), 14:465-75 gives an interesting brief account of that road.

XIII. The Completion of the Northern Transcontinental Roads

References to the Union Pacific and its debt to the government may be found under Chapter VI; Northern Pacific references are in Chapter VIII; pooling references are in Chapter XI. R. T. Colburn, "The Pacific Railway Debts," in *Annals of the American Academy* (1895), 5:684-704 gives a good brief summary of the situation. The genesis of the Oregon railway system is recounted in I. L. Poppleton, "Oregon's First Monopoly—The Oregon Steam Navigation Company," in *Quarterly of the Oregon Historical Society* (1908), vol. 9 and in P. W. Gillette, "A Brief History of the Oregon Steam Navigation Company," in *Quarterly of the Oregon Historical Society* (1904), 5:315-26. The activities of Villard can best be followed in H. Villard, *Memoirs of Henry Villard* (2 vols., N. Y., 1904).

XIV. The End of the Era

Many of the roads discussed in this chapter have no formal history. Stennett, *Yesterday and Today* covers the Chicago and Northwestern. The Great Northern can best be followed in C. H. Grinling, *The History of the Great Northern Railway, 1845-1895* (London, 1898), and J. G. Pyle, *The Life of James J. Hill* (2 vols., Garden City, 1917). References on pooling may be secured under Chapter XI. The attitude of one interested person may be obtained in A. Carnegie, "My Experience with Railway Rebates," in *Century Magazine* (1908), 75:722-8. The best place to find the objections of various classes to railroad pools is in the evidence collected by the Cullom committee, given in *Senate Report* 46 (2 vols.), 49th Congress, 1st Session.

XV. The Labor Supply

The source of the labor supply has never been worked out,

and consequently there can be no formal bibliography for this chapter. The references for the succeeding chapter contain a certain amount of material on the subject, although not in a convenient form. The immigration side of the question can be followed to some extent in such books as J. W. Jenks and W. J. Lauck, *The Immigration Problem* (N. Y., 1913); S. P. Orth, *Our Foreigners* (New Haven, 1920); A. M. Schlesinger, *New Viewpoints in American History* (N. Y., 1922).

XVI. LABOR ORGANIZATION

General histories of labor organization, including that of railroad labor, may be used for a general background—J. R. Commons and others, *A Documentary History of American Industrial Society* (10 vols., Cleveland, 1911); J. R. Commons and others, *History of Labour in the United States* (2 vols., N. Y., 1918); J. R. Commons (ed.), *Trade Unionism and Labor Problems Second Series* (Boston, 1921); F. J. Carlton, *Organized Labor in American History* (N. Y., 1920); J. H. Hollander and G. E. Barnett, *Studies in American Trade Unionism* (N. Y., 1905); R. F. Hoxie, *Trade Unionism in the United States* (N. Y., 1923); S. Perlman, *A History of Trade Unionism in the United States* (N. Y., 1922). The story of the railroad strike of 1877 is told in J. F. Rhodes, *History of the United States from Hayes to McKinley 1877-1896* (N. Y., 1919), pp. 18-43. The official account of the troubles on the Gould lines is told by a bulletin of the Bureau of Labor Statistics of Missouri, under the title *The Official History of the Great Strike of 1886* (Jefferson City, 1887); an excellent account of the strike is F. W. Taussig, "The South-Western Strike of 1886", in *Quarterly Journal of Economics* (1887), 1:184-222. T. V. Powderly, head of the Knights of Labor, tells the story of the organization in *Thirty Years of Labor 1859 to 1889* (Philadelphia, 1890), but does not mention the Gould strike. Accounts of the Pullman strike are contained in H. James, *Richard Olney* (N. Y., 1923); W. R. Brown, *Altgeld of Illinois* (N. Y., 1924); E. Berman, *Labor Disputes and the President of the United States* (N. Y., 1924). By far the best single account of the Coxey movement is D. L. McMurry,

"The Industrial Armies and the Commonweal," in *Mississippi Valley Historical Review* (1923), 10:215-52.

XVII. Equipment

The history of the development of equipment is as yet in a very fragmentary state and the materials are largely unassembled. M. M. Kirkman, *The Science of Railways* (12 vols., N. Y., 1900) surveys the whole field to some extent. C. F. Carter, *When Railroads Were New* (N. Y., 1909) and C. Warman, *The Story of the Railroad* (N. Y., 1899) both contain considerable miscellaneous material. The history of the locomotive can be followed in W. B. Brown, *The History of the First Locomotives in America* (N. Y., 1874); A. Sinclair, *Development of the Locomotive Engine* (N. Y., 1907); R. H. Thurston, *A History of the Growth of the Steam Engine* (N. Y., 1884); S. M. Vauclain, "Locomotives of the Nineteenth and Twentieth Century," in *New England Railroad Club Proceedings* (1901), pp. 4-52; A. Williams, *The Romance of Modern Locomotives* (London, 1905); *History of the Baldwin Locomotive Works* (Philadelphia, 1903). The development of track is presented in J. E. Watkins, "The Development of American Rail and Track," in *House Miscellaneous Document* 224, part 2, 51st Congress, 1st Session, and in J. D. Steele, "Early History of Railways and the Origin of Gauge," in *Transactions of the American Society of Civil Engineers* (1872), 2:53-61. The history of various types of specialized equipment comes in "History of the Railway Mail Service," in *Senate Executive Document* 40, 48th Congress, 2nd Session; A. C. Stimson, *History of the Express Companies and the Origin of American Railroads* (N. Y., 1859); L. D. H. Weld, *Private Freight Cars and American Railways* (N. Y., 1908).

XVIII. The Railroads and Western Settlement

By far the best two volumes on the subject are those by Professor F. L. Paxson—*The Last American Frontier* (N. Y., 1910) and *History of the American Frontier, 1763-1893* (N. Y., 1924). The significance of railroads in the settlement of the

THE STORY OF THE WESTERN RAILROADS

public domain is stated from two points of view in E. Hough, "The Settlement of the West: A Study in Transportation," in *Century* (1902), 41:355-69, and the very suggestive article by F. L. Paxson, "The Pacific Railroads and the Disappearance of the Frontier," in *Annual Report of the American Historical Association* (1907), 1:107-18. F. J. Turner, "The Significance of the Frontier in American History," in *Annual Report of the American Historical Association* (1893), pp. 191-227, called attention both to the importance of the frontier and to its disappearance. Standard works on the public domain are T. Donaldson, *The Public Domain* (Washington, 1884); S. Sato, *History of the Land Question in the United States*, Johns Hopkins Studies, Fourth Series 7, 8, and 9 (Baltimore, July, August, September, 1886); A. B. Hart, "The Disposition of Our Public Lands," in *Quarterly Journal of Economics* (1887), 1:169-84; M. Conover, *The General Land Office* (Baltimore, 1923); Sanborn, *Congressional Grants;* Haney, *Congressional History.* Oberholtzer, *Jay Cooke* gives considerable material on foreign sales. Personal experiences with railroad land sales are recounted in J. R. Buchanan, "Great Railroad Migration into Northern Nebraska," in *Proceedings and Collections of the Nebraska State Historical Society* (1907), 15:25-34; E. L. Lomax, "Work of the Union Pacific in Nebraska," in *Proceedings and Collections of the Nebraska State Historical Society* (1907), 15:181-9; J. B. Power, "Bits of History Connected with the Early Days of the Northern Pacific and the Organization of its Land Department," in *Collections of the State Historical Society of North Dakota* (1910), 3:337-49. J. C. Malin, *Indian Policy and Western Expansion* (Lawrence, 1921) presents sufficient material on Indian policy. A number of works give the situation of the western farmer and his reaction toward it—T. C. Atkeson, *Semi-Centennial History of the Patrons of Husbandry* (N. Y., 1906); S. J. Buck, *The Agrarian Crusade* (New Haven, 1920) and *The Granger Movement* (Cambridge, 1913); J. R. Elliott, *American Farms, their Condition and Future* (N. Y., 1896); H. Farmer, "The Economic Background of Frontier Populism," in *Mississippi Valley Historical Review* (1924), 10:406-27; F. E. Haynes, *James Baird Weaver* (Iowa City, 1919); W. C. Mitchell, *A*

History of the Greenbacks (Chicago, 1903); W. S. Morgan, *History of the Wheel and Alliance and the Impending Revolution* (Fort Scott, 1889).

XIX. REGULATION AND THE INTERSTATE COMMERCE ACT

The history of both state and federal regulation is included in E. Jones, *Principles of Railway Transportation* (N. Y., 1924). Dixon, *State Railroad Control*, Dey, *Railroad Legislation*, and S. W. Moore, "State Supervision of Railroad Transportation in Arkansas," in *Publications of the Arkansas Historical Association* (1911), 3:266-309, treat of state action. Land grant forfeiture is discussed in Sanborn, *Congressional Grants*. The history of all types of federal action is presented in Haney, *Congressional History*. The history and discussion of federal regulation are included in S. M. Cullom, *Fifty Years of Public Service* (Chicago, 1911); S. C. Dunn, *Regulation of Railways* (N. Y., 1918); H. S. Haines, *Problems in Railway Regulation* (N. Y., 1911), and *Restrictive Railway Legislation* (N. Y., 1905); E. R. Johnson and T. W. Van Metre, *Principles of Railroad Transportation* (N. Y., 1916); W. Larrabee, *The Railroad Question* (Chicago, 1893); H. R. Meyer, *Government Regulation of Railroad Rates* (N. Y., 1905); W. Z. Ripley, *Railroads Rates and Regulation* (N. Y., 1912); A. B. Stickney, *The Railway Problem* (St. Paul, 1891). M. B. Hammond, *Railway Rate Theories of the Interstate Commerce Commission* (Cambridge, 1911), and A. N. Merritt, *Federal Regulation of Railway Rates* (N. Y., 1907) both deal in most part with the rate theories of the Interstate Commerce Commission. The Interstate Commerce Act as interpreted judicially and administratively is given in considerable detail in E. H. Martin, *Interstate Commerce Law* (2 vols., Chicago, 1917). References on pooling history may be found under Chapter XI.

XX. THE REIGN OF GIANTS

Most of the reading on this chapter must be done in current periodicals. Financial practices are discussed in F. A. Cleveland and F. W. Powell, *Railroad Finance* (N. Y., 1919); M. G. Cunniff, "Increasing Railroad Consolidation," in *World's*

Work (1902), 3:1775-80; S. Daggett, *Railroad Reorganization* (Cambridge, 1908); J. Gibbon, "Railroad Consolidation," in *North American Review* (1892), 154:251-4; F. H. Graser, "The Voting Trust in Railway Finance," in *Railway World* (1906), 48:547-8; T. L. Greene, "Changes in the Form of Railroad Capital," in *Quarterly Journal of Economics* (1890), 4:449-57, and "Railroad Stock Watering," in *Political Science Quarterly* (1891), 6:474-92; E. A. Harriman, "Voting Trusts and Holding Companies," in *Yale Law Journal* (1904), 13:109-23; A. J. Hirschl, *Combination, Consolidation and Succession of Corporations* (Chicago, 1896); W. Z. Ripley, *How Consolidation Has Worked Out in the Case of One of the Great Common Carriers* (Chicago, 1900). In addition to the works on individual roads cited before there is G. Kernan, *E. H. Harriman, a Biography* (N. Y., 1922); J. G. Pyle, *The Life of James J. Hill* (2 vols., Garden City, 1917); G. H. Coolidge, "Hill Against Harriman," in *American Magazine* (1909), 68:419-29; C. M. Keys, "Harriman," in *World's Work* (1907), 13:8455-64, 8537-52, 8651-65, 8791-8804, and "The Newest Railroad Power," in *World's Work* (1905), 10:6302-13, and "The Overlords of Railroad Traffic," in *World's Work* (1907), 12:8437-45 and "The Shifting Railroad Control," in *World's Work* (1910) 20:13045-56, and "A Corner in Pacific Railroads," in *World's Work* (1905), 9:5816-22; B. H. Meyer, *A History of the Northern Securities Case* (Madison, 1906); H. T. Newcomb, "The Concentration of Railroad Control," in *Annals of the American Academy* (1902), 19:89-107, and "The Recent Great Railroad Combinations," in *Review of Reviews* (1901), 24:163-74; W. Payne, "The Rise of Harriman," in *Saturday Evening Post*, December 8 and 22, 1906, and January 5 and 26, 1907; W. L. Snyder, "The Case Against the Great Northern," in *Outlook* (1907), 85:559-62 and "Harriman, Colossus of Roads," in *Review of Reviews* (1907), 25:37-48; F. H. Spearman, "Building up a Great Railway System," in *Outlook* (1909), 91:435-52, and *The Strategy of Great Railroads* (N. Y., 1905); A. B. Stickney, "A Defense of the Great Northern," in *Outlook* (1907), 85:557-9. The story of the completion of the Chicago, Milwaukee and St. Paul to the coast is told in E. Flower, "Opening up the Northwest," in *Putnam's Magazine*

(1909), 6:387-96, and in W. T. Prosser, "A New Transcontinental Railway," in *Pacific Monthly* (1910), 23:209-15. The building of the Denver, Northwestern and Pacific is recounted in L. Lewis, "A Feat in Railroad Building," in *World's Work* (1905), 11:6859-70. The building of the San Pedro, Los Angeles and Salt Lake City is described in F. Strother, "Swinging the March of Empire Southwestward," in *World's Work* (1906), 11:7072-81.

INDEX

Adams, C. F., Jr., 143, 291.
Albany Evening Journal, 18.
Alcott, T. W., 72.
Allen, T., 20, 49.
Allen, W. F., 267.
American Federation of Labor, 246, 252.
American Railway Association, 267.
American Railway Union, 253-254.
Ames, Oakes, 77-79, 92.
Ames, Oliver, 77.
Anderson, A., 114.
Arizona, 40.
Arkansas, 5, 25-26, 55-57.
Arkansas Central, 135.
Arthur, P. M., 245.
Atchison and Topeka, see Atchison, Topeka and Santa Fe.
Atchison, Topeka and Santa Fe, 42, 43, 92, 116, 129, 134-135, 139, 149, 172, 173, 184-194, 198, 200, 201, 202, 208, 209, 241, 247, 266, 282, 283, 305, 315, 316.
Atlantic and Pacific, 42, 107, 118-119, 172, 173, 179, 189-191, 208, 241, 283.
Atlantic and Pacific (telegraph), 272.

Baltimore and Ohio, 3, 175, 243, 315, 316, 317.
Benton, T. H., 12, 14, 15, 18, 20.
Billings, F., 205.
Blaine, J. G., 81.
Blair, J. I., 96, 97, 98.
Bogue, G. M., 221.
Bowles, S., 125.

Brakes, 270-272.
Bridges, 7, 97-98, 100-101, 103, 106, 263-264.
Brooks, J., 79.
Bross, W., 125.
Brotherhood of Locomtive Engineers, 248.
Brotherhood of Locomotive Firemen, 245.
Brotherhood of Railroad Brakemen, 245.
Brotherhood of Railroad Trainmen, 245-246.
Brotherhood of Railway Bridgemen, 246.
Brotherhood of Railway Carmen, 246.
Brotherhood of Railway Trackmen, 246.
Brotherhood of the Footboard, 244.
Brotherhoods, 244-256.
Browne, C., 256.
Buchanan, J., 69.
Buffalo Bayou, Brazos and Colorado, 24-25, 120.
Burlingame treaty, 234.
Burlington and Missouri River (Iowa), 102-103, 105, 215-216.
Burlington and Missouri River (Nebraska), 103, 105, 215-216.
Burlington and Southwestern, 135.
Burlington, Cedar Rapids and Northern, 135.

Cairo and Fulton, 50, 52, 56, 109, 139.
California, 5, 29, 57, 59.